THE SCALPEL'S EDGE

Frontispiece: **"The Surgeon."** Courtesy of the artist, Dean Meeker.

The artist was undecided for a long time whether to have surgery on his eyes. After successful surgery he entitled this etching, "Indecision." No one was interested in purchasing it. When he entitled it, "The Surgeon," many bought it.

THE SCALPEL'S EDGE

THE CULTURE OF SURGEONS

Pearl Katz
The Johns Hopkins University School of Medicine

Allyn and Bacon
Boston London Toronto Sydney Tokyo Singapore

For Liat, Dvora, and Michael

CONTENTS

ACKNOWLEDGMENTS

~

Many people have contributed to this book. First, I am particularly grateful for the generosity of the surgeons at Meadowbrook University Hospital who gave me virtually unlimited access to information about themselves and their lives, decisions, concerns, patients, colleagues, knowledge, and judgment.

For sharing their expertise during the various phases of writing I appreciate the contributions of Joel Alperstein, Michael Bain, Joan Cassell, Donald Ferguson, Atwood Gaines, Derek Gill, Wolf Haber, Shaun B. Jones, Christopher Kaufman, Frederick Manning, David Marlowe, Bernard Ortiz de Montellano, Haim Reizes, John Richters, Joseph Rothberg, Richard Satava, Jonathan Shay, John Singer, and Louise Yolles.

I especially appreciate the considerable amount of time and wisdom that the following people put into reading various versions of the entire manuscript and providing detailed comments: Thomas E. Beam, Sidney Blair, Gert Brieger, Lawrence Fink, Harry Holloway, Louis Mahoney, Donald Joralemon, Lola Romanucci-Ross, Arthur Rubel.

For the art work I am grateful to Marie C. Guidry, William and Mary Martin, Dean Meeker, and Johns Hopkins Medicine.

For their exceptional editorial skills I thank Sylvia Shepard and Linette Sparacino.

I am especially indebted to Faris R. Kirkland whose skills and judgment have contributed to this book in inestimable ways.

INTRODUCTION

~

[I]t is impossible to understand the problems of medical care without understanding the physician. And it is impossible to make significant changes in the medical field without changing physician behavior.

(Fuchs 1974:560)

An unprecedented pace of change in the health care environment is affecting physicians and patients as the new millennium arrives. Surgery and the rest of medicine has changed from being an art practiced by individuals to an industry involving the management of complex teams of specialists. Medicine has evolved from a calling to a career. Physicians have evolved from practicing full-time healing to devoting increasingly more of their work time to developing business strategies to enable them to continue healing. Business concerns, such as managed care, tax considerations, insurance regulations, and threats of litigation, have assumed burgeoning importance (Angell 1994). As a result, both patients and physicians face new and complex sets of pressures and are compelled to develop new relationships with one another.

Surgeons play a prominent role in the medical system. Most people will have contact with surgeons at some time in their lives. Each year in the United States 24 million operations are performed, and one in nine people undergoes an operation. Half of the patients discharged from hospitals in the 1990s had surgical operations (Rogers and Seward 1996:44).

Surgeons have come under increasing criticism in recent years for their detachment from patients, preoccupation with technology, high incomes — ten times the national average (Goldberg 1989) — the possibility of "unnecessary" surgery, and for a tendency to project blame for failure onto patients or the medical system (cf., Lyons 1994). Despite the prominence of surgeons in the medical system and the frequency with which the general population encounters them, we know little about their day-to-day lives. Our knowledge about how they perceive patients, other physicians, and themselves, how they think they behave, as well as how they analyze problems, communicate with other physicians, and how they make decisions is quite limited.

Surgeons were ranked as the most prestigious occupation in a national survey, outranking college presidents, astronauts, big-city mayors, lawyers, and all other physicians (National Opinion Research Center 1991). Indeed, they are often stereotyped as God-like heroes, as the following joke suggests: Question: What is the difference between God and a surgeon? Answer: God knows that he is not a surgeon. Such stereotypes depict surgeons as heroic men who exude confidence and optimism and who are quick to act and too busy to listen. Although the stereotypes derive as much from movies and television as from real life, there also are many surgeons who behave in a caring manner and place importance upon communicating with and informing their patients.

The kind of work that surgeons do influences their demeanor and behavior with others. What other profession makes decisions and takes risks that literally control patients' lives or deaths on a daily basis? Who but a surgeon routinely and boldly cuts into the most intimate depths of people's live bodies, penetrates their innermost body cavities, exposing blood, guts, and excreta, and cut and remove their organs, burn blood vessels, saw bones, and sew layers of skin? Surgeons' detachment from their patients may be understood as necessary protections from these routine sights, smells, acts, and dramatic confrontations with mortality. Their demeanor of confidence and apparent arrogance may be partially explained by the almost-superhuman requirements of their work.

Until a little more than a century ago surgeons had operated without anesthesia on patients who were in unbearable pain, and often did not survive their surgery. It is only in the present century that patients were most likely to survive surgery. Surgeons' stereotypic demeanor of coldness and insensitivity to patients were likely to have been essential to enable them to distance themselves sufficiently to take necessary risks with frightened patients. Surgeons' reluctance to admit doubt and uncertainty or error was likely to have permitted them to be sufficiently bold to carry out extremely difficult and risky procedures.

Surgeons are trained, and they manage their professional lives, within the constraints of a surgical "culture." The concept of a "culture of surgeons" is used here to represent a specific Western medical tradition. It may also be called a professional "subculture," with its own social organization, values, theories of disease causation, and treatment, and rules of behavior (cf., Helman 1994; Mishler 1981:205; Stein 1990). (See Appendix A for a discussion of culture, medical anthropology, and biomedicine.) This culture of surgeons has its roots in a long historical tradition, and it has been further defined by the specific training environments and hospital systems in which they work. Each generation of surgeons perpetuates that culture and passes it on by recruiting surgical residents who appear to resemble them and training these residents to emulate their thinking and behavior. Gert H. Brieger, the eminent historian of surgery, wrote about the importance of studying the "culture of surgery ... the beliefs, the values, and the society of the surgeons." He stated: "we must begin to view surgeons and their activities in an ethnographic way" (1984:33, 37).

In order to understand any individual surgeon's behavior it is necessary to understand the culture of surgeons. Without such understanding neither patients, other medical professionals, nor surgeons themselves can change the medical cultural system in which the culture of surgeons is embedded.

The organizational structure of the modern hospital contributes to distancing surgeons from their patients. Care of patients in hospitals is fragmented for the patient and the physician. Most hospital patients have many specialists treating their case, and frequently none of them encompass the patient as a whole person. Surgeons, with their focus on mechanical repair of parts of the body, are farther removed from the whole person than many other medical professions. Surgeons see large numbers of people in their offices, the operating room, and the surgical wards. In each case he[1] sees them for a specialized task, such as diagnosing, operating, and supervising post-operative recovery. There is negligible opportunity for a surgeon to become acquainted with and follow a particular patient through his surgical illness. It may be that if a surgeon were to empathize with each of his patients who are in fear, pain, and confusion and are sick and dying, his efficacy as a surgeon may be compromised.

Although many patients wish that surgeons would be warmer, more sensitive, more informative and communicative, and involve them more in decision making, many other patients prefer them to continue to play their customary role of the confident, active, optimistic hero to help them overcome their uncertainties and fears. Consequently, patients' traditional expectations for surgeons' behavior may influence and perpetuate that very behavior. Many patients prefer surgeons to impart an aura of certainty toward their skills for negotiating life and death. Bosk (1979:210) wrote that surgeons' charisma was not simply the result of surgeons' behavior but was also nurtured by patients' needs and desires.

Surgeons' heroic posture helps many patients counteract fears of intrusions into their bodies, of being in a state of near-death under anesthesia, and of relinquishing total control of their body's functions. For most Westerners to give up such control induces fear. However, most surgeons prefer not to be confronted with the fear of their patients. Many aspects of surgical culture, such as some rituals in the operating room and the fragmentation of care, also protect surgeons from identifying with their patients and listening to their fears. The converse side of surgeons' distance from both patients and colleagues is that of isolation. Surgeons are alone with their very weighty decisions; they rarely talk about their doubts or uncertainties to others.

When patients are referred to surgeons by their doctors they are typically frightened, because they usually come for the purpose of determining whether a condition requires surgery. Typically patients prefer a surgeon who appears confident and assured. Such behavior represents to them skill, knowledge, and experience. Many want someone who emphasizes his unique ability to "cure" them. They want someone who radiates optimism, because they want hope to replace their fears. They do not welcome a surgeon who admits doubts and uncertainties about his own ability, the diagnosis, or the surgical procedure, or the results of surgery. Their most frequently asked questions are: "Do I need an operation?" "Is the condition serious?" and "How long will I be sick?" Most patients' fears about the seriousness and intrusiveness of a surgical operation take precedence over their desire to understand the specifics of their disease process and the options that are available to them.

This book presents an in-depth picture of how surgeons in a particular hospital work, think, make decisions, manage their emotions, and communicate, or fail to communicate, with their patients and other doctors. Based upon intensive anthropological field-work, it examines surgeons' actual day-to-day behavior — in the operating room and interacting with other surgeons, physicians, and patients.

These chapters explore how surgeons' culture is molded as much by their historical tradition in which they operated without anesthesia and saved comparatively few patients from death, as it is by recent advances in technology, organizational structures of hospitals, referral systems, and insurance reimbursements. That history has influenced their present predilection for active intervention, risk-taking, and maintaining their heroic image. It has influenced the ways in which they make big and little decisions. Their history has influenced their unwillingness to admit doubts and limitations to their patients and their colleagues. And it has affected how they process information and treat patients. The implications of the surgeons' culture for the well-being of their patients and for their identity as scientists are examined — particularly the effects of the perpetuation of their heroic image by the posture of certainty and not admitting doubts, their penchant for action, and their barriers to communication with patients, other physicians and surgeons. It addresses why the culture of surgeons has been so remarkably tenacious despite considerable changes in surgical technology.

At the beginning of the new millennium major changes will continue to shape the American medical system. Its potentials for change and its limits to changes can be better predicted by understanding the physicians who are the cornerstones of that system. This book is written with the belief that understanding the culture of the surgeons, including the historical and cultural factors which influence surgical decision-making, may help patients, consumers, and all physicians to become wiser and more compassionate decision makers.

NOTES

1. The masculine pronoun is used for surgeons and most patients.

Chapter 1

ENCOUNTERS WITH SURGEONS

~

I've got a girl following me around all the time, taking down everything I say.

(Dr. Jennifer's remark about the anthropologist)

INTRODUCTION

I came initially to Meadowbrook University Hospital[1] in response to the surgeons' request to help them with a problem. The surgical residents were complaining that staff surgeons were not spending enough time teaching them. To help solve the problem the Chief of the Department of Surgery, Dr. White, and the Director of Resident Training, Dr. Jennifer, requested a consultation from the Meadowbrook University's School of Medicine's Department of Medical Education. Two of us from the Department of Medical Education, an educational psychologist, and I, a cultural anthropologist, came to consult with them.

When we arrived for our appointment at the 800-bed Meadowbrook University Hospital at the outskirts of Meadowbrook City, one of Canada's larger cities, we went to the office of the Chief of Surgery, Dr. White. Dr. White's receptionist immediately called Dr. Jennifer to join us. Dr. White was 45-years-old, slightly under six feet tall, with medium build, dark blond hair, and blue eyes. Dr. Jennifer

2

Courtesy, Mary L. Martin, Ltd.

was 48-years-old, about four inches shorter than Dr. White, with a stocky, muscular build, medium brown hair, and brown eyes.

The two surgeons greeted us in a very friendly manner with firm handshakes and engaging smiles. They described their problem briefly, and with little pause Dr. Jennifer continued by suggesting a quick and easy solution to us: "Look at our schedules! Tell the residents how hard we work! Let them know how busy we are — our long hours and dedication! Explain that to them so they will understand!" They thereupon handed us the hospital's surgical manual for residents which included their goals for residency training, model schedules for the residents, and brief descriptions of the 17 surgeons in the Department of Surgery.

My colleague was an educational psychologist with considerable consulting experience about educational problems in many medical specialties, and I was an anthropologist with research experience in a variety of cultural settings, but none in medical settings. My research at that point had consisted of long-term participant-observation, interpreting, and analyzing cultural values and social structure among Southwestern American Pueblo Indians and among immigrants in Israel. Our respective approaches to the surgeons' problems differed significantly, and in large part it reflected our respective professional backgrounds.

Within a few days' time my colleague had obtained the data he believed he needed from the surgeons. He had reviewed the schedules of the surgeons, their written goals for surgical training, and the curriculum of the residents in the department manual. He obtained copies of several surgeons' schedules for the past several weeks and calculated the hours each spent seeing patients, operating, teaching, and attending meetings, rounds, and other activities.

Ten days after our first meeting my colleague presented his recommendations for minor modifications of the surgeons' schedules. His oral and written presentation, accompanied by elaborate and colorful charts which documented representative surgeons' schedules of time and activities, confirmed the surgeons' perceptions that the residents were getting as much time as the surgeons could spare. After some discussion he suggested that because the surgeons' time was limited, he would meet with the residents to explain to them how the senior surgeons were adequately meeting their teaching goals, given their demanding schedules.

My colleague presented solutions based on the surgeons' perceptions of both the problem and solution. He accepted the surgeons' definition of the problem (the surgeon's time) and the surgeons' perspective of the solution (to show the residents how busy they were). He assumed that surgeons and surgical residents perceive and act in accordance with clearly defined rational goals. He also assumed that once the residents were presented with this information by an objective professional they would be likely to accept their definition of the problem and, thereby, accept the recommended solution.

My colleague appeared to identify with the surgeons whose status, both in and out of the medical school setting, was considerably higher than ours as social scientists. In the general style of surgeons he came up decisively and quickly with a concise solution. But identifying with the surgeons did not prevent him from acting like a dutiful patient, following surgeons' instructions and obtaining fast relief from the problem.

In keeping with my anthropological training, I believed I should try to understand the differences in perception between the surgeons and the residents that appeared to be at the core of the problem. To accomplish this I had to learn a great deal more about the surgical culture and the social organization in the Meadowbrook University Hospital where the surgeons and residents interacted. I had first to understand how the surgeons defined themselves, to see "their experience within the framework of their own idea" of what a surgeon is (Geertz 1984:126). I wanted to know how they were influenced by their surgical, national/Provincial, and hospital cultures, and how they contributed to these cultures and perpetuated or changed them. And I wanted to understand the context in which the residents perceived that the surgeons' teaching time was inadequate for their needs. Therefore, in the initial meeting with Drs. White and Jennifer I tried to explain that in order to "solve" their problem I needed to understand what the residents had to learn in order to become surgeons.

Before I finished explaining the way in which I would approach this task, Dr. White interrupted me by restating some of the major goals of surgical education. He reminded me that they had given us a copy of these goals along with their curriculum. He reiterated the details of their schedules, conveying in what I perceived to be a patronizing manner that they were taking time from their busy and important work to repeat information they had already given us. They indicated that I, particularly, was asking questions whose answers were obvious and had already been transmitted in the documents they had given us. As a result, I began to feel intimidated by their response.[2] They appeared to expect appreciation for the time and patience that they had granted us.

My initial responses and perceptions became useful to me in subsequently understanding the perspectives of patients who were frightened and bewildered by their illnesses and were recipients of some surgeons' impatience and ill-disguised condescension.

In order to get them to agree to my conducting anthropological fieldwork with them, I explained to them that since the residents learned largely by behaving like surgeons and doing surgery, I could understand the problem they presented to us by "following" a few surgeons around as they went about their daily tasks, and observing them, and taking notes on their behavior.

Drs. White and Jennifer first responded by stating that the clarity and comprehensiveness of their written schedules and teaching goals should be sufficient for understanding them. Then they appeared to become intrigued and amused by the idea of being the focus of a study in which they would be "followed." They first looked at each other, then at me, and after a pause Dr. Jennifer said in a slightly amused way, "Okay, when do you want to start 'following' me?"

OBSERVATIONS BEGIN

The first morning I arrived at the hospital at 6:30 a.m. I had informed Dr. Jennifer that I would take notes as I observed him attending to his daily tasks, and that he should let me know if he wanted privacy at any time. To my surprise, in the course of six months of field work there were only three occasions in which a surgeon asked to be alone. One was when a priest visited Dr. Michael. The second occurred when Dr. White met with the Dean of the Medical School in the Dean's office. The third was a generic request in the middle of field work with Dr. Gottlieb, the urological surgeon, who suggested that I no longer be present in the outpatient clinic when his male patients were undressed. The only other places where I did not accompany the surgeons were the men's bathroom and locker room.

My first encounters with the surgeons in the presence of my colleague revealed much about the culture of surgeons, particularly some of their thinking patterns, modes of decision making, and approaches to communication with non-physicians and women. For example, they articulated their initial problem as that of the residents' misperceptions. They did not include themselves in their statements of the problem. I wondered why they attributed the cause of their problem to an immediate or symptomatic manifestation and not to an underlying or systemic cause. Why did they embed the cause in the solution? Why did they so actively instruct us how to solve their problem, when *they* had asked *us* for expert assistance? Why did they expect us to act passively by accepting their instructions on how we were to arrive at an efficacious solution?

These introductory encounters revealed some of the surgeons' perceptions of problems. It particularly revealed their proclivity for attributing immediate, concrete causes together with solutions that could be solved by active intervention. The surgeons' discourse was filled with action: They used the active tense with active words: "do," "solve," "fix," "teach" — transitive verbs which had direct objects: "problems," "diseases," "residents," "patients." They rarely used passive words. They gave instructions to us, even though we were the consultants whom they had engaged to assist them: "Tell them ...," "Look at ...," "Let them know ...," "Explain to them ...," or "Make them understand.... " The surgeons transformed us from active consultants who could inform them into passive and uncritical recipients who would comply with their instructions for intervention.

These first encounters persuaded me to examine their penchant for action, a major theme throughout this book, most explicitly in Chapter 2, "The Surgeon as Hero," and Chapter 7, "How Surgeons Make Decisions: Influence of the Active Posture on Decision Making." The initial discourses with the surgeons suggested that in spite of the fact that the residents were those who were distressed and had initially defined the problem, the surgeons' attention was on their own distress. It did not appear that these surgeons included the residents' concerns, perceptions, problems, or demands in their understanding of the problem. They instructed us, the consultants, to find solutions to their problem, not to that of the residents.

One of the images that I held of surgeons before I began the study was that they routinely were immersed in the drama and heroism depicted in American television programs, such as *ER, Chicago Hope, M*A*S*H, Shock Trauma, China Beach,* and *St. Elsewhere.* Surgeons are portrayed in these programs as continuously engaging in dramatic, life-and-death decisions, much of which take place in the operating room. These images reinforce the public's perceptions of surgeons as heroes whose everyday life is filled with formidable death-defying challenges.

Many of the surgeons in Meadowbrook University Hospital also held this image of themselves. The operating room was the central dramatic focus in their lives. They stated that they preferred to spend their time in the operating room. However, I quickly discovered that this image did not represent the actuality of the daily lives of any of the surgeons in Meadowbrook. The surgeons at Meadowbrook were typical of North American surgeons (except trauma surgeons) in that their daily lives were repetitive, mundane, and relatively thankless. To be sure, they dealt in disease, human lives, death, and the intrusive process of operating. But, day after day, week after week, most of their activities were routine and relatively uneventful. They only spent about one-fourth to one-fifth of their working time in the operating room, about fifteen hours in their sixty- to seventy-hour work week

(Fonealsoud 1972:760; Folse et al. 1980). Even the greater drama of operating was, for the most part, quite predictable, standardized, repetitive and, ultimately, ordinary.

BEGINNING UNDERSTANDING

In attempting to understand the surgeons and their culture, their responses to me and my personal reactions to them played as important a role as my observations and documentation of their behaviors with their patients and colleagues. These responses helped reveal their perceptions about male surgeons, non-physicians, and females.

For example, Dr. Jennifer initially introduced me to his colleagues saying, "Look, I've got a *girl* following me around all the time, taking down everything I say." When they introduced me to patients, they told them I was a nurse, addressed as Miss, not Doctor, even though I had asked them (for my own professional ethical reasons) to let patients know that I was a medical school consultant/researcher. They did not appear to regard me as a critical observer who was actively examining, studying, and interpreting their culture, and helping them solve their problems (male characteristics as they saw them). Instead they reversed the reality of my relationship with them and transformed me into an uncritical, passive non-interpretive recorder of their world (female characteristics as they saw them).

My understanding of their culture was facilitated by noting my perceptions and emotional responses during the initial and subsequent encounters with the surgeons. For example, when I wore a white surgeon's coat or green operating room costume surgeons, patients, and other medical staff behaved differently toward me than when I had no identifying costume. Observing my responses helped me understand many aspects of surgeons' roles. These include surgeons' responses to patients' awe and expectations and their way of communicating with patients. These perspectives are particularly discussed in Chapter 2, "The Surgeon as Hero," and Chapter 6, "Communication with Patients."

Initially each surgeon appeared to behave toward me with some condescension and mild distrust. This was combined with curiosity, amusement, and considerable pleasure at being followed and having their every move and statement recorded. These responses initially allowed them to take me and my observations lightly —

which was advantageous for me because they may not have revealed so much if they had taken me more seriously.[3]

However, their curiosity led them to ask me periodically what I was writing and thinking. At first I answered these questions literally, showing them some notes I was taking. Subsequently I realized that by asking me about my writing and thinking they were not requesting substantive information, nor were they interested in my work. Instead they were asking me for some kind of validation and appreciation of them. By asking me what I was doing, they really wanted to know how *they* were doing. Accordingly, I began to answer them with some form of genuine affirmation, such as, "I am impressed with....[the hours you put in; your skill in that operation; the knowledge you have]" or with queries, such as, "I was wondering what you were thinking when...," or "I didn't understand why you did that."

The surgeons' apparent need for affirmation suggested not only that they needed positive feedback, but also that they probably did not receive such affirmation from their colleagues. Cassell quotes a surgeon in her study who said: "A guy who becomes a surgeon rather than an internist is a guy who needs a lot of positive feedback" (1987:7:233). This information facilitated understanding a number of the characteristics of surgeons' traits and behavior, such as their dependency on being active, their heroic posture and its burdens, their isolation, their competition with their colleagues, and their reluctance to admit doubts, uncertainty, and mistakes. It suggested a number of ways in which their culture did not appear to support them adequately.

It became apparent that these surgeons obtained positive feedback from three sources. The first was the performance in front of others of tasks that were risky and dramatic and had significant life-death consequences for patients. Surgeons perform in an "operating theater," which produces immediate and noticeable results. There is always risk when a surgeon operates. Some surgeons' zest for difficult and experimental procedures suggests that the risk enhances their gratification.[4]

The second source of positive feedback was the surgical mystique — a component of the surgeons' culture that convinces non-members of that culture that they should be in awe of the members. The surgical mystique conveys to patients and other non-surgeons that surgeons have special talents that others cannot comprehend and that these talents can work miraculous cures. Beneficiaries of these cures as well as others who revere the surgeons' mystique are the principal sources of praise for surgeons. A corollary of this process is that the behavior of many surgeons serves to protect the surgical mystique by not systematically sharing their knowledge with others. This is discussed in Chapter 5, "Communication with Colleagues" and Chapter 6, "Communication with Patients."

Third, surgeons derived gratification from the process of renewing their ranks. Surgeons themselves are usually not a dependable source of positive feedback for each other. Competition and pride deter them from directly praising their colleagues (although they praise great surgeons of the past in exaggerated fashion) or from acknowledging to their colleagues that they learned from them. Members of each generation of surgeons recruit people who initially resemble them and can be further molded into their image. People who accept initiation into the surgeons' culture are not those who easily give praise or deference. But interns and residents learned quickly to behave deferentially toward the senior surgeons. In the apprenticeship process surgeons-to-be learn by example how to behave toward others so that they get praise from patients and other medical professionals (cf., Brieger 1986).

I did not enter the world of surgeons culture-free. It was easier for me to identify with the patients than with the surgeons. I was initially highly critical of the apparent disregard which the surgeons showed for the concerns of their patients. They referred to suffering, frightened patients as "the breast," "the colon," "that messy, end-stage cardiac failure." However, after a few weeks in which I had seen about a hundred patients I was equally horrified to discover that I too had begun to recognize patients post-operatively by their operative sites, even though I had seen many of these patients several times in the surgeon's office before the operation. By observing the process by which I came to depersonalize the patients, I began to understand some of the cultural mechanisms by which the surgeons protected themselves against the experience of empathizing with the personal anguish of patients.

During the first operation which I observed, a mastectomy, the patient's head was obscured from the surgeon's view while he was operating on her breast. When Mrs. Laue had initially visited Dr. Jennifer, I had identified strongly with her and her fears when she learned not only that she had cancer but also that her breast might have to be removed.[5] During that operation I was startled at seeing her breast without skin, without personal meaning, without erotic or maternal context, and whose removal was so straightforwardly mechanical and routine. Several times I moved first past the curtain toward the anesthesiologist where Mrs. Laue's face was in view and her female personhood for me was revealed. Then I moved back to the other side of the curtain and was horrified to see her personless body, apparently destructively invaded, becoming hideously asymmetrical before my eyes. (In operations that do not involve the head a curtain separates the anesthesiologist's area from that of the surgeon so that the head is not easily visible to the surgeon.)

I later asked Dr. Jennifer if he thought of Mrs. Laue's face or personality even once during the operation. He replied that such thinking at that time would have interfered with the neat, clean breast job he had just completed. Through this process of "feeling-thinking," which Wikan (1991) describes as using emotion and thought to comprehend the quality of lived experience, I learned about the adaptive value of the surgeons' separation of feeling and identification with the patient from that of the operative tasks at hand. I better understood the distancing functions of the surgeons' gallows' humor, their use of objective, active language, and their rituals. I learned that the time, space, and ritual structure of the surgeons' work supported their detachment from patients' suffering. I understood surgeons' preference for patients who were under general (as opposed to local) anesthesia, when it was easier for them to ignore patients' personhood and fears.

Noting my emotional responses at that first operation increased my understanding of the nature and meaning of operations to surgeons, nurses, and patients. I experienced awe and excitement as I observed technologically and scientifically advanced operations. At the same time I observed the surgical staff in the operating room, with their restricted entrance, their costumes, and the tense, almost sanctified atmosphere. The timing, cadence, standardization, and predictability of the staff's movements appeared to be rituals which protected them from unpleasant feelings, such as fear, disgust, anger, and victimization, as well as from eroticism and voyeurism. In Chapter 3, "Are Surgeons Scientists?" and Chapter 10, "Operating Room Rituals," concepts of science and ritual are used to explain how these rituals were necessary to provide the surgeons and nurses with increased autonomy of thought and action.

Observing how the surgeons applied some of their expectations, feelings, and perceptions of people and situations from their past onto me facilitated my understanding the surgeons' culture. For example, in their initial responses to me they appeared to transfer their attitudes from their past and their culture about non-physicians and females onto me.[6]

I was also surprised when in the course of the study on those occasions in which I was absent for a day or a part of a day, each of the surgeons invariably stated to me that I was missed. Their response surprised me, because I felt that the communication of information was one-way: they were sharing their world with me, and I was mostly silent. But their responses suggested that they attributed significance and support to a non-judgmental observer who listened and recorded attentively, rarely spoke, and who was present throughout their working day. Even though I said little, they attributed to me characteristics of understanding, approval, and a measure of companionship. These responses led me to understand the lack of affirmation they obtained from their colleagues and their isolation from, and inadequacy of communication with, others, especially their colleagues. This response, which also revealed the loneliness of the hero and the salience of their wish to be understood, is discussed in Chapter 2, "The Surgeon as Hero," and Chapter 5, "Communication with Colleagues."

Similarly I tried to recognize and interpret my feelings during the field work for the purposes of understanding the surgeons and their culture (cf., Devereux 1967; B. Good and M. Good 1991:194–196; Herdt and Stoller 1990:6; 372–379; P. Katz 1984). For example, I used my feelings in my initial contact with the surgeons to help me understand how easily a lay person can come to be overawed in the presence of a surgeon enacting his powerful role. This understanding suggested ways in which unequal distributions of power, exacerbated by patients' fears of illness and surgery, may function in transactions between surgeons and surgical patients.

Most difficult was examining those feelings that seemed to prevent me from understanding the surgeons. For example, when I recognized my own envy of the surgeons' power, I began to understand how such beliefs could facilitate interpreting their activities as simply exploiting weak patients. I was forced, thereby, to critically examine the "politically correct" diatribes against physicians' power and influence prevalent in the popular mass media and in many social science analyses.[7] This understanding obligated me to analyze the multiplicity of cultural influences on both surgeons' and patients' behavior with each other.

The surgeons I studied frequently asked me for information about other surgeons, particularly about their schedules and operative procedures. Many of their questions about others were subtly phrased to obscure the questioners' intent. Such questions suggested that the culture of surgeons contained significant barriers which prevented them from sharing information with other surgeons. They further suggested that they did not feel comfortable asking their colleagues about themselves and their activities, and that they were uneasy about my knowing how much they wanted the information.

Asking those questions of me was also the surgeons' way of determining my reliability, understanding, and trustworthiness. It was clear that their trust of me was dependent upon how I behaved in response to these and other questions — how well I passed their scrutiny. When they asked me questions about another surgeon that I had studied, I quietly reminded them that I did not convey information about others, regardless of its importance. Then I usually asked the surgeon why he did not know that information and by what other means he could obtain it. I learned more about the barriers to their communication from their questions to me about other surgeons and from their replies to my subsequent questions.

For example, their questions about other surgeons revealed how secretive and isolated they were from their colleagues, whom they regarded as both friends and competitors. They also revealed how anxious, curious, and competitive they were about their colleagues. Their responses, described in Chapter 5, "Communication with Colleagues," also elucidated the ways in which they used residents and operating room nurses for obtaining information about other surgeons.

Meadowbrook University Hospital

Meadowbrook University Hospital is located in a large city in Canada, Meadowbrook City. The hospital has 800 beds, 120 of which were for surgical patients. At the time of the study the surgeons at Meadowbrook University Hospital performed 15,000 operative procedures per year, the majority of which were inpatient procedures.[8] Meadowbrook University Hospital is one of seven teaching hospitals which are affiliated with Meadowbrook University School of Medicine. It had a reputation in Canada among professional and lay people in the Province for providing quality care. Although it had a reputation among surgeons and residents for a good surgery department and a good residency program, it was neither the most nor the least prestigious of the teaching hospitals in Meadowbrook City.

Thirteen years before this study began the hospital affiliated with Meadowbrook University School of Medicine, after having been a community hospital for 58 years. This change from a community hospital to a university hospital entailed adapting to different hospital "cultures."   The culture of a community hospital differs from that of a university (teaching) hospital in the orientation, practices, and training of its medical staff (cf., Cassell 1987:246; Inglehart 1993). The culture of a hospital influenced the behavior and attitudes of the physicians within. The academic culture of a university hospital fostered inquiry, learning, teaching, and questioning. It emphasized the scientific identity of surgeons, and it sometimes influenced the kinds of patients it selected and the kinds of diseases that were treated. It led to proliferation of surgical specialties on its staff and to training programs in these specialties

Community hospitals, on the other hand, were primarily oriented toward service. Treatment was their first priority. Teaching and research were virtually ignored. Fewer surgeons practicing in community hospitals were likely to be Board-certified or to be trained as surgical specialists than in teaching hospitals. Few surgeons who identified themselves as scientists were attracted to community hospitals. Community hospitals fostered surgeons solely as clinicians, not as scientists, academics, or researchers.

For the full-time medical-surgical staff at Meadowbrook the transition 13 years before to a university hospital meant that those who had been trained in an exclusively service-oriented culture were suddenly expected to participate in a university culture and to behave as scientists. Virtually overnight the surgeons were required to teach medical students and surgical residents and to participate in research, in addition to continuing their own surgical practices. Few models of experienced academic surgeons had been available for them to emulate. They had neither the training, skills, nor first-hand experience, for participating in the new university culture.

The Surgeons at Meadowbrook University Hospital

When Meadowbrook Hospital changed to a university hospital all of the physicians who were not Board-certified in their specialties left (approximately half of the medical-surgical staff), and new Board-certified physicians were hired in their places.[9] In the Department of Surgery six surgeons who were not Board-certified left Meadowbrook. Four new Board-certified surgeons were hired immediately, and two more surgeons were hired in the following five years, including Dr. White. Dr. White was first hired as a staff surgeon and then became the Chief. The change resulted in a surgical staff of whom only one-quarter (i.e., some of the new hires) had first-hand experience in academic surgery. However, the most drastic change was that the 10 Board-certified surgeons who remained became university physicians and faculty members overnight.

Many aspects of Meadowbrook's community hospital culture remained after the transition. Most of the surgeons retained much of the old patient-care, non-research, non-teaching beliefs, attitudes, and ideas at the same time that they were obliged to assume the roles of university surgeons. They taught surgical residents and medical students, although they were not trained to teach. They were under increased pressure to keep up with the literature and innovations in their field and to recruit additional Board-certified surgical specialists. They were encouraged to participate in research, although they were not trained to conduct research.

The culture of a hospital can significantly affect surgical outcomes for patients, including mortality and morbidity rates and lengths of stay. Hospital structure, particularly medical staff organization, has been shown to be the major factor influencing the postsurgical mortality rates. Low mortality rates were associated with high volumes of particular surgical procedures, rates of Board certification of its physicians, and with the hospital's medical school affiliation (Flood and Scott 1987; Kelly and Hellinger 1986). Additionally, surgeons who performed larger volumes of particular operations had lower post-operative infection rates, lower mortality rates, and shorter lengths of stay than those who performed fewer of those operations (Arndt et al. 1995; Hannan et al. 1989; Lau et al. 1988).

At the time of the study Meadowbrook University Hospital had 17 surgeons on its full-time staff — all male and seventy-one surgeons on its part-time staff — two of whom were female. Of the 17 full-time surgeons, six were general surgeons, three were orthopedic surgeons, two were thoracic surgeons, two were neurosurgeons, two were cardiac surgeons, and two were urological surgeons. This kind of multi-specialty surgery department can be found in most hospitals in the last several decades. No pediatric surgery or transplant surgery had been performed at Meadowbrook University Hospital at the time of the study.

The history of specialty surgery depicts competitive battles between specialists and general surgeons. Whereas general surgeons used to operate on most parts of the body, the increase in specialties in the last decades has drastically restricted their domain. As surgical specialties developed, surgeons competed for surgical control of specific parts of the body. However, in the words of Dr. Jennifer, a general surgeon, "The gynecologists took away everything except the breasts, and the urologists took away everything but the hernias."

Additionally, there were 15 surgical residents in their second to fifth year and four surgical interns who were in their first year after medical school (called "clerks" [pronounced "clarks"], in Canada). The interns and residents remained on the surgical service for at least one year. There was a revolving contingent of third and fourth year medical students who spent three to six weeks in the Department as part of their surgical rotation.

Because the majority of surgical teaching takes place in the course of carrying out daily surgical tasks, surgeons spent from 40 to 80 percent of their total time teaching residents. Most of their "teaching" time was coterminous with other activities, such as operating, conducting patient Rounds, and examining patients in their offices. Transmission of surgical knowledge and surgical culture occurs both explicitly and implicitly. Surgical residents learn largely by assisting and accompanying senior surgeons. Only a small minority of surgical teaching takes place in formal situations, such as Grand Rounds or lectures in lecture halls to medical students. Students also learn about the culture of surgery through informal banter of surgeons in the cafeteria, the hallways, and the surgeons' lounge.

Surgical residents as well as medical students actively assisted the senior surgeons in their work, as part of their educational experiences. The chief resident, a fifth-year resident, typically assisted in 400–500 cases over a period of six months. Most of these operations were small. Assistant residents, in their second, third and fourth year of residencies, typically assisted in 100 to 200 operations during six months, most of which were small.

CONCLUSION

In the course of the field work with the surgeons, I studied six senior surgeons intensively, including the chairman of the Department of Surgery, the chiefs of two of the subspecialty departments, and the director of the surgery residency programs. All six men were among the most senior members of the Department. Together they represented three surgical specialties: Four of the six, Drs. White, Jennifer, Nordberg, and Roddy, were general surgeons. One, Dr. Robinson, was a thoracic surgeon, and one, Dr. Turunen, was a urological surgeon. With each of these six surgeons I spent approximately three continuous weeks, beginning when they came in the morning (approximately 6:30 to 7:00 A.M.) and ending when they left in the evening (approximately 7:00 P.M.).

All of the surgeons were men. All but one of the surgeons were married; Dr. White was divorced. Dr. Ofir and Dr. Nordberg were in their fifties — older than the other four who were in their forties. Only Dr. Robinson was over six feet tall; the shortest surgeon was Dr. Jennifer at five feet, eight inches. They all appeared to be vigorous and in good health. None of the surgeons, however, resembled superhuman mythic heroes.

In addition to studying each of these six senior surgeons systematically, intensely, and consistently over three continuous weeks, I studied three surgeons, Drs. McCullars, Michael, and Aranow, and four surgical residents (including the chief resident) less systematically and consistently (e.g., three full days to two weeks). I conducted several hours of interviews each with an additional three surgeons, five nurses, and two receptionists, as well as shorter interviews with four other physicians in the hospital, two hospital administrators, and six patients.

I attended numerous formal and informal meetings. The formal ones included departmental meetings, administrative meetings in both the hospital's Department of Surgery and in the university's Department of Surgery (which included other hospital departments), Grand Rounds, Mortality Rounds, residents' meetings, and journal club,. Occasional non-work situations, such as dinner in my home or a surgeon's home and parties in surgeons' homes, provided additional opportunities for studying the surgeons.

I had been warned by friends and colleagues that I would have difficulty getting accurate information on what surgeons did. They feared that the surgeons would drastically limit my access to information and that they would not really "talk" to me. They explained that the surgeons were suspicious of outsiders, worried about being accused of malpractice, and would attempt to obfuscate information and overawe a non-physician, particularly a woman.

However, after the first two weeks with the surgeons, after testing my reliability and getting used to my continuous presence, virtually all barriers to communication ended. Their trust of me was extraordinary. Some of that trust was due to their underestimation of my capacity to understand them. Some was due to the fact that Canadian physicians were not as malpractice-oriented as those in the United States (cf., Estey 1978); Canadian physicians are only one-fifth as likely to be sued for malpractice as U.S. physicians [Coyte et al. 1991]).[10] Some of their trust was due to their desire to be understood and less isolated. However, most of their trust was due to their generous good will. I was also fortunate to be able to take notes openly, and thereby, record their speech verbatim and describe other events as they occurred.[11]

The surgeons trusted me not to harm them when I published my data. Their trust initially resulted in my refraining from writing anything about them until my colleagues, Joan Cassell and Atwood Gaines, suggested that I effectively obscure the identities of the city, hospital, and surgeons. I hope that the surgeons' generosity and my response will contribute to the understanding and appreciation of these fascinating, highly skilled, accomplished people.

NOTES

1. All names and identifying features of the city, hospitals, surgeons, other physicians, and patients are disguised.

2. Cassell too wrote of her responses when surgeons "talked down to me — which many surgeons tended to do to non-surgeons" (1991:xxiv).

3. It was likely to have been an advantage to be a women and a non-physician in this context, because they did not act competitively towards me.

4. A general physician who had practiced some surgery during his internship recalled, "Surgery is like a narcotic! You feel a rush of pleasure!"

5. At the time of the study mastectomy was the most probable option for surgical treatment of breast cancer.

6. The application of the psychiatric concepts of "transference" and "counter-transference" to ethnographic field work was introduced by Devereux (1967).

7. See Appendix A for a discussion of "critical medical anthropology."

8. Many procedures that had been performed as inpatient procedures in the past are increasingly being performed as outpatient procedures (Rogers and Seward 1996:52).

9. The United States and Canada confer certification by the American Board of Medical Specialties for medical specialists, such as general surgeons and specialty surgeons. To receive Board certification surgeons must pass rigorous examinations in their specialties, in addition to fulfilling the residency requirements in their specialties. The following are surgical specialities which offer Board certification after training and examinations: cardiothoracic surgery; colon and rectal surgery; gynecology and obstetrics; neurological surgery; ophthalmic surgery; orthopaedic surgery; otorhinolaryngology; pediatric surgery; plastic and maxillofacial surgery; [general] surgery; urology; vascular surgery. There are also specialties in surgery for which there is no Board certification after training and examinations.

10. Coyte et al. claimed that the malpractice rate in Canada was significantly lower than in the U.S. because of: Canada's universal health coverage, social welfare, limited use of contingent fees, having the losing party bear litigation costs, effectiveness of the Canadian Medical Protective Association (CMPA), and less litigious culture (1991).

11. I was very fortunate to have such access to the surgeons' candid behavior and talk and to be able to take notes as events occurred. As a contrast, Cassell wrote of the long months of time and effort to gain acceptance: "It was months before any of the senior surgeons I wanted to study took public notice of my presence or said a word to me" (1991:223). Both Bosk and Cassell recorded virtually all of their notes daily after leaving the field work scene (Bosk 1979 and Cassell 1991). Cassell wrote that taking field notes made subjects "nervous and self-conscious" (1991:224).

Chapter 2

THE SURGEON AS HERO

~

I wasn't God by a long shot, but as far as power was concerned, I was closer to Him than anyone else at hand.

(Nolen 1968:272)

There is no time to think. There is only time to do or let die.

(Haggard 1935:8)

INTRODUCTION

Most people in Western industrialized countries carry a stereotyped image of a surgeon. This image usually includes an action-oriented male hero who single-handedly performs death-defying feats, acts with certainty, eschews doubts, and maintains an even-tempered optimism. Parsons suggested that surgeons who are usually active, pragmatically oriented, who take decisive action to save lives embody the symbols of heroism in American society (1951). Not only does the lay public hold this image, but also other medical professionals, including surgeons themselves, have this image (See M. Good 1995:67).

The image of surgeons as active heroes originated in the early history of the surgical profession. It is related to the perilous conditions of surgery in the past,

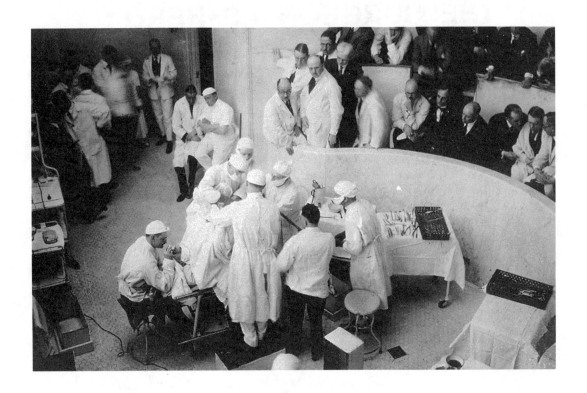

Courtesy, Johns Hopkins Medicine.

to the traditional relationships of surgeons to physicians, and to saving lives in spite of the hazardous hygienic conditions of past times. Although contemporary conditions differ from earlier ones, the present practice of surgery and the demeanor and training of surgeons have many similarities to those of the past. This chapter discusses how the image of the surgeon as an active hero evolved historically and how this image has been perpetuated in contemporary times.

Surgeons express many facets of their heroic and active image in their everyday practice. This image is as much a part of surgical culture as their technical knowledge and operating skills. This image is not, however, explicitly taught as most surgical skills are taught. Instead it is communicated implicitly in informal contexts — in the small talk and banter in the halls, cafeteria, elevators, lounges; in wise-cracking in the operating room; and through surgeons' folklore about patients and other physicians. They reveal their proclivity for action in their use of language which not only prefers using active words and active tense, but also refers to battles and wars, strength and masculinity, while denigrating weakness, passivity, and femininity. Surgeons' jokes are permeated with themes which glorify themselves as decisive, powerful, and "masculine." Their jokes mocked the less interventionist internists as indecisive, weak, and "feminine."

RISING AGAINST ODDS FROM HUMBLE ORIGINS

Until the late nineteenth century surgeons had been accorded a much lower status than that of physicians. That difference in status continues to be reflected in some aspects of contemporary surgical culture. The low esteem accorded surgeons since very early times can be illustrated by a passage from William of Salicet's *Chirurgia*, in 1275, "A wise surgeon will refrain from stealing whilst he is actually in attendance upon a patient" (quoted in Power 1933:16).

Medicine and surgery had been separate professions since the second century A.D., and they comprised two separate healing cultures.[1] They differed from each other in social organization, their relationship to academic learning, and in the social origins and education of their practitioners.

From the early Middle Ages until the eighteenth century surgeons constituted a distinctive profession with a much lower social class than that of physicians. Surgeons were either called barbers or were considered to be in the same lower social class as barbers.[2] Surgeons did not attend universities and, therefore, did not study anatomy. The great universities gave no special degree in surgery.

In contrast, medicine from the eleventh and twelfth centuries was practiced by physicians who were gentlemen from the higher social classes. Medicine was studied in one of the basic university faculties, whereas surgery was learned entirely by apprenticeship. The license of a surgeon allowed him to operate "so long as he does not practice medicine" (Power 1933:22-23).

Surgeons' distinction from physicians, barbers, and itinerant quacks was most manifest in their respective characteristic activities. For example, in the sixteenth century surgeons, who still did not study anatomy or attend university,[3] sutured wounds, reduced dislocations, treated fractures, and amputated when necessary. Barbers shaved, loused, drew teeth, and let blood. Itinerant quacks, who were neither barbers nor surgeons, cured hernias, excised stones (lithotomy), and undertook operations which were liable to end in disaster.

By the seventeenth century those operations which had been done by quacks, such as excision of stones (lithotomy), operations of the eye, and hernias, began to be done by surgeons. Surgeons in North America in the seventeenth and eighteenth centuries were restricted to setting fractures and dislocations, treating superficial ulcers and abscesses, debriding wounds, and for such emergencies as amputation of limbs.

The seventeenth century status of surgeons was depicted by William Harvey in his diary:

> *What, after all, is a barber-surgeon? A man who is sufficiently dexterous to wield the razor when he cuts a beard or opens an abscess. A person who is skillful with his hands, no more. A performer. As soon as the act extends to the inner organs...instructions and control can come only from the physician.* (Harvey 1647, In: Hamburger 1992:73)

Harvey further described barber-surgeons in his diary: "Almost all were former barbers, who for many years had known no more than how to shave a beard and cut hair. They had then become so bold as to use their razors to open an abscess. They had learnt to bandage a wound or use a cautery; a few had some slight knowledge of how to reduce a dislocated bone. But none of this manipulation made them competent to recognise diseases or prescribe their remedies" (Harvey 1647, in: Hamburger 1992:78).

The distinction between the roles of surgeons and physicians and their competition for power continued through the eighteenth century in both Europe and North America.

Some surgeons in attempting to distinguish themselves from barber-surgeons sought to raise the level of their educational and professional competence by developing their own organizational system with a specific course of study, oaths, and distinctive dress. They instituted a system which included systematic teaching of anatomy and pathology, examination for surgical licenses, and specific roles for provosts, masters, licentiates, bachelors, and apprentices. In this system surgeons were permitted to wear a long gown, which imitated academic dress. Known as the "gentlemen of the long robe," they contrasted with the "gentlemen of the short robe," the barber surgeons (Power 1933:23). That distinction between surgeons and other physicians which began in the second century A.D. is still reflected symbolically in contemporary Britain where surgeons are addressed as "Mister" instead of "Doctor"[4] (Eibel 1988).

By the mid-eighteenth century when surgeons formed a new organization that was separate from the barber-surgeons, they established that criteria for membership would be obtained either through a seven-year apprenticeship with a senior surgeon or through experience in serving as a surgeon in the army or navy. Even when the House of Commons passed the bill authorizing the Company of Surgeons, one member is reputed to have said, "There is no more science in surgery than in butchering" (Halsted 1904:74).

By the early nineteenth century, however, surgeons routinely operated on impending blindness, bladder stones that were incapacitatingly painful, hernias, and occasional superficial tumors. They sometimes removed small organs, such as the thyroid gland. Even though by the early nineteenth century many instruments and techniques were available for complex and invasive operations, surgery rarely invaded the deep body cavities because of the dangers of shock and fatal infections and because of the pain which the conscious patient experienced (C. Rosenberg 1987:25-28).

Unlike physicians who learned medicine through a course of formal study in universities, surgeons learned their profession entirely by doing surgery or by watching and assisting another surgeon who was practicing surgery. Until the late nineteenth century a surgeon learned by becoming an apprentice to a master-surgeon who was often a relative. He had the possibility of becoming a master-surgeon when his own master died or retired. In England, for example, even by the mid-nineteenth century a vacancy on the surgical staff in the older hospitals was usually filled by a favored apprentice of a retiring member — who was frequently a relative. Surgeons were virtually unpaid until 1948, because only the sick poor went to hospitals (Cartwright 1968:9-ll). Many surgeons and those barbers who did not become surgeons became specialists as cutters for stones, herniotomists, amputators, bone-setters, wound surgeons, cataract removers, and blood-letters.

The image of the uneducated, unrefined surgeon persisted in Europe and in America until the early nineteenth century.[5] In the early nineteenth century in the era before anesthesia the men who practiced surgery were, according to Cartwright: "of little culture or refinement. Sometimes they were quite uncouth, rude, and rough with their patients to the point of brutality" (1968:20). Halsted wrote that "The *maculalevis notae* [suggestion of disrepute] clung to surgeons the world over until the beginning of the nineteenth century" (1904:69).

The prestige of the surgeon, however, rose from the middle of the nineteenth century and remains high today. In late Victorian and Edwardian England surgeons became national heroes (Lawrence 1992:2). In contemporary North America surgeons' prestige has surpassed that of physicians. As the results of surgery became more apparent after antisepsis reduced infection and therefore mortality, and anaesthesia relieved pain, the prestige of surgery and surgeons rose precipitously (Brieger 1972:163). In 1905 Dennis, a surgeon, viewed the progress of surgery and surgeons as analogous to the progress of nineteenth century America and its heroes:

> *There is no science that calls for greater fearlessness, courage, and nerve than that of surgery, none that demands more of self-reliance, principle, independence and the determination in the man.   These were the characteristics which were chiefly conspicuous in the early settlers of this country. And it is these old-time Puritan qualities, which ..., have passed into surgeons of America, giving them boldness in their art, and enabling them to win that success in surgery, which now commands the admiration of the civilized world* (1905:84).

SURGEONS AS COURAGEOUS, RISK-TAKING, DECISIVE INDIVIDUALISTS

The heroic qualities of courage, risk, and daring, and decisive action were essential attributes of surgeons' roles. Throughout most of surgical history performance of any operation was risky. For example, in Babylonian times the Code of Hammurabi stipulated both the rewards and risk and dangers for the surgeon who attempted to preserve a patient's eyesight: If the patient's sight were preserved, the surgeon received an enormous monetary reward. However, if the patient's sight were destroyed, the surgeon's hands were to be cut off.

Surgeons performed activities in which the patient was very likely to undergo hemorrhage, intense pain, infection, shock, and a high probability of death. The virtue of courage, often described in the form of surgeons being impervious to patients' sufferings, combined with the special surgical skills to save the patient's life was extolled by surgeons and historians of surgery alike. For example, in the first century Celsus wrote in *De Medicina* about the courageous qualities of a surgeon: "[A surgeon should have] a spirit undaunted; filled with pity, so that he wishes to cure his patient, yet is not moved by his cries to go too fast, or cut less than is necessary; but he does everything just as if the cries of pain cause him no emotion" (Book VII, quoted in Brieger 1986:2). It took a particular kind of decisiveness and daring to operate when pain relief was minimal, and the probability of mortality from shock and infections was high. Nevertheless, many surgeons were affected by the pain. Many were physically sick before or after an operation.

Before the general use of anesthesia in mid-nineteenth century pain was considered to be an integral part of surgery. To be a surgeon it was psychologically necessary to shield oneself from identifying too powerfully with the suffering of patients. For example, the biography of the surgeon, Sir Charles Bell, emphasized his demeanor during his service in the Battle of Waterloo:

> *While I amputated one man's thigh .... It was a strange thing to feel my clothes stiff with blood.... It was ... more extraordinary still, to find my mind calm amidst such a variety of suffering. But to give one of these objects access to your feelings was to allow yourself to be unmanned for the performance of a duty. It was less painful to look upon the whole than to contemplate one* (In Pichot 1860:81).

The patients' suffering put a premium on surgeons' boldness, speed, deftness, and decisiveness in operating. A speedy operation also reduced the possibility of shock for the patient. In the thirteenth century Henri de Mondeville wrote that a "surgeon ought to be fairly bold" (Power 1933).

Surgeons also had to be able to act decisively, without doubts. The quality of certainty was characteristic of surgeons. Brieger wrote: "For the most part, surgeons and their art were exempted from the doubts and criticisms applied to their nonoperating colleagues" (1972:163). A popular anecdote states: "A surgeon is sometimes right, sometimes wrong, but never uncertain."

In the mid-nineteenth century America surgery was a minor aspect of the procedures of hospitals, even though anesthesia had been invented. Most of the surgical admissions were for minor wounds and lacerations, fractures, hernias, or persistent skin lesions (C. Rosenberg 1987:144). Similarly, in nineteenth century England surgical admissions were few. A large teaching hospital would have fewer than 200 operations a year, and only one day a week was an operating day (Cartwright 1968:12).

By the mid-nineteenth century, surgeons were still judged by the numbers and magnitude of the operations they performed, despite the grim and hazardous obstacles that existed in performing any surgery, particularly major surgery (Bigelow 1850, cited in Brieger 1986:6). For example, Robert Liston, who had performed the first operation under ether in England in 1846, had been known to chase an unwilling patient down the hospital corridors (Richardson 1964:13). Because of the value placed on the number of operations, surgeons rarely reported their failures (cf., Brieger 1987:1182). Surgeons' reputations, therefore, were based on anecdotal case reporting. Success-failure ratios were not reported.

By the last half of the nineteenth century surgeons treated a much wider range of injuries and diseases as a result of increased knowledge of antiseptic procedures and increased vigilance in applying them. The use of general anesthesia, begun in 1846, drastically altered the conditions under which surgery could be performed. Patients no longer suffered from unbearable pain. Yet, the other conditions — shock, infection and hemorrhage — remained. By the late nineteenth and early twentieth century pathology was not yet a science, and transfusions were dangerous. But surgeons, nevertheless, remained cautious in expanding their traditional repertoire and only infrequently performed major surgery.

Heroic Surgeons as Exaggerated Exemplars

According to scholars of American culture and its heroes (e.g., Hsu 1983; Klapp 1962; Parsons 1951; Williams 1963), heroic archetypes in North American culture include the following, all of which can be ascribed to the image of surgeons:

- Competitive winners who achieve high status by rising against odds from humble origins.

- Confident, optimistic, self-assertive, physically strong males who act courageously and decisively, often in dangerous situations.

- Independent, self-sufficient rugged individualists who act and stand alone.

- Splendid performers who shine in front of an audience.

The heroic image of surgeons was perpetuated by numerous writings through the centuries about surgeons and surgery. Typically writers, many of whom were surgeons themselves, used exaggerated, idealized language as they described surgeons as exemplary characters and even deities who were beyond reproach. Some of these writers wrote surgical textbooks in which they modestly and dispassionately described technical aspects of operations. However, when writing about the surgical profession these same writers switched to an exaggerated mode, frequently using the words, "progress," "perfection," "triumph," and "courage," Two examples follow: "In applied science nothing so beneficent has ever occurred, nothing surely of greater advantage to humanity, than the progress of surgery." (Moynihan 1928:38).

> *That there must be a final limit to development...our profession there can be no doubt.... Like every other art...it can only be carried to a certain definite point of excellence...it cannot be perfected beyond certain attainable limits...That we have nearly, if not quite, reached these final limits there can be little question.*
> (John Eric Erichsen 1873, quoted in Brieger 1986:10)

After the Napoleonic wars Alexis Boyer is supposed to have said that surgery had then reached almost, if not actually, the highest peak of perfection of which it was capable (Halsted 1904:70).

For Haggard, surgeons were virtually gods: "Surgery has a noble heritage. Its disciples are the intellectual descendants of all of the great minds who have glorified time. There has been an apostolic succession in surgery from the Father of Medicine to each Bishop in our Priesthood to the latest devotee who enters the sacred portals" (Haggard 1935:25). "Our art is illumined in the arsenals of history by an unbroken chain of inspired workers, captained by the occasional heaven-endowed genius, imbued with great purpose" (Haggard 1935:10-11).

Although some of the form of their writing can be attributed to a common literary style of the time, particularly the romantic language of Victorian histories, surgeons' preference for using superlatives, exaggerations, and unqualified descriptors in describing themselves and their abilities reflected their perceptions of themselves as unique heroes who are free of doubts, imperfections, and error.

The Surgeon as Performer

The heroic image of the surgeon is enhanced by the visible, performing nature of surgery. Surgery is drama and has often been referred to as a performance or a pageant. For example, Moynihan wrote, "In medicine the whole pageant is as noble and splendid as in any of the sciences or arts..." (1920a:44). Despite the solitary nature of their work, surgeons perform before an audience, even if their audience consists only of those who assist in the operation. Like the heroic soldier who triumphs on the battlefield, the surgeon's triumphs are highly visible. His actions are accessible to public scrutiny and admiration.

The operating theater provided an audience to view surgeons. The mere name of "theater" imparts the performance- and exhibition-like quality of a surgeon's work. Bigelow wrote in 1850:

> *Why is the amphitheater crowded to the roof,... on the occasion of some great operation, while the silent working of some well-directed drug excites comparatively little comment? Mark the hushed breath, the fearful intensity of silence, when the blade pierces the tissues, and the blood of the unhappy sufferer wells up to the surface.* (Bigelow, cited in Brieger 1972:164).

Most surgeons love the adulation of an audience. Schwarzbart wrote: "[a surgeon's] triumphs partake of every facet of adulation and applause so beloved of the performing artist on the stage" (1982:22). Richardson described: "...green-gowned students gathering in awe-inspired reverence round the master. In his hands he holds the balance between life and death; his skill and judgment are on trial" (Richardson 1968:3).

However much that surgeons loved to perform before an audience, by the late nineteenth century a trend toward conserving the body vied for surgical attention (Brieger 1992). Conserving limbs and organs and preserving the integrity of the body "moved away from the drama and theatricality of the operation itself to the drama of the results" (Brieger 1992:217).

The Surgeon as Masculine Hero

The active posture of surgeons embodies an exclusive masculine connotation. The surgical profession, including its priest and barber-surgeon predecessors, rarely included women until very recent times.[6] The exemplary characteristics used to describe surgeons were either explicitly stated as masculine or were implicitly understood within each historical period to be male characteristics.

An example of the explicit masculine characteristics contrasting with feminine ones is illustrated in the description of a good surgeon in the Middle Ages, as described by William Bulleyn of London in 1579. He wrote that the: "propertyes of a good Chirurgian [were that he] must be clenly, numble handed, sharpsighted, preganant witted, bolde spirited, ..., but not womanly affectionate to weepe or trimble when he seeth broken Bones, or blouddy Wounded" (quoted in Peterson 1972:xv).

The opposition of the heroic male to the sinful female is illustrated in the following passage: "When sepsis, the maternal analogue of sin, stalked up and down the haunts of men, the science of Pasteur and the art of Lister came as the Redeemer came. It was by absolute asepsis that surgery was exalted to a plane in unbroken continuity with morality and religion" (Haggard 1935:7).

The heroic image of surgeons as rescuers of females is implicit in the surgical image. For example, Haggard, a surgeon, wrote: "Surgery has given its greatest endeavors to woman....The victim of vesicovaginal fistula is no longer a prisoner in her own house. She is rescued from her wretchedness by the most delicate skill and the gentlest artisanship" (1935:10).

Although the most exaggerated characterizations of male heroic surgeons and female helpless patients were found in older writings, contemporary surgical culture has continued to perpetuate such images. For example, in 1985 Schumacker wrote in a leading surgical journal about the selection of a surgical chairman: "He should be a superman [and] have an attractive understanding wife who will help him achieve all his objectives..." (1985:291). In 1991 a senior female surgeon, Dr. Conley, resigned from a prestigious institution because of "gender insensitivity" (L'Hommedieu 1991:52). Her male surgical colleagues, Dr. Conley said, "cannot see me as a peer....They have to establish a relationship that makes me inferior to them.... where the man is supposed to be dominant and the woman subservient" (L'Hommedieu 1991:52-53).

All of the surgeons in Meadowbrook were male. They often told jokes which denigrated women and implicitly or explicitly elevated men, especially surgeons. They minimized the statuses or accomplishments of female colleagues. These surgeons at Meadowbrook University Hospital consistently referred to female medical colleagues, including those highly esteemed in their professions, as "girls."

Battle and war metaphors have permeated the culture of surgeons (as well as the culture of medicine) and have contributed to the image of surgeons as masculine heroes (cf., Martin 1994). Edmund Andrews, a nineteenth century surgeon wrote: "Among the particular traits which go to make up a manly character, one of the first, and one which is eminently necessary to a good surgeon, is courage" (quoted in Brieger 1972:178). Deaver and Reimann were more specific:

> *The modern surgeon...is like a general armed ...for the battle against insidious disease. Surrounded by an efficient and intelligent corps of uniformed assistants, nurses and orderlies...his is but to command and his orders are obeyed with military precision. But, like a general, he himself must bring to the operating-table a detailed knowledge of every strategic point not only within the limits of the immediate field of battle but of the surrounding area as well.* (Deaver and Reimann 1923:104; 112)

Similarly, an article entitled, "The Romantic Aspects of Being a Surgeon," ended with the statement that a surgeon is "above all else a soldier. For this healer greets every day as a day of battle" (Schwarzbart 1982:22). When surgeons, or those who write about surgeons, use war metaphors they always refer to the heroic aspects of war. They never depict themselves as helpless, wounded, or defeated victims of war.

Like their predecessors, the surgeons of Meadowbrook University Hospital referred to their activities as "battles," "conquests," "victories," and "triumphs." They spoke of their surgical armamentarium as "weapons" and "defenses." They made "strategic offensive plans" and executed "rescue missions." They referred to themselves as "warriors" and "heroes" on the "battlefield" who deserve "medals" for "courage."

Wars have played an important role in the history of surgery and have been integrally connected with the ancient and contemporary cultures of surgeons. Furnishing unparalleled training for surgeons from earliest recorded history, wars provided access to a great assortment of wounds as well as opportunities to study anatomy and to experiment with treatments and healing techniques.

Before the eighteenth century and especially during the Middle Ages military service was essential for any man wanting to practice surgery. Prospective surgeons were expected to go to war to treat injuries in order to obtain surgical experience. Many famous doctors were military surgeons. The Napoleonic wars provided opportunities for military surgery and contributed to the advancement of French surgery, which, in turn, influenced American surgery. Military surgery was ghastly, however, because surgeons frequently amputated without anesthesia. This practice supported the prevailing belief that the heart was better able to stand the strain of surgery in this state because surgical shock (lowering blood pressure) contributed to surgical success. Many casualties resulted from infections from filthy instruments which were often borrowed from kitchen tables (Richardson 1964:170). For example, of the 13,000 amputations performed by French army surgeons during the Franco-Prussian War (in 1870-1871), 10,000 were fatal (Shyrock 1936:280). In spite of their horrors, wars also contributed significantly to the development of surgical advances. For example, in World War I the techniques of blood transfusions were developed to meet the challenge of shock.

The Solitude of the Surgeon

A surgeon, like other heroes, bears the burdens of his activities and decisions alone. The practice of surgery is perceived by the surgeons to be a very solitary activity, despite the many situations in which they are not alone. Surgeons practice in hospitals, frequently have an audience, and participate in sharing of information through formal Rounds and professional meetings. Most conduct their surgery with an operating room team in which they are usually the only qualified surgeon (although an increasing number operate in teams). Yet, their perception is that they alone are responsible for the fate of the patient.

Surgery is a solitary activity also because surgeons only minimally share the burdens of their profession with their colleagues. Most surgeons do not talk intimately with their colleagues (See Chapter 5, "Communication with Colleagues"). The competitive structure of surgical practice makes it precarious to reveal too many weaknesses to colleagues with whom they are competing for patients. Their penchant for independence, certainty, individualistic action, and optimism also discourages introspection, doubt, and admitting fears and failures. Surgeons have an additional burden of maintaining a strong, decisive, optimistic, and action-oriented public posture to sustain the morale and confidence of their collaborators and assistants, as well as of their patients.

Cutting someone's body and having some control over their subsequent life or death are inherent in the surgical profession, and they entail burdensome responsibilities and risks. Feelings associated with these responsibilities and risks are not easily shared by, nor communicated to, those who are not surgeons. Aird acknowledged the emotional burdens when he wrote:

> *When all appropriate advice has been taken from his colleagues, and when all aspects of the problem have been discussed with his own staff, it is the surgeon himself who must make the final decision, and in making it he necessarily stands apart from his colleagues in a kind of loneliness....it is inevitable that he should speculate somberly on his peculiar solitary responsibility....A young surgeon should keep his affections in cold storage.* (1961:18; 20).

THE ACTIVE POSTURE OF SURGEONS

Surgeons maintain an active, interventionist posture toward conquering disease and curing patients. Their active interventionist posture is manifest in virtually all of their activities — from operating (e.g., incising, retracting tissues, chiseling and sawing bones, extracting, sewing), conquering disease, and interacting with their patients and medical colleagues. Their active interventionist posture is not merely that which is entrenched in Western medicine (See Muller and Koenig, 1988; Jordan 1993; Ortiz de Montellano 1980). It is embedded in the very origins of the surgical profession. The words "surgery" and "surgeon" originate from *"Chirurgia,"* which is derived from the Greek words, *cheiros*, meaning hand, and *ourgia*, meaning action. Thus, a surgeon acts with his hands.

Textbooks of surgery define surgery by action and intervention. Surgeons' penchant for acting is reflected in their defining surgery by what they do, such as, for example, repair, reconstruct, excise, alter, and correct. This contrasts with other medical practitioners who define their profession by their field of study. For example, surgical textbooks have defined surgery as "what surgeons do" (Atkins 1965:vii), "a branch of medicine which uses manipulative and other modalities" (Gius 1972:1), "planned anatomic alteration of the human organism designed to arrest, alleviate, or eradicate some pathologic process" (LeMaitre and Finnegin 1975:3). The handbook for surgical residents at Meadowbrook University Hospital defined surgery in a tautological manner as "the study of all aspects of those diseases which may be treated by operative methods."

A preference for acting over not acting has been part of the culture of surgery since it was distinguished from medicine in the second century. The active, interventionist posture of surgeons is based upon three cultural beliefs: 1) it is possible to influence and control events and processes through one's own action; 2) it is good to intervene and less good to refrain from action; and 3) important in modern Western medical tradition is direct human intervention and control — as opposed to divine intervention and abrogating control.

Unlike most physicians, surgeons do not see themselves merely as healers; they see themselves as curers. They are not only frequently convinced that their active interventions may cure or save a patient, they are also convinced that they are the only medical practitioners with the ability to make such heroic interventions.

Surgeons' use of the word "cure" is one example of their active posture. "Cure" assumes a different meaning in surgery from that in internal medicine. In medicine "cure" is used much more cautiously than in surgery. In medicine "cure" refers to a state in which all clinical and laboratory evidence of the disease is eliminated, and it is unlikely that the disease process will continue. In contrast, in surgery "cure" refers solely to the interventions that surgeons can do. Cure is restricted, for example, to those surgical interventions in which visible tumor is removed (cf., Cochrane et al. 1980; Attiyeh and Stearns 1981). The surgeons at Meadowbrook spoke of surgical "cure" when they believed they had removed all of the disease that was surgically possible. One surgeon in Meadowbrook University Hospital said that when he said he did a "curative resection" he meant, "I think we have removed all of the disease." This perspective does not verbally acknowledge, for example, that removing all the *visible* malignant tumor may not remove all the malignant cells that were not visible and inaccessible to surgical removal and which could continue to invade the body.

Even though contemporary surgeons are aware that disease processes may remain after surgery, they continue to use the word "cure." The frequent use of that word perpetuates their optimistic stance and their belief in the efficacy of their active interventions. By calling such interventions "cures" surgeons avoid acknowledging the limits of their surgical activities. It suggests that surgeons see themselves as having more power over disease, and perhaps life, than they actually have. Surgeons at Meadowbrook readily used the word, "cure" not only when speaking to, or writing for, their colleagues but also when talking to their patients.

This led their patients to believe that a "cure" was permanent. It offered them hope, because they believed that their disease was eradicated. Patients did not perceive that the surgeons' view of cure was different from theirs. For surgeons invoking powerful images of heroic curing contributed to their sense of omnipotence by impeding them from admitting their limitations and failures when their patients failed to get well and/or died.

Optimistic Stance

Surgeons' active posture is manifest in their optimistic stance. A positive attitude toward the future and certainty implied that the surgeon could control future outcomes for the patient. Bosk refers to surgeons' optimism as the denial of the possibility of failure (1979). Surgeons' demeanor of optimism and confidence was believed to aid in the healing process. For example, in the eighteenth century Sir Ashley Cooper wrote on the demeanor of a surgeon in his *Lectures on Surgery*: "It is the surgeon's duty to tranquilize the temper, to beget cheerfulness, and to impart confidence of recovery" (quoted in Schwartz 1983:13).

The active posture of surgeons entails a more passive posture for patients. Surgeons conveyed their belief in the efficacy of their actions by consistently expressing optimism, even when the medical situation of the patient gave little room for optimism. Surgeons' optimism gave patients much-desired hope. However, surgeons' penchant for optimism frequently created barriers to their communication with their patients, particularly when they were required to communicate unfavorable or pessimistic information, such as about terminal illness or death. Cases illustrating such communication are discussed in Chapter 5, "Communication with Patients."

Surgeons acclaim the value of their decisiveness and optimism by denigrating physicians, such as internists, radiologists, and anesthesiologists. They portray these physicians derogatorily as hesitant, contemplative, introspective, and prone to wait to make decisions and act until it is too late to save a patient (cf., Bosk, 1979:105). They accuse them of appearing indecisive, in the words of Dr. White, Chief of Surgery at Meadowbrook, "like an internist, who puts his hands in his pockets and thinks instead of acts." Deaver and Reimann wrote: "We daily have it in our power to be the means of correcting mistakes in the interpretation of the language of living pathology, and thus save an otherwise condemned sufferer from medical procrastination" (1923:115).

Surgeons' focus on action is focus on the present, not on the past or future. Performing before an audience takes place in the present, and it results in immediate recognition by the audience. It creates immediate results: the surgeon cuts through layers of skin and other tissues, takes out an organ, connects parts together, and sews a patient back up.

Surgeons perpetuate their active image by depicting themselves as spending long dramatic hours in the operating room. However the reality of Meadowbrook University Hospital was different. The surgeons there spent significantly more time examining patients outside of the operating room than they did in the operating room. They rarely admitted that the time they spent in the operating room constituted only approximately one-fourth to one-fifth of their time (See Figure 1, page 36). Dr. Robinson, explained, "I don't like offices. I can't sit in an office to see patients. I am a surgeon!" Indeed, the surgeons in Meadowbrook University Hospital stated that they preferred the action in the operating room.

The Meadowbrook surgeons repeatedly asserted their active posture. For example, during a lecture on portal-caval shunts given for surgeons and internists in which an internist asked a question about the necessary gradient for a portal-caval shunt, the lecturer commented that he could tell the question came from an internist, because "an internist asks for numbers and gradients to guide future decisions, and a surgeon just makes decisions *ad-hoc* in the course of surgery."

In another example the following communication took place between an internist and a surgeon:

The internist said, "Mrs. M. is growing a bunch of stuff. She's now two months post-operative and has infection." The surgeon responded: "The least we can do is to put in a naso-gastric tube. We can tell if anything is happening." The internist stated, "I bet it's not serious. I asked Jim [an internist] about it. There is no question that something happened to her bowels last week." Whereupon the surgeon said: "I'll look into her bowels."

The internist used passive verbs and negatives (i.e., "I bet it's *not* serious." "There is *no* question that something *happened*. ..."). The surgeon used positive and active verbs (i.e., "I'll *look* into her bowels," "*put in* a naso-gastric tube")[7] (cf., Weintraub 1982).

Figure 1
Proportion of Surgeons' Time in Activities

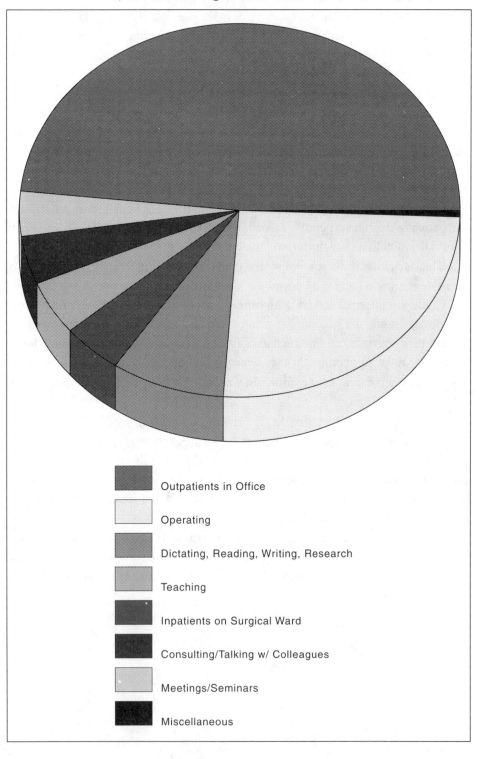

Outpatients in Office

Operating

Dictating, Reading, Writing, Research

Teaching

Inpatients on Surgical Ward

Consulting/Talking w/ Colleagues

Meetings/Seminars

Miscellaneous

The Active Posture in Teaching Residents

A surgeon-teacher criticized the resident because he spent too much time thinking about a course of action. The surgeon commented, "You can stand around and meditate all day with your hands in your pockets, but to save his life you've got to act!" In a surgical teaching seminar at Meadowbrook University Hospital in which a hypothetical case of an acute abdomen was presented by Dr. White, the Chief of Surgery to the residents:

The Chief said: "Whenever you make a diagnosis where the implications are important, like an operation, you have to think of the complications. How sure do you have to be about appendicitis in order to operate?"

The resident answered, "Ninety percent?"

The Chief responded, "Eighty percent correct in a diagnosis of appendicitis. From the story you have told on this patient do you agree that the patient has appendicitis?"

The resident replied, "I don't agree. I think that further investigation is necessary."

The chief exclaimed in a ridiculing voice, "You want to be an internist, don't you!"

The resident continued, "I'd want an x-ray of the bowels."

The Chief persisted in a ridiculing voice, "What is the purpose of x-rays? Is it going to help your diagnosis of appendicitis? There are no radiological signs of appendicitis. The purpose of an x-ray is if you suspect something else."

The Chief persisted to question and lecture the resident, "What is the mortality rate for an untreated appendicitis? It is around five to ten percent. It is extremely important to keep this perspective in mind when you make a decision. You've got to arrive at a diagnosis. Nothing in this world is certain. You can stand around and wring your hands and worry if it's right. But there comes a time when you've got to treat that person."

Implications of the Heroic Active Posture

Surgeons' belief in the virtues of heroic action may have serious implications in the treatment of patients. Surgeons' heroic action may result in intrusive treatment even when it will not cure the disease. Heroic action may prevent a surgeon from offering palliative solutions to alleviate a patient's suffering. Such belief frequently results in surgeons' choosing action over inaction, even where inaction may be medically indicated. It may result in deceiving the patient about options, and sometimes in deceiving the surgeon himself.

An active focus may lead a surgeon to neglect other interventions which may help heal a patient. For example, a surgeon who focuses on his primary role as curer may not realize the importance that his patient may place on his role as listener. Or a surgeon may not acknowledge the importance of his role in alleviating fear for the patient by explaining the nature of the illness.

That surgeons' active posture leads them to impose a passive posture on their patients was reflected in their participation in patients' decision-making, in withholding of information from patients about conditions which the surgeon could not "cure," and in their inability to admit failures and instead suggest that failure was an attribute of patients. (See the chapters on decision making, Chapter 7, "How Surgeons Make Decisions: Influence of Active Posture on Decision Making," Chapter 8, "Surgical Decision Making: Referrals, and 'Keeping' Patients," and Chapter 9, "Implications of the Culture of Surgeons for Modern Medicine.")

The active heroic posture was manifest in surgeons' preference for intervening with highly sophisticated technologies, rather than desisting from intervention. The surgeons' active heroic posture encourages active testing with increasingly more sophisticated technologies instead of waiting until symptoms either disappear or develop (cf., Reiser 1978:191).

The active heroic posture also affects the way in which surgeons think, interpret, and participate in research. For example, in an investigation of published opinions of surgeons and other physicians about the benefits of coronary bypass surgery it was found that surgeons were more inclined to be "enthusiastic" that surgery reduced mortality and improved angina than non-surgeons (Chalmers and Sacks1979).

The active heroic posture of surgeons affected the ways in which surgeons made decisions in the course of their work. These include decisions on when and whether to operate, which operative procedures to use, what to tell patients, how to make diagnoses, how to interpret data, how to interpret risks, how much risk to expose patients to, how and what to teach surgical residents, and how to participate in research (cf., P. Katz 1984). This is discussed in detail in Chapter 7, "How Surgeons Make Decisions: Influence of Active Posture on Decision Making."

The interventionist ethos of surgery (and medicine) has contributed toward the prolific rise in cost of medical treatment in the United States, and to a lesser degree in Canada, without showing a corresponding similar improvement in morbidity and mortality rates. The interventionist ethos has also influenced medical organizations, such as hospitals, the AMA, the American College of Surgeons, medical school curricula, and student selection, as well as medical insurance funds and research allocations, all of which are more oriented toward active intervention than to waiting (See Ortiz de Montellano 1980).

CONCLUSION

Contemporary North American surgeons possess the qualities of American heroes. As descendants of the heroic traditions of surgeons of the past, particularly from England and France, they have interpreted and molded their histories in a uniquely American heroic mold. Although the individualist cultures and the geographical distances in the United States and Canada promoted the development of surgery along individualistic lines that were somewhat different from those in Europe, surgeons' heroic interventionist posture persisted (cf., Ravitch 1981:605).

American surgery was particularly known for its introduction of anesthesia. It was also known for the development of difficult operations that were rarely attempted in European practice (cf., Shyrock 1936:177). The American surgeon had to practice every branch of medicine. He had to rely upon himself and was forced to take risks.

Surgeons portrayed themselves as active heroes in their oral accounts and in their articles and books. They are also perceived as active heroes by the general public. The public audiences and the paintings of surgical scenes in clinics of Gross, Agnew, and Billroth (which also portrayed the audiences) contributed to the heroic image of surgeons (cf., Brieger 1987:1188). More recently, characters in the contemporary mass media and the publicity surrounding transplant and artificial organ surgery have presented the surgeon's working life as consisting of a continuous procession of dramatic, crises-oriented actions. These images obscure the mundane daily and weekly routine of most surgeons.

However, while the characteristics of the surgeons as active heroes may have been adaptive in the past, they could have disadvantages for the contemporary practice of surgery. For example, the new technologies of CT scans, PET scans, MRIs, sonograms, lasers, fiber-optic scopes, and the non-surgical means for crushing bladder and gall stones have made some of the surgeons' quick life and death decision-making skills less necessary and sometimes inappropriate (See Appendix C, "Cybersurgery: The New Surgical Technologies").

Whereas bold, risky, quick decisions that surgeons rendered independently of internists were necessary for saving lives in the past, at the present most patients are likely to be better served by a posture focusing more upon searching for medical alternatives in consultation with internists. Surgeons' traditional isolation from, denigration of, and competition with internists has had the effect of reducing communication among specialists and constraining surgeons from learning more about the practice of internal medicine.

The surgeons' heroic image has discouraged them from communicating with their patients, who are essential ingredients in the decision-making and healing process, particularly in contemporary America. Surgeons' optimism and absence of doubts may prevent them from asking critical questions of themselves and others and from learning from their mistakes.[8]

The subsequent chapters examine how the heroic image of the surgeon evolved and was expressed in Meadowbrook University Hospital. They explore how this image may influence surgeons' behavior toward their colleagues and patients. It particularly focuses on how their heroic active image has affected their communication with their colleagues and patients, and how it influenced their decision making.

NOTES

1. Some of the most distinguished surgeons through the ages, such as Celsius in the first century, De Mondville in the fourteenth century, and Cushing and Albutt in the early twentieth century, have proclaimed the similarities between surgery and medicine, and they have advocated for their unification.

2. In London before 1540 there were two separate organizations, the Company of Barbers and the Fellowship or Guild of Surgeons. In 1540 they merged and developed

examinations and licenses for their members. In 1744 they again separated, and in 1745 founded the Company of Surgeons and the Company of Barbers (Dobson and Walker 1979).

3. The histories of the various centers of surgery in medieval Europe differed in their associations with physicians, organizational status, and relationships to university training. For example, in the twelfth century surgeons were well organized in Florence, Padua, and Montpelier, but not in Paris where they were excluded from universities (Parker 1920:12).

4. In Great Britain surgeons are more likely to be referred to as Mister. They may, however, be addressed as Doctor (Sidney Blair, personal communication, 1997).

5. The predominant image of surgeons as uneducated has obscured the reality that some medieval and Renaissance surgeons were knowledgeable in the theory of medicine and saw themselves as at least the equals of physicians (Lawrence 1992:3).

6. There are notable exceptions in the past of women surgeons. The early organization of barber-surgeons stated: "no carpenter, smith or woman shall practice surgery." After the sixteenth century French women belonged for a time to the "Corporation of Surgeons" (Geer 1993:47).

7. At the present time an internist who is a gastroenterologist would recommend the same procedures as a surgeon and be able to observe and take biopsies with a fiber optic endoscope (Harry Holloway, personal communication).

8. The emphasis in this chapter upon the heroic image of the American surgeon masks the dynamic interplay of many different subcultural trends within American surgery. The history of surgery in the last two centuries reveals a constant interplay between radical (heroic) and conservative trends. In the mid-nineteenth century in America, for example, the conservative surgeon attempted to preserve the integrity of the body (Brieger 1992). In 1862 Flint claimed that the brilliant and daring surgeon was no longer invested with the *éclat* belonging to the hero of the battlefield: "We hear now comparatively little of terrible operations and of that sort of heroism which is associated with bloody deeds. What once was considered as courage was now stigmatized as rashness" (quoted in Brieger 1987:1195).

Chapter 3

ARE SURGEONS SCIENTISTS?

~

Many surgeons continued to hold that their clinical judgments, and not the pronouncements of laboratory scientists, were the ultimate arbiters of practice.

(Lawrence 1992:33)

INTRODUCTION

Are surgeons scientists? Do they think like scientists? How does their behavior reflect their thinking? This chapter examines surgeons' thinking and behavior as they enact their roles in actively applying the findings of scientific medicine to the bodies of their patients.

Surgeons have been described as scientists, artisans, and artists since the Middle Ages, when the profession of surgery first became distinguished from that of medicine. However, the scientific identity of surgeons became most salient since the 1880's. This was largely due to the advances in microbiology, namely to the impact of Lister's, Pasteur's, and Koch's discoveries of the pathological mechanisms of bacteria in wounds. These, in turn, led to procedures for preventing and treating post-operative infections. Over time these and other scientific advances led to broader domains for surgical intervention and to decreased surgical mortality.

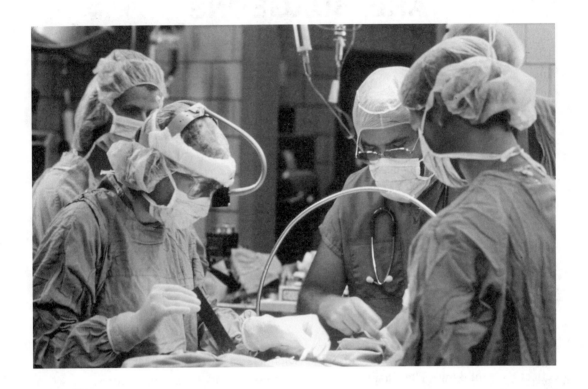

Courtesy, Johns Hopkins Medicine.

SCIENTISTS AND CLINICIANS

The question of surgeons' scientific identity depends upon the activities and thinking of scientists and of clinicians. A theoretical/basic scientist is one who discovers rules, creates conceptual formulations, and builds orderly, abstract, impersonal schemes which represent new ways of thinking about and interpreting phenomena. Their generalizations clarify many details of actual situations (F. Katz 1971). A scientist in a scientific medical or surgical setting attempts "to acquire knowledge about human anatomy and physiology and about the cause, prevention, and treatment of diseases" (Siegler and Osmond 1974:123). Some physicians fall into this category of scientists. However, many, perhaps most, surgeons do not. Surgeons are clinicians. Hereafter in this chapter they are called "clinicians" to distinguish their thinking and behavior from those of theoretical/basic scientists, who are hereafter in this chapter called "scientists."[1]

As an example of the different approaches between a scientist and a clinician, a scientist may seek to understand the mechanisms of pathogenesis of bacteria in open wounds. A surgeon may apply scientific concepts in order to understand why a particular patient became infected after a particular procedure is performed by a particular surgeon in a particular hospital. The surgeon may not only treat the patient for the infection, but he may also use this information to help prevent and/or treat infection in subsequent patients.

A scientist is a skeptic. He questions theories and hypotheses and investigates anomalies and exceptions. Carl Sagan stated: "Science is a way of thinking, asking skeptical questions" (1996). A scientist gathers data and subjects them to rigid and systematic examination, challenge, refutation, reformation, verification, and analysis. Huxley stated: "In scientific inquiry it becomes a matter of duty to expose a supposed law to every possible kind of verification" (1896).

The scientist emphasizes impersonal, objective criteria in subjecting knowledge to systematic testing. Claude Bernard, a scientist who was a pioneer in medicine for advocating rigorous experimental criteria for testing theories, wrote: "When we meet a fact which contradicts a prevailing theory, we must accept the fact and abandon the theory, even when the theory is supported by great names and is generally accepted" (1865). Although in reality all knowledge, including basic scientific knowledge, is interpreted culturally, the objective nature of the scientific knowledge is emphasized in this discussion in order to contrast it with its clinical applications. Because clinical knowledge is applied to specific patients in specific situations, myriad factors, including biological, cultural, and psychological ones, can influence their application.

Clinicians practicing scientific medicine derive their authority from applying their scientific knowledge to treating patients. For example, scientists discovered that most sources of infection were microorganisms. They identified which microorganisms were harmful and the ways that these microorganisms could be transmitted to the patient in the operating room (e.g., through the air, by physical contact, through moisture). Surgeons, as clinicians, established procedures by which these microorganisms could be effectively prevented from contaminating the patient in the operating room, such as, for example, maintaining sterility and preventing contamination in the operating room (P. Katz 1981; P. Katz and Kirkland 1988). When the same procedures were repeated at each operation, they became clinical rituals which were based upon science (See Chapter 10, "Operating Room Rituals").

Scientists consider their subject matter in terms of probability, algorithms, and outcome measures. They are comfortable with uncertainty in knowledge and outcomes. In contrast, clinicians, especially surgeons, are trained to think more in categorical or absolute terms (cf., Eddy 1982b; Kassirer 1989). They act to solve problems about which complete knowledge rarely exists (Trotter 1946:163; F. Katz 1971). Scientists are concerned with abstract relationships between hypothetical patients, diseases and treatments (F. Katz 1971; Siegler and Osmond 1974:125; Trotter 1946:163). Clinicians are concerned with real patients and diseases for which decisions have to be made about treatments. A surgeon is immersed in a particular concrete situation with an actual patient to which he applies knowledge based on many principles from many disciplines. The surgeon amalgamates those sources of knowledge and applies them to the specific characteristics of the patients' psychological, cultural, and economic situation in order to devise practical strategies for solving concrete problems for that patient.

Clinicians in Traditional Societies

Clinicians can be found both in modern scientific settings as well as in traditional/non-literate societies. In modern scientific settings clinicians have medical or nursing certifications which attests to their grounding in systematic empirical science. In traditional/non-literate societies clinicians are usually philosophers, priests, shamans, or medicine men. The clinicians in the traditional/non-literate societies are frequently the same people who are the theorists. Instead of being concerned with empirically determined causes of disease, these clinicians are concerned with the "ultimate" causes, that is the interpretive meanings of the diseases. Such causes are often supernatural, and they are inherently unverifiable.

Traditional practitioners and their clinical practices are typically greeted with awe in their societies, and their theories are likely to be accepted as statements of undisputed fact. Often these clinicians diagnose etiologies using moral rather than medical criteria (cf., Foster 1976). In contrast to clinicians who are rooted in scientific knowledge, the traditional clinician's etiologies and clinical outcomes are not subject to systematic examination, challenge, refutation, verification, or significant reformation.

However, medical practice in traditional/non-literate societies resembles that in modern scientific societies in that the clinicians apply knowledge that was empirically obtained. For example, the Aztecs had found a superior way of handling wounds that is valid today.[2] However, while empiricism may be present, and its results may be effective and reproducible, its methods and findings are not *systematically* subject to empirical testing. Traditional medicine uses cures that have been found to be effective, but fundamentally they are based upon established, untested traditions which frequently depend upon belief in the personal, and often spiritual, powers of the clinical practitioners.

Yet, traditional clinicians have great insight into many of the causes of distress of their patients. They usually share the culture of their patients, know their kinship and friendship networks, and can apply the medical knowledge that is known in their society to the specific characteristics of the patient. They are frequently effective in alleviating suffering of patients, particularly those suffering from chronic diseases and psychological distress. Shamans, for example, have been found to have a number of qualities in common with clinicians, such as surgeons. Furthermore, in comparison with non-shamans they have been found to have: the ability to impose form on diffuse, unstructured sensory data; a richer repertoire of categories for classifying stimuli (Shweder 1972); and greater psychological integrative and adaptive capacities (Boyer et al. 1986). Also, in common with surgeons, shamans are performers with the ability to have "communicative interplay with spectators" (Peters and Price-Williams 1980).[3] Some characteristics of traditional priests/shamans/medicine men can be found in those surgeons who are excellent clinicians. One of these characteristics is "intuition," and it is described in the following section.

The Culture of Surgeons and Clinical Effectiveness

The application of scientific principles is the nominal basis of surgical practice in North American hospitals. However, other skills, some of which are characteristic of all effective clinicians, including surgeons, shamans, priests, and medicine men, are also included in modern surgical training and practice. Some of these skills enhance surgical efficacy and contribute to surgical progress. Some, however, interfere with surgical efficacy and hinder surgical progress. All, however, affect surgical outcomes.

The hallmarks of the culture of surgeons, and, in fact the core of the identity of a surgeon — namely the heroic active posture, demeanor of certainty, absence of doubts, optimism, and focus on the person of the surgeon — both contribute to surgeons' clinical effectiveness as well as detract from their claim to be scientists.

Intuition

The effectiveness of surgeons as clinicians does not solely depend upon their ability to understand and work within the paradigm of science. To a greater degree it depends upon the ways in which they translate their knowledge into action to heal specific problems of specific patients. Some of the basic characteristics of the culture of surgeons, their propensity for action and their confidence, certainty, and optimism, contribute to their ability to heal. Additionally, the emphasis upon the person of the surgeon gives them the authority to use their intuition in making decisions about patients.

Intuition is a characteristic of the "art" of surgery. Although intuition is commonly thought to be separate from knowledge and logic, it is instead a different process of using expert knowledge with different kinds of "logic." It is a method of thinking about a problem which involves listening closely, weeding out false leads, with a measure of playfulness (cf., Wartofsky 1986:91). It is characterized by sudden insight, seeing problems in a new way, making new connections, and recognizing patterns when those patterns are not obvious (Abernathy and Hamm 1995). It is clinical judgment tempered by knowledge based on experience in interpreting statistical data (Romanucci-Ross and Moerman 1991).

Intuition uses thought and feeling — often visceral — to detect subtle clues from which the surgeon can make inferences that are drawn from his total experience. It is manifest in surgeons' ability to recognize diseases quickly and accurately, to decide what additional information to look for, what actions to take, and when to wait, as well as how to prioritize their actions (Abernathy and Hamm 1995:22). Intuition has a feeling of certainty — a deep, incontestable truth (Hilden 1991). In many cases the expert surgeon cannot explain his intuition and claims, "I just knew." (Abernathy and Hamm 1995:3). These characteristics of intuition reflect its compatibility with surgical culture, particularly its emphasis on the heroism, the personal characteristics of the surgeon, and the surgeon's demeanor of certainty.

The most effective surgical clinicians use intuition to make diagnoses and other clinical decisions (Abernathy and Hamm 1995:19). However, most scientists denigrate clinical intuition as a too elusive, "fuzzy," non-analytical, and ultimately non-scientific trait, even though the most creative scientists depend upon their use of intuition in creating and testing theories (cf., Barrows and Mitchell 1975).

Surgical intuition uses all the senses, especially the eye and touch. For example, an anesthetist observed that when a surgeon has a difficult problem:

> *The senior surgeon will ask the junior to change positions at the table. Often, apparently suddenly and unexpectedly, the senior, previously at a loss to put the data together, will arrive at an answer, just from feeling the tissues or viewing the situation from a new angle. Although a previously unobtained answer or formulation has appeared, the surgeon is hard put to describe how he got it.* (McPeek 1991:83)

Experienced surgeons use intuition in making most of their decisions, and virtually all of their decisions in the operating room or in emergency situations. They weed out false leads and discard irrelevant data. They do not make decisions in those situations by logically examining alternatives; they do not wait until their information is more certain or more complete (Abernathy and Hamm 1995). Their reliance upon intuitive thinking has been informed by scientific knowledge, past clinical studies, and the situation with live patients they have encountered and handled during the own years of experience.

Scientists use analytical thinking, computer-like algorithms, "expert systems," and outcomes data in their quest for advancing the science of medicine. However, such knowledge can only be accurately applied to a probability sample of patients, not to any individual patient, where a multiplicity of factors influence cause, treatment, and outcomes (cf., Goldman et al. 1988; Posen et al. 1984). Clinical practice differs from clinical research: "In good clinical practice, treatments are prescribed on the basis of various individual patient characteristics. In good clinical research, patients are assigned to treatment groups by a process explicitly described to pay as little attention to individual patient characteristics as medical ethics will allow" (Yancy 1992:365).

INFLUENCES WHICH DETRACT FROM SURGEONS' IDENTITY AS SCIENTISTS

Historical Separation of Surgery from Medicine

One of the reasons that surgical culture differs from many aspects of scientific culture is because of its historical separation from medicine. Chapter 2, "The Surgeon as Hero," described how surgeons for most of their history were prevented from attending universities and studying the "sciences" of anatomy and physiology. This obstacle to their participation in the "culture" of medicine shielded them from the advances in science of the day and also from exposure to the traditions of scientific thinking. Some legacies of this history remain today as surgical culture is transmitted to new surgeons. These include their emphasis on action, the high value they place upon apprenticeship in training, and the pervasiveness of denigrating physicians for thinking instead of acting.

Since surgeons were historically deprived of opportunities to learn the postulates and postures of theoretical/basic science and to participate in the scientific tradition of medicine, they focused on other ways of thinking and developed other skills to meet the demands of suffering patients. They emphasized speed, decisiveness, and risk-taking in operating to save lives, alleviate suffering, and reduce morbidity.[4] Surgeons not only focused upon the characteristics of the interventionist posture of the hero-surgeon, they also emphasized such characteristics, as certainty, absence of doubt, and optimism.

Heroic, Active Posture, and Propensity for Certainty

The centrality of the active and heroic posture for the culture of surgeons distinguishes them not only from scientists, but also from many other modern clinicians, such as internists. The active and heroic postures entail thinking styles that are in many ways antithetical to scientific thought and method. The active posture of surgeons, expressed in the semantic, historical, and behavioral culture of surgeons, embodies thinking that is oriented to action rather than to analysis. It is oriented to certainty and in eschewing of doubts in order to find immediate solutions rather than to understanding problems. Thinking that emphasizes certainty diverges considerably from (scientific) thinking which emphasizes skepticism, questioning, knowledge-seeking, reflection, analysis, and verification.

Surgeons' categorical thinking was described by a surgical resident who stated, "Surgeons in general don't like theoretical or psychological problems. Things are either black or white. If they don't understand something, they try to put it out of their minds" (Bosk 1979:48). Categorical and certainty-oriented thinking is not conducive to statistical, probabilistic thinking about risks. It is also not conducive to considering multiple factors in disease causation, even though "most medical problems are extremely and deceptively complicated" (Eddy 1982b:344).

Surgeons' certainty-oriented thinking is not compatible with the kinds of questioning or examining of subtleties, ambiguities, and anomalies that characterize scientists' thinking. Concentrating on curing by surgical means detracts from looking for disease causes. Where medical scientists link etiological and diagnostic thinking to that about therapeutics, surgeons often ignore causes in favor of noticeable, dramatic, and often short-term, therapeutic results. Their communication and decision-making processes were often based on short-term perspectives, and they emphasized quick, certain, and decisive action.

The active and heroic postures of surgeon may have deterred scientific discoveries in the field of surgery, and it may in some cases have vitiated their effectiveness as clinicians. The data on Meadowbrook University Hospital suggest that surgeons made decisions that frequently resulted in outcomes that were not optimal for their patients (See Chapter 7, "How Surgeons Make Decisions: Influence of Active Posture on Decision Making," Chapter 8, "Surgical Decision Making: Referrals, and 'Keeping' Patients," and Chapter 9, "Implications of the Culture of Surgeons for Modern Medicine").

Emphasis on the Person of the Surgeon

The emphasis upon the person of the surgeon in the culture of surgeons has detracted from surgery's identity as a science. It is reflected in most historical writings about surgery. Most histories of surgery that are written by surgeons (as opposed to those written by historians of medicine)[5] have emphasized great surgeons. They are defined as great in most cases because they have discovered or advanced technical innovations (cf., Ravitch 1981; Brieger 1986). Such surgeon-authors focus as much attention upon the person of the surgeon as they do upon their surgical innovations. Brieger described this as "the medical mandarin syndrome" (1966:34-35). The personal orientation is at variance with the emphasis in the sciences on impersonal, reproducible, objective criteria in evaluating and testing data (cf., Merton 1968:607–610; F. Katz 1976:125).

The apprenticeship system of surgical training contributes to the perseverance in surgical culture of focusing upon the person of the surgeon. The apprenticeship system is ensconced to a greater degree in surgery than in other fields of medicine. In the early fourteenth century De Mondeville (1260-1320) wrote: "The surgeon ... should first frequent the places where able surgeons often operate; follow with care their operations; fix them in his memory; and then practice by operating with these surgeons..." (Zimmerman and Veith 1961:141). The concepts underlying the apprenticeship system are present in the training of modern surgeons. Apprenticeship emphasizes the personal experiences of specific surgeons as well as their innate endowments. For example, Deaver and Reimann wrote: "The surgeon like the poet is born such" (1923:105). The apprenticeship system favors the clinical judgment and surgical techniques of senior surgeons, regardless of outcome or scientific verification. It perpetuates the belief that the individual surgeon with his individual, and often genetically endowed, skills is more important than scrupulous attention to application of scientific principles.

The focus upon the person of the surgeon had its counterpart in the focus upon the personal attributes of the patient. Before the 1880s surgeons and other physicians believed that disease was not caused by non-personal causative agents, but rather by the personal "constitution" of the patient (cf., Christakis 1997). The individual characteristics of the patient determined the outcome of an operation rather than activity of microorganisms, or poor technique which facilitated the pathogenesis of those microorganisms.

The designation of the operating room as a "theater" highlights the personal performance aspect of surgical practices. Until the end of the nineteenth century operating theaters had been stages which were modeled after anatomical theaters which existed in university faculties of medicine. They were stages for dramatic public spectacles in which the audience not only consisted of surgeons and medical students but also of members of the general public (Cartwright 1968:12; Wangensteen and Wangensteen 1975; Brieger 1987).

Through the theater the surgeons' performance was made accessible to public scrutiny and admiration — although Brieger has questioned how much students actually learned about surgery in a crowded surgical amphitheater where few were near enough to see much of value (1987:1201). The disproportionate emphasis upon the personal operating skills of the surgeon, even in modern times contrasts sharply with the small proportion of their time (20-25 percent) that most present-day surgeons actually spend in the operating room (see Figure 1).

The emphasis upon the person of the surgeon influences surgeons to discount the results of objective clinical trials or results of their own work which have been subjected to objective evaluation. They discount these trials because the experiences that are reported are either remote in time and/or place from their own experience or because they refer to a probability of occurrence of events for a large number of people, but not to the details of any one particular patient. For example, Wangensteen and Wangensteen wrote: "The slow progress of surgery before the full acceptance of prophylactic antisepsis was owing in large measure to the reluctance of surgeons to subject suggested innovations to trial, preferring debate and argument" (1978:553).

The following example illustrated Lawrence's statement, "Many surgeons continued to hold that their clinical judgments, and not the pronouncements of laboratory scientists, were the ultimate arbiters of practice" (1992:33). The event took place in a research institute during an objective review of a proposed new technique in surgery. The review panel rated the research design highly, including the competence of the surgeon who proposed and intended to carry out the innovative procedures. However, there was no mention of the person who was to evaluate the results. When questioned by the review panel, the surgeon replied, "I will evaluate the results." When asked which objective criteria were to be used for the evaluation, the surgeon replied: "My clinical judgment!" (Fred Tyner, personal communication 1997)

Emphasizing the personal experiences of specific surgeons over objective criteria contributes to a culture that is at variance with that of science. While using personal experience in intuition can contribute to clinical efficacy, it can lead to surgeons' ignoring or undervaluing the contribution of other surgeons, particularly those who are geographically distant. The focus on the person of the surgeon can foster reverence for, and preservation of, established ways of surgical thinking and behaving. Procedures based on the personal experiences of respected surgeons may have contributed to the reluctance of surgeons to change their ways of thinking and behaving even in the face of overwhelming scientific evidence. Examples of this are presented in the last section of this chapter.

A logical consequence of focusing attention upon the person of the surgeon is that of attributing the success of an operation to the personal characteristics of the surgeon (and, concomitantly, attributing failure to the personal characteristics of the patient). In Meadowbrook University Hospital it was commonly known that the patients of particular surgeons were more likely to become infected, regardless of the nature of the operation. In contrast, highly successful surgeons were known to have a "special touch." The personal reputation of the clinician sometimes intruded into explanations for a cause or a cure of post-operative infection.

Some older surgeons at Meadowbrook University Hospital, for example, claimed superior knowledge by virtue of having had a long history of personal experience with diagnosing and treating a specific disease. They used their personal auspices as a basis to advocate, or impose, their methods, irrespective of the currency or efficacy of their therapy, and irrespective of systematic empirical testing.

Some surgeons, for example, attributed specific post-operative infections to the fact that the surgeon (usually a surgeon apart from themselves) had operated at the end of a long, busy day, or was irritable and less careful as a result of specific personal problems. Similarly, many surgeons choose personalistic reasons for performing an operation in a particular manner. In Meadowbrook University Hospital several surgeons explained that their reason for performing a particular procedure was because it was the way in which their teacher(s) performed that operation, or the way with which they were used to performing it (cf., Fielding et. al. 1978). Some of these same surgeons admitted that an alternative procedure was likely to be (or had been empirically determined to be) superior to that which they performed. Israel wrote: "in the overwhelming majority of instances a therapeutic decision was arrived at in direct relation to what happened in the last similar case the doctor was familiar with" (1982). Such a tendency to place greater weight upon personal experience and thus to draw sweeping conclusions from a few observations (cf., Eddy 1982b) detracts from surgeons' scientific identity.

Attributing disease causes to personal characteristics of patients was used by surgeons at Meadowbrook University Hospital when they pointed out to patients that their diseases resulted from their deliberate indulgence in poor health habits. Rather than being objective statements of causality, these statements carried a disapproving moral tone to them. Indictment of the patient served to exculpate the surgeon when a patient presented with a disease the surgeon was helpless to correct. An example of the surgical literature attributing post-operative infection to the personal characteristics of the patients is contained in Hardy's *Total Surgical Management* (1959), in which the author attributed post-operative infection in a hypothetical elderly man as "no will to live."

The personalistic idiom explains disease causes by answering *why*, not how? (Foster 1976). Asking *how*, for example, post-operative infection occurs in a large sample of cases leads to scientifically determined objective laws which may have been systematically tested on many patients. In contrast, asking "*Why* does operative infection occur?" leads to untested, personal, and frequently moral explanations. Clinicians in traditional/non-literate societies, such as priests/shamans/medicine men, as well as laymen in modern societies, are more likely to ask "why" than "how."

Emphasis upon the special personal characteristics of specific surgeons favors evidence based upon the experience of individual clinicians, such as case studies, rather than evidence gained through the more generally applicable universalism of controlled clinical trials (Armstrong 1977:601). For example, Robson, in a highly technical article on the biology of infection, wrote, "an experienced surgeon can rely on his past experience ..." (1980:16). Emphasizing the person of the surgeon also favors senior surgeons who have more experience and more power to influence other surgeons (Armstrong 1977:601). This not only reinforces a conservative power structure within hospitals and the profession, but it also discourages surgeons from instituting or accepting innovations. It may result in creating barriers against learning new ways of thinking, against implementing technical innovations, and actively identifying causes of disease.

The personal intrusion into scientific examination was illustrated in two highly technical writings on surgical infections. The language in each of these writings abruptly changed from that of a precise technical/scientific tone to one which conveyed a sense of personal hurt and betrayal by factors outside the surgeon's control. For example, a scientific book, entitled *Surgical Sepsis*, began with: "Sepsis is a slight upon surgical virility" (Alexander-Williams 1979:1). Another technical article on surgical infection stated: "All surgeons appreciate how difficult things can be when the infection converts a superior technical result into a disaster" (Polk 1977:3).

The first quotation makes a revealing link between surgical competence as measured by a successful cure with the masculinity of the surgeon. "Virility" is equated with active, successful cures. Many surgeons who do not like to admit that their cases have septic complications, in the event of a patient becoming post-operatively infected may "blame" the infection on shortcomings of the patient. Their rivals may, on the other hand, "blame" the infection on the surgeon himself.

Surgeons' focus upon their unique personal characteristics has another consequence that is antithetical to science in that it leads them to resist thinking in terms of probability. They may discount data that suggests that many factors may influence surgical outcomes and decline to explore such factors. Chalmers and Sacks claim that if proper and sufficient randomized clinical trials had been performed as soon as operative treatments were devised we would now know much more about which patients would benefit from each kind of operation (1979).

The attribution of personal causation to surgeons' successes and failures has contributed to barriers toward their accepting the value of theoretical/basic scientific knowledge and applying that knowledge to their practice. Wangensteen and Wangensteen wrote: "Testing the worth of a proposed remedial measure by argument rather than by trial was common in earlier times, a practice unfortunately continued throughout most of the 19th century university medical academies and the profession generally" (1978:556). Although the scientific literature has replaced personal experience as the accepted medical-surgical authority, even when randomized clinical trials are available surgeons do not always pay attention to their results (Chalmers and Sacks 1979).

SCIENTIFIC KNOWLEDGE AND APPLICATION IN SURGICAL PRACTICE

The history of surgery is replete with examples which illustrate surgeons' resistance to both accepting findings of scientists and to subjecting their own practices and results to scientific scrutiny. Surgeons' initial resistance to accepting the principles of Lister for preventing contamination and infections, discussed below, is the best known historical example. However, even the introduction of anaesthesia, which many historians have heralded as an example of American ingenuity for both its discovery and application to surgery has instead been demonstrated to have been an innovation which was resisted in America. Anaesthesia in the 1840s and 1850s made less of an impact upon surgery than has been claimed; its introduction made little difference initially to the types of operations that surgeons performed (Lawrence 1992:24).

Three examples of surgeons' barriers to acceptance of scientific knowledge and surgical practice are described. They are a) Lister's germ theory; b) drainage after cholecystectomy; and, c) preoperative shaving.

Resistance to Lister's Germ Theory

Lister's papers describing a series of cases demonstrating the effects of antisepsis in wound infection and healing first appeared in the scientific literature in 1867. Yet, the acceptance of Lister's ideas into the surgical literature did not take place until well into the 1880s, and the integration of his ideas and methods into surgical practice did not take place on a large scale until after the 1890s. The sequence of events from Lister's and others' (e.g., W. W. Cheyne and A. Ogston) publications until surgeons integrated the principles of Listerism into their surgical practice, was complex. The initial resistance of surgeons to accepting Lister's germ theory may be attributed in part to the difficulties surgeons had understanding the relationship between its etiological basis (i.e., the scientific posture), and its practice (i.e., the applied scientific posture).[6] One of the reasons for the difficulty was that the tradition of systematically subjecting theories to empirical testing had not yet been established in surgery. The surgical culture accepted or rejected ideas on the basis of the authority of the surgeon who proposed them.

Even when certain antiseptic practices were adopted, it was not necessarily in response to Lister's recommendations. Few surgeons had real understanding of the underlying theoretical foundation of Listerism regardless of whether they rejected or attempted to practice Listerism. For example, surgeons' misunderstanding of the empirical basis of this theory was demonstrated by their common argument that the germ theory was merely a theory and not a demonstrable fact (Brieger 1966:138).

The application of antiseptic techniques was not always attributed to specific antiseptic properties of agents. For example, the antiseptic capabilities of carbolic acid were attributed to its anti-inflammatory properties. Many surgeons adopted practices based on Listerism because it worked and not because they understood or believed in the theory. For example, Lawson Tait (1845–1899) steadfastly opposed Lister and denied the existence of bacteria. Yet by applying the principle of scrupulous cleanliness, he nevertheless reduced infection and mortality for ovariectomy (Blalock and Nanson 1954:1748).

In another example of the lack of understanding of the theoretical principles underlying Listerism, the renowned Johns Hopkins surgeon, Halsted, initiated the use of surgical gloves not for the primary purpose of preventing infection, but rather to protect a nurse's hands from dermatitis. Halsted wrote: "It is remarkable that during the four or five years, when as an operator, I wore them occasionally, we could have been so blind as not to have perceived the necessity for wearing them invariably at the operating table" (1913). The practice of using the gloves to protect hands was adapted for general use in the operating room out of habit (Miller 1982). The ritual of using surgical gloves acquired a scientific basis only after Halsted and others recognized that using gloves reduced infections.

Although surgeons as applied scientists systematically emphasized antiseptic techniques in some contexts, they did not do so in all contexts. This may have been because they were applying practices without being cognizant of the empirical basis for their application — as in Halsted's case. For example, many surgeons who worked in carefully cleansed operative sites and used instruments dipped in carbolic acid also held their knives between their teeth, wiped their noses, or picked up instruments from the floor without redipping them in the acid (Brieger 1966:140).

Surgeons' lack of understanding about the nature of germs is revealed by their fallacious belief that operating in "the pure Virginia country air" did not require antisepsis as did operating in the cities (Brieger 1966:140). This belief suggests that their conceptualization of germs was that the air had an overall quality that was either clean or dirty, a conceptualization based on social and moral attitudes (e.g., pure country versus contaminated city), and not on theoretical/basic scientific findings by the bacteriologists of the time. Brieger explained: "There is a significant difference...between discussing the role of germs and really understanding their part in the process of wound infection" (1966:137).

The discoveries in the laboratory by the bacteriological scientists of staphylococci and streptococci in 1880–1883 presented the surgeons with clearer theoretical bases for causes of infection that were easier to understand. From these bases they could not only devise more effective aseptic strategies, but they could also understand the processes by which wounds healed and/or became infected.[7] The bacteriological discoveries presented surgeons with information that enabled them to understand that bacteria, not pus, was the cause of infection, and that pus was the result of infection by bacteria.

Adherence to Accustomed Practices: Drainage after Cholecystectomy

Many surgeons continue to routinely drain after performing a cholecystectomy (gall bladder removal), even though every available study has demonstrated the safety and advantage of not draining in many, if not the majority, of cases (Criado 1982). Many surgeons continue to ignore the large number of reports which show that *routine* drainage after cholecystectomy is unnecessary. It may be dangerous, and it increases post-operative morbidity. Studies documenting increased wound infection rate, postoperative fever and pain, respiratory complications, incision herniating, prolonged length of hospital stay, and poorer cosmetic results with drainage have not discouraged the majority of surgeons from continuing to routinely drain after cholecystectomy.

One of the reasons for the reluctance of surgeons to abandon draining in cholecystectomies in the large number of case in which it is unnecessary may be a consequence of their preference for an active posture which differentially evaluates errors resulting from omission as more egregious than those of commission (cf., Ortiz de Montellano 1980). In 1905, Yates writing about surgeons' preference for draining wounds despite increased risk for post-operative infections, stated that there was a "tendency always to attribute fatalities in undrained cases to sins of omission, whereas the many evil results of the sins of commission are given much less consideration" (1905:473).

Science versus Custom: The Case of Preoperative Shaving

Another example of recent empirical, scientific evidence not being fully incorporated into surgical practice involves the presence or removal of hair before surgery. According to Cruse (1977) and Seropian and Reynolds (1971), shaving may cause increased infection rates. Cruse found that the infection rate was 2.5 percent in patients who were shaved, and was reduced to 0.9 percent for those not shaved. Based on 406 patients, Seropian and Reynolds found that the infection rate was 5.6 percent among those who were shaved, and 0.6 percent on those who were not shaved (1971).

Although Seropian and Reynolds' article appeared in 1971, there was little notice of it in the surgical literature until the 1980s. It is a reasonable inference that few surgeons ceased shaving on the basis of their article. Cruse reported that, based on the empirical findings of others and their own, the surgeons at his hospital shave as little as possible (1977:80). In June 1983, 12 years after the Seropian and Reynolds' article appeared in *The American Journal of Surgery*, the editors of *The Lancet* recommended that surgeons stop shaving patients. Yet, in 1998, 27 years after the Seropian and Reynolds' article was published, many hospitals still continue to shave much beyond the immediate operative areas of their patients.

The reluctance to change practices based upon massive empirical evidence is described in a physician's autobiography. Rosenbaum wrote: "I know that therapy is changing, but I am slow to change.... I know that is not the way it is done today, and I understand all the reasons, but so far I am not convinced that the new way is better. I read the favorable statistics, but I remain uneasy" (1988:76).

CONCLUSION

Most contemporary surgeons are primarily clinicians rather than scientists. They apply science to their patients. Their thinking differs from that of scientists. In medical school they are taught the theoretical and empirical bases of the biological sciences. In their residencies and subsequent training and practice they are expected to apply these sciences to clinical situations with patients. Most of their activities — diagnosing, treating, and particularly their decision making and operating — emphasize applying their scientific knowledge integrated with their clinical experience and skills to treat patients. Yet, the culture of surgeons, both in the past as well as the present, has raised and continues to raise substantial barriers to accepting and applying scientific knowledge.

The history of surgery is replete with examples that demonstrate the resistance of the culture of surgeons to accepting scientific results, applying scientific knowledge to their patients, and especially subjecting their own practices and the results of their practices to scrutiny. Surgeons' resistance to accepting the principles of Lister for preventing contamination and infections is the most dramatic, well documented historical example. It is, however, by no means unique.

The emphasis upon the person of the surgeon appears to result in reluctance to accept innovations that they only read about, without having personal experience of its efficacy — whereas they appear to be more receptive to accept innovations that are transmitted face-to-face [cf., O'Connor et al. 1996]). For example, a recent study evaluating face-to-face education outreach endeavors found surgeons more likely than internists to change their behavior as a result of face-to-face educational interventions (Soumerai et al. 1993).

A small minority of surgeons, most of whom are in university medical centers, engage in scientific research that is relevant to surgery. These surgeons are as much scientists as their counterparts in medicine, pathology, or any other "pure" science. Nevertheless, these surgeons are threatened by a perception among their fellow academicians who view them as operating room technicians incapable of laboratory research (cf., Souba et al. 1995).

Cultural barriers continue to exist which restrict surgeons' applying scientific discoveries to their practice. Surgeons continue to adhere to their revered practices, even in the face of scientific evidence which indicates the contrary. Such behavior stems from sources which are embedded in the culture of surgeons — surgery's historical separation from medicine; the active, heroic, certain, and categorical postures of surgeons; surgery's emphasis on the person of the surgeon. Some of surgeons' resistance to applying scientific knowledge to their practices may be attributed to the organizational culture of surgery. Surgeons differ in their institutional ties and their links to surgical and medical scientific research (cf., Ravitch 1981). In America during the past hundred years surgery has been organized in several overlapping tracts which include hospital surgeons, private practice surgeons, and academic (i.e., scientific, research) surgeons, each of which has different kinds of links to science and scientists.

Additionally, many surgeons' resistance to accepting scientific knowledge can be attributed to the different "styles" of surgeons (the subject of the next chapter). Specific surgeons can be characterized as having stronger interest in scientific findings than others. Others see themselves as pure clinicians, and yet others can be characterized as "entrepreneurs."

Some surgeons insist that they are engaged in a scientific profession. The evidence indicates that some actually are. A small number of (usually academic) surgeons will bridge the gap between science and clinical practice; all will eventually make use of scientific discoveries. But the patient population would be ill served to depend on a bacteriologist and physicist to set bones and excise tumors.

Virtually all surgeons, nevertheless, are primarily clinicians who eclectically utilize scientific knowledge in their practice. Because the culture of surgeons is so based upon their practicing their clinical skills, they value active doing over analytical thinking. Because they depreciate analytical thinking, which they regard as passive, they have been resistant to accepting new scientific findings and applying them to their practice. Thus, however much the science of surgery is embedded in the contemporary practice of hospital surgery, the culture of surgeons retains pockets of influences which have detracted from surgery's identity as a science.

In many respects the culture of surgeons is incompatible with the culture of scientists. But surgical techniques are ultimately based on scientific findings. Surgical culture can delay the integration of new scientific material into clinical practice, but ultimately science prevails. The next chapter describes how many surgeons continually cross the boundaries between science and clinical practice; they are surgeons with a distinct scientific style. Their penchant for action, the heroic aura, the posture of certainty, and the objectification of patients have made it possible for surgeons to manage the challenging experiences inherent in their calling.

NOTES

1. The terms "scientists" and "clinicians" are used here, even though surgeons are "applied scientists." They are applied scientists because they apply basic, systematically empirically-derived scientific knowledge. Clinicians in traditional, non-literate societies do not. This is described in subsequent sections of this chapter.

2. Thanks to Bernard Ortiz de Mandolin (personal communication 1997).

3. The cited references on shamans reflect dissent from earlier perspectives that shamans are mentally unstable.

4. Speed was even more essential in the pre-Listera and pre-anesthesia era. However, careful handling of tissues, adequate homeostasis, and cleanliness have played significant roles in surgery since medieval times (cf., Wangensteen and Wangensteen 1978).

5. Brieger (1966, 1984, 1986, 1987, 1992), Lawrence (1992), and Wangensteen and Wangensteen (1978) are exemplary historians of surgery who have studied the historical culture of surgery. At least one (O. H. Wangensteen) is a surgeon.

6. Another barrier to acceptance of Lister's ideas was that some of Lister's premises about the causes of wound infection and healing were at first based on erroneous assumptions (e.g., of wounds healing by suppuration) (Lawrence and Dicey 1992).

7. Brieger (1966) and Temkin (1951) also stress the role of surgery in furthering the science of bacteriology.

Chapter 4

STYLES OF SURGEONS

~

[An] important factor to consider in describing the
culture of surgery is the marked differences between
surgeons.

(Brieger 1984:40)

...a great surgeon cannot be recognized by the public.
They have no way of judging between a good doctor
and a quack or between a real surgeon and a mere
pretender.

(Bernays 1906:19)

INTRODUCTION

All surgeons are not alike. They treat their patients differently, operate differently, think differently, make decisions differently, take risks differently, and communicate with other physicians, patients, and patients' families differently. Surgeons differ considerably in the ways in which they interpret the meaning of being a surgeon and the ways in which they manage their surgical practices. They have different surgical styles (cf., Brieger 1984:40; Cassell 1991:13; Salem-Schatz et al. 1990:477). A patient may be either the beneficiary of a particular surgeon's style or the unfortunate victim of another's. The consequences of specific surgical

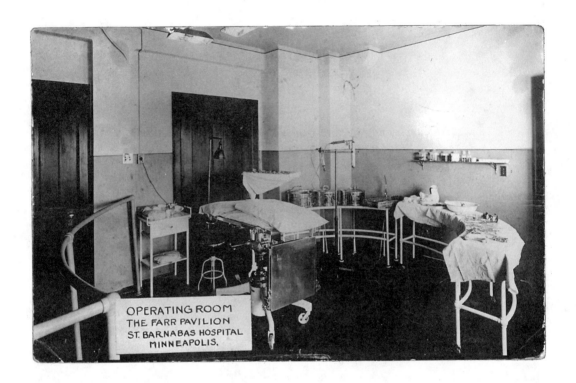

OPERATING ROOM
THE FARR PAVILION
ST. BARNABAS HOSPITAL
MINNEAPOLIS.

styles are often critical for the lives of patients, but they are rarely critical for the lives of the surgeons.

Although all surgeons are immersed in a general surgical culture and each hospital modifies that culture, each surgeon further interprets the ambient surgical culture in his own way. A number of factors influence an individual surgeon's style. One influence may be his personality type. The most important influences, however, are the cultures of the institutions in which he has participated, particularly where he attended medical school, internship and residency programs, and those hospitals in which he served as a staff member. These institutions influence the image of the surgeon he aspires to become as well as the way he interprets the practice of surgery.

At Meadowbrook University Hospital each surgeon's particular style consistently manifested itself in all his professional activities — operating, decision-making, teaching, doing research, conducting daily Rounds, and talking with patients, colleagues, and residents. The consistency of each surgeon's style offered a modicum of predictability about how a given surgeon would approach and execute surgical duties. Although accredited residency programs and Board certification with examinations have provided institutionalized standard criteria for learning and practicing surgery during the last sixty years, the culture of surgery and public mystique place high value upon the personal character of the surgeon. Individual differences in surgical styles may be more pronounced than those of other professions because of the legacy of the highly personalized process of one-to-one tutoring   — during surgical apprenticeship and the focus on great surgical heroes. The culture of surgeons has highly prized the individualized person of the surgeon and his particular style.

SURGICAL STYLES IN GRAND ROUNDS

The following illustration of style was demonstrated in Grand Rounds at Meadowbrook. During a discussion in Grand Rounds the staff surgeons were asked whether they used a particular optional diagnostic procedure. The varied responses to this question reflected the style of each surgeon. Each surgeon's response was predictable on the basis of his consistent style that was also manifest in his other surgical activities.

In one of the Grand Rounds in the Department of Surgery at Meadowbrook University Hospital the question was raised whether the surgeons present routinely used cholangiography, an x-ray of the common bile duct. Cholangiography was an *optional* diagnostic procedure that took place during the course of one of the most common operative procedures, a cholecystectomy (gall bladder removal). Almost 20 percent of surgical admissions at Meadowbrook University Hospital were for cholecystectomies. Cholangiography takes place during the operation after all the stones are believed to have been removed and while the abdomen remains open. Its purpose is to determine if any stones remain in the common bile duct (which could cause subsequent problems for the patient and require another operation).

Each of the surgeons attending that Rounds were essentially aware of the contemporary data on intraoperative cholangiography. At that time[1] that data indicated the following: a) Approximately 95 percent of the cholecystectomy patients did not have stones remaining in their common bile duct (Kitahama 1986). b) Cholangiography was the only certain way to determine if a patient were among the five percent who had stones remaining (Kondylis et al. 1997). c) Using cholangiography added 15 to 35 minutes to an operation; d) Not undertaking the procedure was not life-threatening.[2] e) Neither patients nor referring physicians were likely to inquire about, or to discover whether, cholangiography was undertaken or whether the possibility of stones remaining in the common bile duct was not thoroughly investigated. f) If stones remained in the common bile duct, the patient was highly likely to have a recurrence of gallstone trouble at a later time to require another operation for removal of gallstones (Carroll et al. 1996). g) Detection of remaining stones and returning for removal would take place at a much later time and could not definitively be attributed to the absence of cholangiography.

A surgeon's decision whether to use an intraoperative cholangiogram had no immediate consequences for either the surgeon or the patient. It had no subsequent consequences for the surgeon, because remaining stones would be discovered long after the operation. However, it had serious subsequent consequences for about five percent of the patients at a later time (Shievely et al. 1990).

The following discussion illustrates the Meadowbrook University Hospital surgeons' responses to this issue in the Grand Rounds:

Surgical Resident: (presenting Rounds): "Is there anyone who does not use an [inter-operative] cholangiogram?"

Dr. Ofir: "I don't use it on all my patients — only the ones whom I am worried about and suspect stones are left in. It's not necessary for most."

(There are no known indications or tests which could predict the presence or absence of common bile duct stones (Koo and Traverso 1996).

Surgical Resident: "Are you surprised often enough to warrant this procedure?"

Dr. Nordberg: "I only need to be surprised once, and that's enough for me to warrant it. I do it on each patient."

Dr. Aranow: "I never do a routine cholangiogram, and I'm satisfied with the results."

Dr. Robinson: "Most of us do it, because there is a higher incidence of recurrence of stones when it is not done. It is enough for me that I may miss one stone by not doing it."

Dr. Jennifer: "There was a clinical trial here a few years ago on 600 cholecystectomies and their follow-up in which intra-operative cholangiograms were taken. They found 15 in which stones were missed. At that time I had two cases where I later found I missed a stone. Now I do a cholangiogram routinely."

Dr. Haber: "I'd like to compare the percentages, and I bet there is not much difference."

Dr. Turunen: "Is there a legal problem if we decide not to do it?"

Dr. White: "The courts make a judgment based on what is a routine practice in the community."

Dr. Ofir: "Legally it is reasonable if we don't do a cholangiogram."

Dr. Turunen: "I guess the scrutiny is becoming greater."

Dr. Roddy: "Most patients probably don't need a cholangiogram. But we don't know who the ones who do are. So I believe in doing it."

Dr. Jennifer: "Many patients have jaundice post-operatively. It would be nice to know that it is not due to retained stones in the common bile duct. Sometimes these stones do not show up for a long time."

Dr. White: "Doing a routine cholangiogram gives us another indication of what's going on — of our operative effectiveness. [He presented a case in which a cholangiogram was crucial to the patient's post-operative recovery.] There is enough evidence in the literature that would warrant us to adopt routine cholangiogram as policy here."

Each surgeons' style was expressed in the responses to the Grand Rounds cholangiography issue: The surgeons who had a predominantly scientific style, Drs. Nordberg and Jennifer, could be predicted to respond in a consistently informed, questioning manner. They offered a careful, empirically-based response. Other conservative surgeons, some of whom were also known for their artistic style, Drs. Michael, Russell, Roddy, and Robinson, predictably offered cautious, vigilant responses. Less careful ones who frequently short-cut careful precautions, Drs. Aranow and Ofir predictably tried to avoid doing extra work, even when it may have been more advantageous for the patient. An older and less careful surgeon, Dr. Haber, predictably opposed innovations, particularly those that involved new techniques. The surgeon who was considered by the other surgeons to be the most negligent in the Department, Dr. Turunen, was only concerned with the legal risks involved in his decisions. Dr. White, the Chief of Surgery, whose style was both entrepreneurial and artistic, acted decisively in this example, and became immediately willing to explore and implement new ideas.

Another illustration of the consistency of style over many aspects of their professional lives occurred during a film shown to the Meadowbrook University Hospital surgeons in Grand Rounds. The film suggested a new, more effective technique for preventing post-operative infection in colon surgery. Their responses to this innovation were similar to their responses to the cholangiography question. Those surgeons who consistently short-cut careful precautions in their surgery (Drs. Aranow, Ofir, Turunen, and Haber) were reluctant to adopt the new technique. They complained that the new technique involved more coordination of nursing staff and too much extra vigilance than they were prepared to exercise. They also claimed that the implementation of the new technique would only cause more problems, and they predicted that the new technique would never take hold in their hospital.

Some of the older surgeons, such as Dr. Haber, who were consistently threatened by new surgical technology and were reluctant to try new techniques, predictably spoke about the efficacy of the old ways. In contrast to the older surgeons and the less careful ones, one of the surgeons with a scientific style, Dr. Jennifer, quoted a study from the surgical literature which supported the innovation. He suggested that the surgery department implement a clinical trial to see if it would be effective in the hospital. Dr. White, the Chief, represented an entrepreneurial style. He was interested in modernizing the department, in instituting innovations, and in participating in research trials. Predictably, he said in response to the suggestion that they implement a clinical trial to test this innovative techniques, "It looks good. Let's try it!"

Each surgeon's style was consistently expressed not only in discussions or in their acceptance of new technologies, but in virtually all their behavior as surgeons — in their responses to patients, patients' families, referring doctors, and other colleagues. Their respective styles also affected the nature of their decisions about treatment and care of their patients. For example, the research surgeons, Drs. Nordberg and Jennifer, were scientific, introspective, questioning, and cautious. Their style not only extended to their research activities but also to the way in which they interacted with patients, residents, and colleagues, in the operating room, in the office, and in Rounds.

Most of the surgeons in Meadowbrook University Hospital emphasized their clinical, artistic style in their relationships with patients and approach to decision-making, while retaining pride in both their manual dexterity (artisan's qualities), and scientific orientation. However, the ways in which each individual surgeon chose to emphasize his clinical, artistic, scientific, or entrepreneurial aspects of his roles determined his specific style. Significantly the expression of each style had important consequences for patients.

SCIENTIFIC STYLE

Dr. Nordberg was known by his colleagues in the Department of Surgery at Meadowbrook University Hospital to be the most knowledgeable and up-to-date on general surgery topics. During discussions in Rounds he predictably was the surgeon who best knew the contemporary surgical literature. He would ask penetrating questions about the rationale behind surgical decisions.

Dr. Nordberg maintained a serious interest in research in histology. He had collaborated with a histologist on a surgical research project and claimed to love working in the laboratory almost as much as he loved operating. He managed his schedule so that he worked one day a week in the histology lab, even though he earned less as a result. He published in major surgical journals and was invited to speak on his research at national and international meetings.

Dr. Nordberg considered himself to be, and others saw him as, a research surgeon with a scientific style, even though he spent most of his time with surgical patients. His scientific style was expressed in the way in which he interpreted and carried out his surgical activities, taught, made decisions, as well as how he behaved with patients, colleagues, residents, and other hospital staff. Dr. Nordberg' scientific style was one in which questioning, inquiring, verifying, and learning entered into all his activities. He believed that decisions must be made on the basis of substantial, in-depth, broad knowledge and on careful consideration of the meanings and implications of those decisions. His behavior appeared to confirm that belief.

Although Dr. Nordberg was known and respected by the national and international surgical research community, he was not particularly respected in Meadowbrook University Hospital. Most of his surgical colleagues at Meadowbrook University Hospital made jokes about the time he "wasted" in asking questions, reading, and doing research. Their jokes made fun of his thoughtful, non-decisive style, that he was interested in the autopsies of his patients, and that he didn't delegate his surgery for the residents to do for him. They said, for example, that he "didn't act like a surgeon," or that, 'he thinks he's a pathologist, the way he goes for those autopsies." The original community hospital culture of Meadowbrook expressed itself in their reactions to Dr. Nordberg. A more established university hospital "culture" would probably have appreciated his scientific style. One of the consequences of his colleagues' depreciation of Dr. Nordberg, and his working one day a week in the laboratory, was that he had fewer patients than the mean number of patients in the Department of Surgery.

In the Operating Room

Dr. Nordberg's careful style was evident by the way in which he carried out a mastectomy.[3] The first part of the operation was standard for all surgeons who planned for a likely mastectomy: Dr. Nordberg made a small incision at the site of the tumor (which he had discovered by needle biopsy in his office and which the lab had determined to be malignant) and removed a small part of the tumor and sent it for immediate diagnosis to the [stat] pathology laboratory which adjoined the operating room. There the tissue section was frozen, examined under a microscope, and a pathologist diagnosed the tissue. Sometimes at this stage of the operation Dr. Nordberg would leave the O.R. and go to the pathology laboratory to see the cells himself under the microscope. He said, "I am always visualizing in the OR what things look like under a microscope."

After making the first incision to remove part of the tumor for microscopic examination, he first sewed that incision closed. He removed his gown and gloves, and rescrubbed, regowned, and regloved. (These procedures are described in detail in the Chapter 10, "Operating Room Rituals.") He carried out these extra procedures because some of the literature on cancer suggested that cancer cells may be reintroduced into the body through the circulatory or lymph system. The evidence as to the danger of reentry of cancer cells was indeed theoretical. That information was known by most of the surgeons at Meadowbrook University Hospital. However, Dr. Nordberg was the only surgeon in the Department who decided to take these extra time- and labor-consuming precautions on the remote chance that it might prevent recurrence of cancer. Notably, when the other surgeons were asked if they knew of the existence of the practice of rescrubbing, regowning, and regloving, none were aware that one of their own colleagues practiced it (See Chapter 5, "Communication with Colleagues"). Additionally, neither Dr. Nordberg's patients, their families, nor the doctors who referred them were aware that he carried out a number of extra precautions.

The Autopsy

Dr. Nordberg's scientific style was illustrated in the way in which he managed the care, operation, death, and autopsy of his patients. When one of his patients was near death from cancer of the liver and gall bladder Dr. Nordberg attempted to prepare the family to agree to an autopsy. He did that because he believed that it was his obligation to understand as much as possible of the reason for his patient's death. He wanted to learn whether he could have done something that would have helped or saved that patient, so that he would improve his care of subsequent similar patients. Dr. Nordberg was puzzled and curious by the sequence of events which led to that patient's death. The sequence of events did not coincide with that which he had predicted from his clinical observations in the operating room or from the results from the lab and from x-rays. The only way he could learn about the final course of his patient's disease was through a careful autopsy. Yet, autopsies were not routinely undertaken at Meadowbrook University Hospital. Families of the deceased patients had to be persuaded to give permission, and most surgeons did not spend the extra time with the families to build a relationship in which such a request was likely to be granted.

The question of the cause and course of the disease made no difference to the fate of the patient or her family. But the question engaged Dr. Nordberg's mind. It was typical of his scientific style — to question anomalies and unknowns to discover why his patient died. Dr. Nordberg was so obsessed with understanding why his patient was failing that before the patient died he talked frequently to her son. Those conversations were not only because of his humanistic orientation to the patient and family. They set the stage for a request for an autopsy to be granted. In Dr. Nordberg's experience patients' families were more like to grant permission if there was good communication with the family, and if he had mentioned the possibility of an autopsy before the patient died.

Dr. Nordberg wanted the autopsy to indicate whether the cancer in the gall bladder or the liver was the primary cancer. He went over his reasoning about the patient's developments in his mind a number of times: "She had [last] come to the hospital with liver abscess. There was no gross evidence of cancer. We couldn't tell whether she died from sepsis or progressive malignant infiltration. However, her cholangiogram [x-ray of the gall bladder and bile ducts] showed persistent jaundice deterioration. That is why we called about an autopsy. In her last two weeks, we had to decide whether to subject her to surgery."

When Dr. Nordberg came in to work the morning after his patient died he informed those surgical colleagues, residents, internist, and radiologist with whom he had discussed the case. With each of them he raised the question of why she died. However, no one else was interested: The patient was dead. It was likely that he would have been interested, even if she were not his patient; he often showed interest in causes of death of patients of other surgeons. The questions about the cause of death intrigued him as a scientist and as a clinician.

Dr. Nordberg requested that the senior pathologist do the autopsy to determine the cause of death. He suggested that he should pay particular attention to the liver. When he spoke to the pathologist his voice tone was casual, as he hid the urgency of his interest. Nevertheless, later that morning he dropped by the pathology lab and continued in a casual manner to engage the pathologist's interest in the case. He described the case and the way in which it progressed. He emphasized the questions that remained unanswered.

When the pathologist's report finally answered those questions Dr. Nordberg obsessed over the results for days: "She had two big tumors in the gall bladder," he said. "The necrosis of the liver was secondary." He said excitedly: "That explained why it never healed! The size of the tumor masses suggests that the cancer had to be growing when we took out the gall bladder." He continued in an elated tone: "Now I remember an article on the gall bladder which stated that 65 percent of the patients with cancer of the gall bladder died of intra-hepatic metastasises. I think we had it chronologically wrong. The reason her liver was mushy was secondary necrosis. She died of pulmonary edema." Then he said: "I'm so glad we put pressure on the son about the autopsy."

Dr. Nordberg's scientific style of asking questions and pursuing the answers was transmitted to all the people he communicated with about his patient — the radiologist, pathologist, internists, other surgeons, and most important, the surgical residents and interns. Although most of those with whom he spoke were not interested in the course of the disease leading to the patient's death, the residents and interns nevertheless learned from his way of thinking and behaving.

Few other surgeons in the department took time or interest to request autopsies of any of their patients who died. It required an interest in the pathology of disease and death. It required time to achieve a level of communication with the family before the patient died in order to prepare them for the idea that an autopsy would be requested. It also took time to discuss the questions to be addressed with the pathologist in order to analyze the results of that autopsy. And most important, many surgeons did not encourage autopsies because autopsies could reveal their mistakes or failures. Moreover, autopsies had no immediate results: They did not save the patient's life, increase the surgeon's referrals, or enhance the surgeon's reputation in the Department of Surgery at Meadowbrook. However, autopsies increased the knowledge of the disease and of the immediate and proximate causes of death.

Dr. Nordberg pursued his interest in the cause of the patient's death and course of disease for more than a week after the death. His interest was due solely to his scientific style. The case had been routinely discussed in Surgical Mortality Rounds. There was no other person in the department, the hospital, or the family that questioned the cause of death. No one had suggested that any other form of care would have been preferred. Yet Dr. Nordberg had persisted in discovering the cause of death of this patient. The only rewards that Dr. Nordberg obtained for these efforts was his own satisfaction at trying to be a better surgeon. Dr. Nordberg was the only surgeon at Meadowbrook University Hospital who carried out these unique series of activities after his patient died. The obsessive pursuit of these questions merely for the sake of understanding was the most distinguishing characteristic of his scientific style.

Dr. Jennifer, the Director of Resident Training, was the only other surgeon in the Department who had a predominantly scientific style. That style was reflected in his dedication to teaching residents, his interest in emphasizing diagnoses in teaching, and his inquiring and persistent approach to understanding the problems of his patients. Dr. Jennifer was dogged in following his diagnostic intuitions, even when preliminary evidence indicated otherwise. Although he is illustrated here as representing a scientific style because of his scientific knowledge and approach to solving problems, there was much in Dr. Jennifer's style that was also artistic; he was a model clinician. These characteristics include his intuitive sense about patients and their disease course, and his adventurousness, and the actions which ensued from these traits. Both of these qualities, however, are characteristic of both scientists and artists. Dr. Jennifer first showed his adventureness when he was the first to agree to submit to being the subject of an anthropological study (See Chapter 1, "Encounters with Surgeons").

An example of Dr. Jennifer's scientific approach to diagnosis occurred when he suspected that a 35-year-old female patient had diverticulitis. Although her symptoms also suggested the possibility of bowel cancer, and she had a family history of cancer, Dr. Jennifer's experience and clinical intuition suggested to him that she had diverticulitis. When the blood test returned with no signs of diverticulitis, Dr. Jennifer did not give up his conviction. He suggested that the blood test be repeated. The test was repeated, and it came back positive for diverticulitis. He explained: "Most of my practice consists of standard cases, and I do them without much thinking. When you've been a clinician as long as I have you know these well. But you also smell an unusual situation. When something doesn't fit, you can't sleep. You pursue it. You ask what it is."

THE CLINICIAN

Dr. Roddy was a 54-year-old general surgeon who had served on the surgical staff at Meadowbrook University Hospital for 18 years. He was an optimistic, active, and gregarious man. He liked to talk with his colleagues, to engage his patients in conversation, to operate, and to teach.

When Dr. Roddy was with a patient, he listened carefully, examined, and made decisions carefully. He concentrated on the patient and the patient's problem.

Although he had good relationships with referring physicians and sent them the usual progress notes on their patients, he concentrated more on being an excellent clinician to his patients than in writing detailed referral notes.

Dr. Roddy made diagnoses with care, study, and analysis, even though it slowed his decision-making process. In the operating room he was present throughout all his operations. He said, "I consider it a breach of contract with my patient if I am not present all the time." Like Dr. Nordberg, Dr. Roddy prided himself that he gave each of his patients the best possible care that was available. However, the referring doctors were not particularly aware that Dr. Roddy gave all their patients exceptionally careful, concerned, and high quality care.

Dr. Roddy's behavior, particularly his use of surgical intuition (cf., Abernathy and Hamm 1995), characterized his combination of an artistic and scientific style. The following case describes the way in which he formulated a difficult diagnosis. It illustrates Dr. Roddy's intuition and his obsessiveness, traits which are characteristic of both scientists and artists:

The Case of the Difficult Diagnosis

This case illustrates how Dr. Roddy intuitively recognized an anomalous symptom pattern and persisted in his attempts to correctly diagnose the disease. Even when the tests did not support his intuitive clinical reasoning, he ordered repeat tests, which subsequently supported his hypothesis.

The patient, Mrs. Ings, had had an oophorectomy (removal of the ovaries) five years previously for cancer of the ovaries. She originally presented to Dr. Roddy's surgical colleague, Dr. Aranow, with distal peripheral neuropathy (nerve damage of the extremities). She had inguinal lymphadenopathy (abnormally enlarged lymph nodes in the inguinal region of the abdomen). For diagnostic purposes Dr. Aranow ordered an inguinal lymph node biopsy, a bone marrow scan, and lymphography of the hilar nodes. He demonstrated no particular intuitive skills when he ordered a standard battery of tests for the symptoms.

Dr. Aranow had been puzzled by the results of the tests, because they were not consistent with the results which he had expected to find if the original cancer had spread. He did not pursue other diagnoses. Rather, he consulted with his colleague, Dr. Roddy: "I have an interesting patient. The family doctor called me about her. She's got a belly ache and gallstones. The chest x-rays showed pleural effusion. I think it is a benign ovarian tumor. I thought it was chronic pancreatitis. I want her to have an ERCP (Endoscopic retrograde cholangio-pancreatography — an invasive diagnostic tool to examine the pancreas) (cf., Scheeres et al. 1990). "She has the biggest inguinal lymphadenopathy I've ever seen and distal neuropathy too."

Dr. Roddy recognized an anomaly in the symptom pattern, which Dr. Aranow hadn't noticed. Dr. Roddy was suspicious that the patient had lymphoma. He suggested to Dr. Aranow that he do another node biopsy which he expected to be consistent with a diagnosis of lymphoma. Despite the pathology report which showed he was wrong, he remained convinced that the symptom pattern indicated lymphoma. He explained his intuition and obsessive conviction: "Even when the node biopsy showed [sic] negative for lymphoma, I felt it doesn't fit with the clinical picture."

Because Dr. Roddy wanted to understand the inconsistency between his intuitive diagnosis and the diagnosis indicated by the pathology report, he consulted with the pathologist. He told the pathologist, "There must be something going on in the lymph glands." He explained the clinical picture and the problem to the pathologist and suggested that the pathologist reexamine the specimen. When the pathologist did reexamine the lymph nodes he indeed found malignant cells. This finding confirmed Dr. Roddy's original diagnosis of lymphoma.

Although the diagnosis was a critical and pessimistic one for the patient, Dr. Roddy was elated at making such a difficult diagnosis correctly. He explained his persistence in diagnosing the present case. "There were a number of indications in the clinical picture, and she was clinically too sick to have nothing. She was weak. Also, her pattern of neuropathy was wrong."

Obtaining Informed Consent

When Dr. Roddy wanted a patient to sign an informed consent form either for surgery or for entering a clinical research trial, he consistently took time to explain the forms to his patients. (Many of his colleagues left this task to the nurses.) He told the patients that they should know the meaning of the form and that they had options to refuse to participate (cf., Hahn 1982; Tancredi 1982). For example, Dr. Roddy attempted to explain the consent form to a lady who was barely literate in English and to her daughter who was literate. He carefully described the patient's current medical status, the nature of the clinical trial, and the experience she could expect. He was careful to ensure that the consent requested was fully understood. He emphasized that she could stop at any time:

Dr. Roddy: "You had a tumor in your bowel and it was the kind of tumor that can spread. It doesn't look as if it has spread. But it could get into your blood. We give medicine that kills tumors in the blood. We do not know if it is working good [sic] or not. We are asking your permission to be in a clinical research trial. We are randomizing who gets the medicine and who doesn't. That means that some people will get the medicine and some will not. They don't know who gets what, and we don't know either. We don't know if the medicine is working on the blood. If the medicine is working for sure, we would give it to everybody. We will be watching you closely. And you can refuse to stay in it at any time."

Patient: "If the medicine does not work is there any harm?"

Dr. Roddy: "No. Some medicines are harmful and can make people sick. But there are no harmful effects with this kind of medicine.[4] You would come in once every two weeks for three times and then every two months for six times. We have a permission slip. Read it and talk it over with your daughter and if you have any other questions just ask."

Dr. Roddy waited for several minutes while the daughter read it and discussed it with her mother.

Dr. Roddy: "Are there any other questions? Do you understand it? Tell me what you understand."

Dr. Roddy listened as they repeated their understanding of the consent form, and when he was satisfied that they understood he gave the pen to them to sign.

THE ENTREPRENEURIAL SURGEON

Dr. John White, the Chief of Surgery at Meadowbrook University Hospital, had a style that combined attributes of both a talented artisan — for his manual dexterity in the operating room — and that of an entrepreneur — for his readiness to commit his department to participation in innovative programs. Although he was immersed in surgical science as were all the other surgeons in the hospital, his ambition and his penchant for wheeling and dealing, and his proclivity for quick decision-making frequently took precedence over surgical science. The results were often to the detriment of his patients.

Dr. White's posture toward his professional activities was characteristic of an artistic and an entrepreneurial style (cf., Lyons 1994; Pear and Eckholm 1991). He could manage many complex tasks in an organized and administratively innovative manner. He had considerable ability to influence the hospital and medical system to increase the power of the surgery department and of himself. Dr. White used his talents in engaging, charming, and influencing friends, colleagues, patients, and university and hospital officials. Frequently his choice of behavior toward a person depended upon the status of that person. He was perceptive about people's interests, strengths, and weaknesses, and he used this knowledge in many situations to manipulate them.

Dr. White's entrepreneurial style was manifest in virtually all of the activities in which he engaged — in interactions with patients and their families, with residents, with surgical and other medical colleagues, and with others in the medical and non-medical community. He expressed his style in the way in which he organized his schedule, made decisions, mediated conflicts, and interacted with colleagues, residents and patients. He also expressed it in the way in which he taught, operated, and initiated research for the Department of Surgery.

Dr. White spent comparatively little time with his patients. However, he spent a large proportion of his time in communicating with other physicians in his hospital and outside who were actual or potential referral sources. His informal conversations with colleagues in the cafeteria and the halls were more likely to involve administrative plans and management and organizational problems than his patients or surgical procedures. He frequently let residents substitute for him during surgery, a practice that was not legal at Meadowbrook University Hospital.

Because he was Chief of Surgery and was skillful in seeking referrals, he had the largest number of patients among the surgeons in the department. As Chief his power and access to resources permitted him to carry out more activities than the other surgeons. He had the chief resident at his command to assist him, and frequently to substitute for him in the O.R. and in all aspects of care for his patients. He was able to arrange operating room times for his own convenience.

Dr. White was typical of most of the surgeons at Meadowbrook University Hospital, including the scientific surgeons, in one respect: He appeared to thrive on interruptions. He deliberately arranged his time so as to be frequently interrupted. If he were not interrupted by others, he interrupted himself. For example, while writing or seeing patients he would suddenly go to a colleague's office to talk. Even though he was not very sensitive with patients and spent very little time with each patient, he occasionally agreed to see a patient who appeared in his office unannounced because he welcomed interruptions.

Dr. White spent more time communicating with potential or actual referral sources than he did with his patients. He was intent on portraying himself to other physicians as a caring physician, even though he spent little time or effort in communication with, or sustained care of, his patients. When physicians referred patients to him he immediately wrote to that referring physician to inform him of the patient's visit, his surgical decision, and the patient's progress. He always ended his letter with "thank you for referring this patient to me." He was acutely aware of the significance of other physicians' impressions of him for his reputation and subsequent referrals. He deliberately cultivated the impression for other physicians that he attended to his patients as carefully as he attended to them. The referring physicians were not aware that Dr. White assigned communicating with and caring for patients a low priority in his hierarchy of tasks.

Dr. White often missed "daily" rounds of his patients who were on the surgical ward, leaving those patients for the residents to see. Dr. White's arbitrary scheduling methods and his haste when he saw patients appeared to affect those patients adversely. For example, Dr. White typically had approximately twenty of his patients at a time on the surgical ward, more than any other surgeon. On those days in which he made rounds he spent less than a minute with each patient. He often did not remember who they were, nor why they were in the hospital. Before or after entering a patient's room he frequently asked the chief resident, "What did we operate on him for?"

Dr. White assumed a very active posture when he made decisions. He believed in acting, doing, and deciding. When he became aware of a reasonable innovation, such as the new procedure for treating colons mentioned previously, he was very likely to decide to implement that innovation. Once he made a decision he proceeded to carry it out. He expressed no doubts about his decisions. For example, when a film from a drug company illustrating a new way of managing abscesses was shown to the members of the surgery department (the surgeons' responses to this film are discussed in Chapter 6, "Communication with Patients"), Dr. White suggested that they implement that new method. Some of the surgeons complained that implementation would be fraught with problems and that it would not succeed. Older surgeons, such as Dr. Haber, spoke about the efficacy of the old ways. Drs. Nordberg and Jennifer, the scientific surgeons, suggested that they first implement a clinical trial to determine its effectiveness. But Dr. White decisively said, "It looks good. Let's try it!" And without inquiring further about the pros and cons, Dr. White immediately made all the arrangements for the innovation to be implemented — without a preliminary clinical trial.

Dr. White's penchant for decisiveness and absence of doubt was illustrated by an incident with Dr. Deborah. Dr. Deborah was participating in a departmental clinical research trial in which he was to place women into one of two categories, pre-menopausal or post-menopausal. Dr. Deborah was unable to decide into which category to place a particular patient whose clinical signs were neither clearly pre- nor post-menopausal. He decided to ask Dr. White how to classify this patient. After hearing the clinical data from Dr. Deborah, Dr. White immediately decided upon the category, even though he was less of an expert on that subject than Dr. Deborah.

It was quite likely that if Dr. Nordberg, the scientific surgeon who probably was best informed on the research topic, were asked this same question by Dr. Deborah, he would have recommended that the patient be taken out of the research trial because she belonged definitively in neither category. Dr. Deborah asked the Chief instead, because he knew that he would give an immediate, definite, and non-ambiguous answer and because he initiated the trial and wanted to recruit patients. Dr. White most likely also realized that the patient should probably not be included in the study, because she belonged in neither category. Yet his decisiveness combined with the desire to have his Department recruit patients for research led him to make such a decision. This example illustrates not only Dr. White's decisiveness and his priorities in making decisions, but also how his surgical colleagues recognized and utilized his decisiveness.

As Chief of the Department of Surgery, Dr. White was responsible for assuring that all of the surgical staff were serving the optimum number of patients. On those occasions when there were too many patients for the number of beds, Dr. White telephoned the head nurse on the inpatient surgery ward to discharge other surgeons' patients: "Is there anyone you can kick out? Look at the list and see whom you can throw out. Give them the big boot!" He added, "My patients are okay!" (cf., Mizrahi 1986).

On these occurrences Dr. White usually suggested that the nurse particularly scrutinize the patients of four of the surgeons in the department to chose their patients for discharge. The four surgeons he chose were those who had the least power. They were those whom he could most easily manipulate. He did not choose those who were known to keep their patients longer than others. The Chief did not ask nurses to determine which of all the patients were well enough to be discharged, because it was not decided solely on medical grounds. He ordered patients "thrown out" according to the statuses of their surgeons, not according to the medical status of patients. Also, Dr. White never considered his own patients when he needed beds. They had special status with regard to their length of stay in the hospital. He earned additional income from their extended time in the hospital.

Dr. White frequently referred to medical problems of patients as if they were the fault of the patient. He expressed anger about (not directly toward) the patient who had unexpected medical problems. For example, when Dr. White talked about one of his patients who had developed a post-operative wound infection he said, "He's been giving me a lot of trouble." When he asked the residents about the status of the patients on his ward, he said, "How are the patients on B? Any grief from them?"

The position of Chief gave Dr. White power. In addition to having his patients stay longer in the hospital, he had power to grant privileges to others in the Department. He also had the power to request the services of the chief resident at any time. He scheduled operating times for himself and other surgeons. He assigned himself more, and more convenient, operating times. His position as Chief brought him an increase in the number of his patient referrals, including many from doctors whom he did not know. He commented that his colleagues treated him with greater deference and respect soon after he was selected to be Chief.

Dr. White performed only about one-third of his own surgeries. Two-thirds of his patients were operated on by a resident, usually the chief resident. Although this practice was illegal in Meadowbrook, he managed to get away with it because he was the Chief of Surgery. The residents were dependent upon him for their future careers. He managed to be present in the operating room when the patient was awake and was able to see that he was there. As soon as the patient was unconscious he usually left the operating room. He remained in the hospital, within reach through paging or telephone. In this way he managed to do many other tasks while his numerous patients were being operated on by a senior resident.

The residents, however, were critical of Dr. White's operating room practice. Although they were pleased to obtain experience, they said that they had to make many small decisions without his input because he only wanted to be interrupted for major decisions. The absence of surgeons in the operating room and on the wards was the major source of complaints by residents who felt that the surgeons were not spending enough time teaching them. This was the problem for which the surgeons had requested the consultation that led to this research.

Dr. White was also predictably present during particularly difficult or complex operations. But, of course, unexpected complications may arise in the most apparently simple operation. It was in these situations, which did occur, that his frequent absences affected patients' lives. The patients, however, were never aware of the risks they were taking. They assumed the surgery would be performed by the Chief, and, if necessary, could verify it later by the hospital record which he signed.

Dr. White's entrepreneurial style was manifest in his attempts to obtain more power for the Department of Surgery. In one of these attempts he devised a plan for his department to take over a cancer ward from the Internal Medicine Department. In making this move he sought to replace the medical oncologist, Dr. Lehrer, whose several years of specialty training and Board certification had made him an expert on the treatment of cancer. His purpose in enhancing the power of the Department of Surgery had critical negative implications for patients with cancer: Oncology is a recognized subspecialty in Medicine requiring several years study of the etiology, pathophysiology, and therapeutic options for treating cancer. At the time of the study it was not a subspecialty in surgery, and few surgeons had comparable training or knowledge.[5] Some of the implications of a surgeon practicing as an oncologist instead of the Board-certified medical oncologist in Meadowbrook University Hospital are discussed in Chapter 8, "Surgical Decision Making, Referrals, and 'Keeping' Patients."

Dr. White's entrepreneurial style was manifest in virtually all of the activities in which he engaged — in interactions with patients and their families, with residents, with surgical and other medical colleagues, and with others in the medical and non-medical community. His style was also reflected in the way in which he taught, operated, and initiated research in the department, as well as in the way in which he organized his time. He combined the general surgical culture of decisiveness and absence of doubts with his unique style through which he was able to use the power he had obtained in order to manipulate his hospital and medical school. The result of his style, however, was one in which thoughtful concern for the patients in the department, including his own, was relegated to a low priority. He assigned enhancing the power of his department to a much higher priority.

CONCLUSION

Knowledge about surgeons' different styles of practicing surgery was largely concealed from patients, referring doctors, and even from most of their medical and surgical colleagues. Most physicians, with the exception of surgical residents, had limited information about their surgical colleagues' styles of decision-making, operating, or bedside behavior. They were not present when the surgeons were making decisions, operating, or making Rounds. The physicians who referred their patients to surgeons were only able to evaluate the surgeons by their personal communication with them, their own observations, and the surgeons' explanations of their patients' outcomes, and the limited information available from patients. Most physician referrals are based on criteria other than first-hand knowledge about the expertise of the other (Freidson 1976; Shortell 1974; Shortell and Anderson 1971).

A surgeon's style directly affects the decisions he makes about his patient. Style affects, for example, the ways in which he makes diagnoses and acts upon those diagnoses. Style affects whether the diagnoses are based upon a careful or careless assessment of the evidence; whether diagnoses and treatments are based upon serious concern and caution and care about the total circumstances of the patient or whether they are based upon concern for expediency for the hospital or for himself; and whether decisions are based upon knowledge or ignorance, experience or naiveté, habit, or awareness of contemporary knowledge and the latest research.

The surgeon's style affects the tests he recommends for the patient, his interpretation of the test results, his decision about the treatment — including whether he should be treated medically or surgically, aggressively or conservatively, or with known experimental techniques. Salem-Schatz et al. found great variation among physicians in the decision making which they attribute to "practice style" or the physician's "clinical personality." They emphasize traits such as "degree of interventionism" and "tolerance for the undesirable consequences of therapy itself" as important components of style which affect decisions about their patients (1990:477).

The surgeon's style affects the ways in which he communicates information to the patient and to his family about the patient's illness, the risks which he subjects the patient to in intervention, and most important, about the choices that are available to the patient. Surgical style, therefore, is not an incidental or negligible attribute of surgeons.

NOTES

1. At the present time laparoscopic cholecystectomy (removal of the gall bladder via an endoscope) is the most common procedure for removing gall bladders; it was first adopted in the 1980s, and most surgeons had adopted it by the early 1990s (Escarce et al. 1997). Its introduction has resulted in increased rates of cholecystectomies (Legorreta et al. 1993). It has changed a major surgical procedure to a minor one. This procedure is

significantly less intrusive (e.g., an inch-long incision and three tiny puncture wounds), requires a shorter hospital stay, results in less post-operative pain and discomfort, and is less expensive than operative cholecystectomies (Berggren et al. 1996; Roush and Traverso 1995). However, increased bile duct injuries are found in laparoscopic cholecystectomies (Mirza et al. 1997; Berggren et al. 1997), likely because of the surgeons' failure to routinely perform intraoperative cholangiographies. Such injuries occur despite the fact that two of the U.S. pioneers of laparoscopic cholecystectomy, D. Olsen and E. Reddick, recommended that this radiographic procedure (i.e., intraoperative cholangiography) be routinely performed in order to better identify the common bile duct before cutting (Thomas E. Beam, personal communication 1998).

2. Undertaking the procedure held a small risk of traumatization by a catheter in those patients for whom the common bile duct was small (cf., Welch and Malt 1987:1004-05). Another procedure used during surgery to determine whether stones remain (in the common bile duct) is that of choledoscopy. In choledoscopy either a rigid or flexible fiberoptic instrument is inserted in the common bile duct. This procedure is considered to be equally effective both in determining the presence of residual stones and in affecting post-operative morbidity (Scheeres et al. 1990; Apelgren et al. 1990; Wheeler et al. 1990).

3. At the time of this study the data on the outcomes of lumpectomy vs. mastectomy were not known. Additionally, it was common practice in Meadowbrook University Hospital to perform the mastectomy once a definitive diagnosis of cancer were made histologically while the patient remained under general anesthesia.

4. Although this is presented as an example of informed consent, it is clear that to deny any "harmful effects" is not full disclosure.

5. Surgical oncologists are likely to be more knowledgeable about surgical treatments than about medical or radiological treatments for cancer. Although at the time of the study oncology was not a Board-certified subspecialty in surgery, as it has been in internal medicine, it is presently a respected surgical subspecialty.

Chapter 5

COMMUNICATION WITH COLLEAGUES

~

Hardly ever does any doctor on the staff approach any other doctor and question his practice methods. It just isn't done.

(Nolen 1970:179)

Gossip has been the only means of communication that we've had here.
(Dr. Michael's comment to the Chief of Surgery)

INTRODUCTION

The surgeons in Meadowbrook University Hospital saw each other almost every working day. They shared the same office areas, operating rooms, and lounges. They attended hospital and department rounds together. For years they worked with the same colleagues and surgical residents and met many of their family members in social contexts. Notwithstanding their shared specialities, offices, and professional and personal social networks, the surgeons at Meadowbrook knew very little about the actual ways in which their colleagues conducted many aspects of their professional lives. They were quite ignorant of their colleagues' patient loads, diagnostic approaches, or surgical techniques. Yet, ironically, they were immensely interested in those aspects of their colleagues' lives. Substantial barriers to

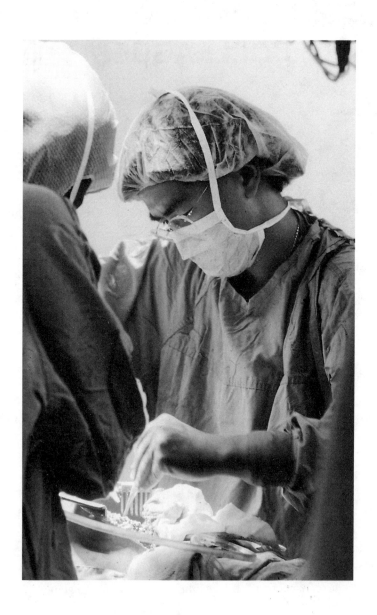

Courtesy, Johns Hopkins Medicine.

communication restricted the exchange of important information among the surgeons.

The surgeons' lack of knowledge about their closest colleagues' professional practices was not due to their shyness. On the contrary, these surgeons were a gregarious lot. They were highly verbal, acted friendly with each other, and appeared to enjoy talking to each other. Informal communication, such as talking, bantering, and gossip, played an important role in their professional lives. Moreover, they were intensely interested in the professional activities of their colleagues. Because the information they received directly from their surgical colleagues was remarkably limited, they were innovative in their efforts to obtain information about them indirectly. They communicated in ways that withheld information about themselves, while seeking to obtain information about their colleagues.

The surgeons' communication patterns created barriers which separated them from each other personally and professionally. Despite their overt friendliness and comaraderie, they maintained distinct distance and secrecy from each other. Such varied and often contradictory styles of communication can be understood as strategies for negotiating processes of cooperating while competing, of sharing some information while concealing other information.

This chapter focuses on the role that communication plays among surgeons in both unifying and promoting solidarity, as well as dividing and encouraging disunity. It describes how the culture of surgeons, in general, and the culture of the surgeons in Meadowbrook University Hospital, in particular, influenced the patterns and substance of communication both among surgeons as well as between surgeons and other physicians. It emphasizes both the informal and indirect ways in which the surgeons obtained substantive surgical knowledge about each other and about other medical specialists.

A friendly but superficial collegiality exists among the surgeons, and a strong community spirit can be activated if they are threatened by outsiders (cf., Bosk 1979:5; Cassell 1989; 1991). This discussion focuses upon barriers to communication and the specific ways in which these barriers affect how the surgeons practiced surgery. It follows Durkheim who stressed that divisive forces exist within every collective group ([1933] 1947:152-54;168-73). It is based on the premise that understanding surgeons' communication styles, communication barriers, and communication efficacy is important for understanding how professional information is transmitted and is prevented from being transmitted. Subsequent chapters analyze the implications of these barriers for surgeons' communicating with their patients, disseminating surgical knowledge, and making decisions. Together these chapters describe how communication barriers ultimately affected the quality of care that the surgeons provided to their patients.

LANGUAGE CONVENTIONS

The surgeons at Meadowbrook University Hospital shared many specific informal, mutually understood unspoken communicative conventions, a trait common to many groups of people with the same occupation and who work in close proximity within the same organization (cf., Bernstein 1971). One of the Meadowbrook surgeons explained: "The system works very much in a nonverbal kind of way."

The surgeons also used informal codes to communicate with each other about relatively unimportant information, such as greetings, as well as for substantive information, including that about patients, colleagues, techniques, or schedules. Their code included some conventional forms which were typically shared by most other medical professionals, such as "stat" (for immediately), or PRN (for as necessary), OR, ICU, ER (for places in the hospital), and nicknames for medical specialists, such as "shrinks" and "orthopods." They also typically referred to patients by names of their operative sites — "the breast," "that colon," their pathological conditions — "the hernias;" the name of their diseases — "the oat cell" (referring to oat cell carcinoma of the lung), the "lipoma" (cf., Estroff 1993); or the name of the operative procedure — the "trach" (referring to a patient who had a tracheotomy). Identifying patients by their operative site represents a form of disembodiment (cf., K. Young 1989).

They also referred to patients by randomly chosen nicknames, usually initiated in the operating room. Humorous linguistic codes described patients with terminal conditions, such as "Going to Chicago," "Don't buy her any L.P.'s," patients who were dead, such as "She canceled her dancing lessons;" and "The lady didn't stand when called," referring to the anecdote about telling the wife that her husband died, "All the married ladies stand up. Not so fast, Mrs. Hayes."

In everyday conversation with each other the surgeons frequently used profanity in the form of commonly forbidden words. The words most frequently used were those explicitly relating to the body and body functions (to which they were constantly being exposed). They used them most often as nouns or expletives, rather than as adjectives. For example, they used the word "shit" frequently as a noun or expletive, but they rarely used it as an adjective or adverb.

In the operating room the surgeons made many joking remarks about patients' bodies and body parts, and the process of operating. They joked about the appearance of the patients' bodies, about leakage of bodily substances, such as excessive bleeding or spilled feces (for example, "Don't you bleed all over me, Agatha"), and joked in graphic fashion about their activities (for example, "I can't wait to get my hands on that esophagus," and "Watch him sports fans, he's got the scissors") (cf., D.P.Gordon 1983).

They made joking remarks more often about those parts of the body related to excretory or sexual functions than to other parts of the body. For example, "Mr. Ryan [a colon surgery patient] is the king of the bowels." They joked about body parts ("Can you believe she has hair on her breasts! But that'll be gone soon") and they sometimes referred to their difficulties in locating those parts. For example, "Dave, where is your rectum? There is a rumor about you that you have a rectum. Yeah, Dave, we've finally found it;" or, "Where the hell's that stomach?" Or, "I'm not sure what this organ is? Is it an organ?" They joked about parts of the body they excised. For example, when a 14-pound lipoma was excised, one of their jokes included, "Send for a large pathologist, one that has had all his hernias repaired."

In the operating room surgeons and anesthesiologists frequently used humor to criticize each other. It most likely occurred because of the potentially conflictual relationship between two equally qualified physicians with distinct and separate responsibilities for the patient. For example, Dr. White addressed the anaesthesiologist indirectly by stating, "If the patient would only stop moving around we would have it easier." "When will he [not you] stop using a local?" or "Let me know if he turns blue or anything."

Day-to-Day Informal Communication

Most studies on surgeons have focused on explicitly surgically-related behaviors (Bosk 1979; Millman 1976) or depend heavily upon interviews in which surgeons talk about their behaviors and attitudes toward surgery and surgeons to the interviewer (Cassell 1981). Most studies on communication among other physicians also focus on explicit physician-related behavior (cf., Freidson 1976; Weinberg et al. 1981). Explicit surgical behavior is more accessible than is the day-to-day, informal, banal, and apparently trivial and not surgically-related talk that is exchanged among surgical colleagues. However, systematically examining these informal verbal exchanges over a continuous time period facilitates under-standing additional aspects of the culture of surgery, precisely because surgeons (and other physicians) rely heavily upon informal means for much of their professional communication. Their informal communication channels underlie, in the words of one of Meadowbrook surgeons, "the way the system works."

The surgeons at Meadowbrook preferred to communicate in a light and frequently funny style. Rather than a more serious, heavy, and direct style, this had the effect of encouraging indirect communication of important matters. They greeted each other in informal, friendly ways during the day. They used nicknames, asked about each others' welfare, spent time bantering, and occasionally patted particular friends on the back. Most of the surgeons behaved in an extroverted, gregarious, and friendly manner. Their light communicative style was compatible with their historically-derived active posture. A surgeon could count on meeting by chance each of his full-time surgical colleagues in the course of one or two days. They met in the hallways, elevators, cafeteria, and surgeons' lounge, The "chance" nature of these informal meetings existed only in the exact timing and exact place, not in the fact of meeting. The surgeons optimized their opportunities for "chance" meetings by frequently moving from one task to another and from one location to another. They rarely remained in one place, or became involved in a single activity for a long period of time.

In every situation in which surgeons were observed, with the exception of the operating room, they interrupted their activities (including activities normally requiring prolonged concentration, such as reading, writing papers, and consulting with patients) by either initiating or responding to diversions. Perhaps this orientation to changing place and activity was a manifestation of their active posture, or an amelioration of their otherwise lone tasks. The previous chapter described how Dr. White deliberately arranged his time so as to be frequently interrupted. The surgeons depended upon such "chance" meetings not only to exchange greetings and banter, but, more important, to convey substantive messages about patients and procedures. These included events of the highest degree of importance to them. Freidson wrote: "the request for and granting of advice or information, ... would probably not have taken place ... if they had not happened to come together when they did. It was often embedded in social non-functional talk. Much corridor or luncheon-table interaction was of this nature,..."(1976:157) Surgeons explicitly sought each other out to speak directly to each other only when there was considerable urgency to the communication.

The following example illustrates how important information was communicated informally and indirectly: Dr. Michael wanted to cancel a procedure on his patient which his resident had initiated. Although he disagreed with the resident's decision about the procedure, he did not want to appear to criticize him by simply instructing him to cancel it. For this reason he did not to seek out the resident explicitly, but instead he chose to wait until he "chanced" to meet the resident in the course of the day. This occurred when they met in the elevator in the afternoon. They exchanged light talk for more than a minute, and as they departed from the elevator, Dr. Michael casually mentioned, "Oh, Mr. Borg has been through so many tests, maybe an IVC is less risky than the ERCP" (Endoscopic retrograde cholangiopancreatography — an invasive fiber-optic diagnostic procedure to examine the pancreas). The resident immediately understood that although the context and style of the communication were casual, Dr. Michael had communicated a message that was clear, serious, and substantive. The resident replied, "I think I'll cancel the ERCP." Dr. Michael's use of an indirect communication style had the effect of giving the resident autonomy to respond, both as to the timing and the substance of the response. They, thus, shared the myth that it was the resident's idea. By not going directly to the resident's office and directly telling the resident what to do, both Dr. Michael and the resident could behave as if they were relative equals and that the resident initiated the change.

Communication Barriers

While these normally extroverted, gregarious, jovial, vocal surgeons talked frequently with each other, they were quite guarded in the information they exchanged. They carefully protected information about themselves, their patients, their operating loads, operative techniques, referral sources, levels of specific knowledge, specific expertise (particularly deficits in knowledge and expertise), income, and doubts and concerns about medical decisions. As a result, surgeons at Meadowbrook University Hospital knew relatively little about the practices of their surgical colleagues, even those who were in the same surgical specialties, who shared offices and/or receptionists, and who had been in the same surgery department together for years. An exception to sharing some knowledge occurred in those cases in which surgeons were "close friends." But even close friends kept much information from each other.

Even during surgical rounds which were designed to provide opportunities to learn by communicating knowledge, exchanging information about specific cases, and identifying errors and gaps in surgical practice, communication among the surgeons was cautious and guarded. Millman's (1977) and Bosk's (1979) books on surgeons' behaviors in Mortality and Morbidity Rounds in their respective hospitals described details of their behavior in hospital rounds that were similar to those found in Meadowbrook University Hospital.

The barriers to communication restricted the surgeons' awareness of their own limitations. They limited their accessibility to new information. This affected their ability to think in new ways. Most important, the barriers to communication and the isolation which resulted from these barriers affected their awareness of the options for making decisions, the nature of decisions, and the consequences of their decisions for patients. Their effects upon decision-making are discussed in Chapter 7, "How Surgeons Make Decisions: Influence of Active Posture on Decision Making," Chapter 8, "Surgical Decision Making, Referrals, and 'Keeping' Patients," and Chapter 9, "Implications of the Culture of Surgeons for Modern Medicine."

Freidson's book, *Doctoring Together*, which studied physicians in a group practice (most of whom were not surgeons), described patterns of communication, particularly barriers to communication that were similar to those used by surgeons in Meadowbrook University Hospital (1976). He discussed the difficulties in evaluating medical colleagues' competency, given the paucity of information about them (cf., M. Good 1995). Freidson wrote about "serious barriers to the transmission of information about critical areas of physician performance" (1976:165). In the group medical practice Freidson studied evaluation was based largely upon gossip of other colleagues, including house staff of another hospital and personal experiences in working and talking with specific physicians, and upon hearsay by either patients or colleagues. "[In group practice] not all physicians agreed that they could really observe and evaluate one another,..." "Many secrets about physician performance were kept rather well" (1976:148;165). Freidson's study confirmed the difficulties in obtaining information about colleagues, even in a group practice which shared more information than in a fee-for-service practice, such as existed in Meadowbrook University Hospital.

Freidson explained that although his research revealed that a number of physicians in the group practice were guilty of dangerous neglect, falsifying records, and outrageous and criminal behavior, "most physicians [in that group practice] did not seem to know of even serious cases of repeated poor performance which occurred in their own specialties, let alone in others" (1976).

Manipulative Communication

Most of the surgeons in the Department of Surgery at Meadowbrook University Hospital learned about proposed amalgamation plans between their hospital and Provincial Hospital through informal channels of communication. The amalgamation would significantly affect the practices of all the surgeons.

For eight months Dr. White, the Chief of Surgery, had been heavily involved in negotiations with the administration of Meadowbrook, its Board, and with the Chief of Surgery at Provincial Hospital. Dr. White did not discuss the plans with any of the other surgeons at Meadowbrook University Hospital. He decided to present the information about the merger to the surgeons in his department eight months after most of the basic decisions about specialties and surgeons had been agreed upon and after a Memorandum of Understanding had been signed by officials of both hospitals. Dr. White announced the amalgamation plans to the full-time surgical staff present at the monthly "Surgical Mortality Rounds." His indirect style for discussing important information was illustrated by the fact that he did not organize a specific meeting on this topic. Dr. White explained the change from Mortality Rounds to Department Meeting by announcing, "There haven't been any interesting deaths this month." He requested all people who were not on the full-time surgical staff to leave the room, including the residents, interns, part-time surgeons, and other physicians. (The author was permitted to remain and take notes.)

Dr. White began the meeting by saying that he wanted to "clarify some of the gossip that has been going around." Although the details had already been worked out, and the hospital officials had made definite decisions about the merger, Dr. White falsely[1] told the staff that they had just begun negotiations with Provincial Hospital, and "We have an agreement in principle that the two hospitals should combine our surgery services in some ways. We haven't worked on any details of implementation."

Because rumors about the negotiations and Dr. White's involvement had been circulating for months, with no direct discussion with any other surgeons on the staff, the surgeons responded angrily to his announcement at this meeting. They shouted, "How come we weren't told about it?"

Dr. White answered, "There are no facts to discuss. We don't know the details, just the principles."

The other surgeons present proceeded to confront Dr. White with those rumors they had heard which spelled out relatively accurately which specialties and which surgeons would operate in which hospital.

Dr. White responded, "This is gossip. These details are just pipe dreams. This meeting has not been called for you to stand up and be critical. If I want to have a meeting to criticize people in the department, I'll call an official meeting."

Dr. Michael called, "We have a right to criticize you just as we wish. `We don't want to be informed after you have made your decisions."

Dr. White continued, "The criticisms are totally invalid."

Dr. White falsely told them: "There is no information to discuss. No details are decided. No decisions have been made."

Dr. Michael stated, "The first time I found out what is going on is from the anesthesiologist in the parking lot. It was described as being a *fait accompli.* Knowing the communication in this department, I had no reason to believe that it hadn't taken place. Then I spoke to my friend, Lou [an internist], and he filled me in on it too. "

Dr. White shouted him down. He addressed him formally: "Dr. Michael, you don't have the floor! Nothing has been formally decided. It is totally unofficial. I called this meeting to decrease the effects of a lot of hallway gossip. That's all it is — hallway gossip."

Subsequently, in response to additional protests from the surgeons Dr. White changed the tone and content of his speech. He outlined the specifics of the agreement, including the distribution of services and surgeons.

He commented, "You are being unjustifiably critical. If there has been a mistake made, it was a mistake of method. If we have erred, it was an error of timing."

The surgeons present were angry. They made statements such as, "You have decided for us. You owed us the right to make these decisions ourselves." (Chapters 7, 8, and 9 on decision making describe similar ways in which some surgeons tended to assume decision making powers for their patients.)

Dr. White continued, "You don't have the floor," or "That's just gossip. We'll set up a meeting to discuss these subjects."

Dr. Michael replied, "Gossip has been the only means of communication that we've had here."

Dr. Roddy said, "I think historically in our department we've had poor communication. We don't speak to each other in the right ways, right times, or right context."

Dr. Robinson ended the meeting by stating, "No one puts down the plan. The only problem is that we would like more involvement. There has to be better communication in our department. Occasionally, we feel left out. To avoid problems in the future and gossip in the hallway, I'd advise you to keep us informed."

During the few weeks after that meeting, the surgeons learned more about the ways in which the amalgamation plans would work when the Meadowbrook cardiac surgeons began collaborating with Provincial Hospital's cardiac surgeons. Other Meadowbrook surgeons asked those working with Provincial, "Are you getting enough help?" "Does their chief resident scrub with you?" "How much [business] are you giving away to them?" "How's the bed situation?" "Have there been any problems about cardiologists here taking care of sick patients there?" "Is there any more word about the neurosurgeons or head and necks [surgeons] moving?"

ACQUIRING INFORMATION ABOUT COLLEAGUES

Much of the Meadowbrook University Hospital surgeons' communication with their colleagues was oriented toward obtaining information about them. They were hungry for information on those very subjects that were hidden from them. They obtained information about their colleagues not only through gossip, but also by using more secretive means. For example, they checked the operating room schedule to see how busy their colleagues were and the kinds of surgery they were performing. Most often they obtained information from intermediaries, such as operating room nurses, residents, pathologists, and radiologists. They were, however, not direct with them. They deliberately engaged them in light conversation — bantering, small talk, joking and gossiping. They attempted to create the impression of having more knowledge than they actually had, while endeavoring to mask their need to know more. One form of their indirect style of inquiry began with bantering about aspects of their own lives in order to appear to offer information, and subsequently, carefully and obliquely, attempting to find out about others.

For example, during a period of several months in which many of the physicians in Meadowbrook University Hospital had progressively fewer patients, their isolation and anxiety made them curious to learn if others were also experiencing a slump. Three surgeons and a pathologist began joking at lunch in the cafeteria that preventive medicine was their enemy and had ruined their practices. One surgeon said, "Health is the enemy. More people should be sick!" The general surgeons joked about how the specialized surgeons were their enemies. The older surgeon spoke of the younger surgeons as their enemies, because they knew more technology. They joked about the way in which surgical research and new technologies made their skills obsolete. (See Appendix C, "Cybersurgery: The New Surgical Technologies.") They continued to crack jokes about some of the new innovations in medicine that competed with their surgical skills, such as the increasing use of scans by radiologists and endoscopes by internists. "Did you hear that even Rippling Brook Hospital (a non-university affiliated hospital in the city) bought a [CT] scan." "Yeah, too much preventive medicine's around." [laughter] Their conversations challenge Aird's statement about surgeons: "No surgeon will ever complain if medical research renders an operation or a series of operations unnecessary and obsolete, and deletes them from his operative repertoire" (1961:3).

As the physicians laughed together at lunch, one surgeon turned to the pathologist sitting next to him and said, "Is Wally [referring to Wallace Roddy, a general surgeon] still filling up your day?" The pathologist answered, "If my income depended on Wally's sections, I couldn't afford this lunch." The conversation changed when one of the surgeons said, "It worries me now when I take a two-week vacation and I get no money coming in. But it's not only no money for two weeks. You have to wind things down for a week before and pick things up a week afterwards."

Communication Through Residents

Surgeons found that their most useful sources of information about other surgeons were the residents. This section discusses some of the roles that residents performed in acting as communication links among surgeons.

The surgeons used their residents to find out how busy their colleagues were, their operative techniques, and their mistakes. The surgeons found it easier to ask for information about other surgeons from their surgical residents than to ask for that information from the surgeons directly. They also found it easier to admit ignorance or doubts to their residents than to their colleagues. Because the residents assisted many different surgeons in the operating room during the course of their training, they had a wider and more accurate range of specific, timely information about the surgeons in their hospital than the surgeons had about each other. Similarly, Freidson found residents to have more access to information about senior physicians than the physicians had of each other. He reported one physician saying, "It was easier for me to judge the ability of people when I was a resident in the hospital than it is [now]" (1976:149).

The residents believed that they had little choice but to provide information that the surgeons wanted, because they were dependent upon the senior surgeons for their future careers. They were also free to reveal information because, unlike the relationship among the surgeons, the residents were not in direct competition with the surgeons while they were still residents. The residents also had greater access to information about the surgical practices and techniques of other hospitals' surgery departments because most of them spent some of their four to five residency years at other hospitals. The senior surgeons at Meadowbrook University Hospital utilized the residents' access to other surgeons in their hospital and other hospitals in various ways.

The residents occasionally revealed mistakes which occurred in other hospitals. For example, while sitting in the Meadowbrook University Hospital Surgery Lounge, a resident who had just finished a year's residency at Riefton Hospital reported an incident about Riefton's Chief of Surgery to two senior surgeons, Dr. Jennifer and Dr. Roddy.

Resident: "They're no good at Riefton Hospital. Dr. Marlowe was doing a right lobectomy for lung cancer. Then he did a shoveling procedure, and then, without thinking, he cut the artery of the upper lobe. After that he said, 'What did I do? I have to take out that lobe.' But he didn't do it. He figured that there was still some vascularization."

Dr. Roddy: "Did the patient die?"

Resident: "Not right away. A week later he had to perform another operation. Then the patient went home. But two months later the patient died, pneumonia, sepsis, etc. But *his* [Dr. Marlowe's] *record is clean.*"

The surgical mistake which was responsible for the patient's death did not count as a surgical mortality because the patient died two months after the first operation. Even though the death was clearly caused by a surgical error, it was not attributed to the surgeon or the hospital in the patient's records. The only reason that the surgeons at Meadowbrook University Hospital knew about it was because the resident had been present and spoke about it to Drs. Roddy and Jennifer. The information was, however, subsequently communicated to other surgeons at Meadowbrook University Hospital. For example, during lunchtime on the following day, Dr. Roddy told several of his colleagues about the incident. Two weeks later Dr. Roddy, who was performing a lobectomy, told the resident who was assisting him, "They had a mortality over at Riefton last month when their Chief was doing one of these."

This incident not only reveals how residents communicate information to surgeons to which they would otherwise not have access. It also reveals some of the ways surgeons are able to conceal important information about surgical morbidity and mortality, particularly if the patient does not die immediately after the operation. (It is not known how the surgeons at Riefton Hospital discussed that problem in *their* surgical Rounds.) Surgical errors that resulted in mortalities were observed in Meadowbrook University Hospital, and the cause of death was "carefully" and indirectly discussed in order to avoid pointing a direct finger at a surgical colleague. Millman's book, *The Unkindest Cut* (1976) presents detailed case studies of how surgeons protected each other during discussions in Mortality Rounds.

The most typical way in which residents provided information about other surgeons occurred when a senior surgeon showed a resident in the operating room how to do a procedure and casually asked, "Does Dr. Nordberg use this?" During one operation, for example, Dr. Aranow noticed that the resident used a particular suture and knotting technique. Dr. Aranow casually asked, "Whom did you learn this from?" Another resident, who had the previous year been trained by the Chief of Surgery at Brooklyn Park Hospital, was performing a hiatal hernia operation through the abdominal cavity. Dr. Russell noticed that the resident performed the operation differently than he performed it. He asked the resident, "Is that the way in which Dr. Holloway at Brooklyn Park does it?" The resident answered, "Yes."

Surgeons frequently asked residents, rather than other surgeons, to demonstrate a particular technique so that they could learn that technique. For example, Dr. McCullars asked his resident, "Before you go I want you to show me how this kind of staple works. I don't want to bother Mike or Wally [senior surgeons at Meadowbrook University Hospital] about it."

The surgeons at Meadowbrook University Hospital also used two other kinds of circuitous techniques for acquiring information — arranging for a resident to act as a spy, and having a resident substitute for the surgeon.

Using the Resident to Spy on Another Surgeon

An example of spying occurred when Dr. Robinson wanted to know what techniques Dr. Nordberg used in particular operations. He did not ask Dr. Nordberg directly. Instead he first arranged to have a resident assist Dr. Nordberg in that kind of operation. Dr. Robinson subsequently arranged to have that resident perform that operation under his "supervision." By watching, and/or directly questioning the resident, Dr. Robinson learned Dr. Nordberg's techniques without either having to ask Dr. Nordberg directly or even to let Dr. Nordberg know that he did not know or was interested in knowing.

Knowledge of other surgeons' procedures was useful to the surgeons in their efforts to be effective practitioners, but their culturally defined ways of relating to each other forced them to resort to labyrinthine ways of learning about them. Surgeons wanted to know about their colleagues both to strengthen their own surgical skills and to reassure themselves about their competitive positions. But their unwillingness to admit their own lack of knowledge or experience, and their competition with other surgeons for patients often either overrode their quest for substantive surgical knowledge or led them to highly indirect and inefficient ways of obtaining that knowledge.

Residents Substituting for Surgeons

It was not uncommon for residents in Meadowbrook University Hospital to substitute for some (not all) of the senior surgeons by performing surgery on that surgeon's patient. Substitution by residents occurred in two situations — in the absence of the senior surgeon and in the presence of a senior surgeon.

In Meadowbrook University Hospital residents were not legally permitted to operate without an attending surgeon present during the operation. Nevertheless, some surgeons at Meadowbrook University Hospital, most notably the chief, Dr. White, had his resident regularly carry out surgery for many "routine" surgical procedures while they surreptitiously absented themselves from the operating room and worked in another part of the hospital. "Routine" did not necessarily mean minor; routine referred to familiar procedures of which they do many. Many of the procedures the chief resident performed for Dr. White were major surgery.

The surgeons who engaged in this practice first greeted the awake patient in the operating room, signed the operative orders, and instructed the resident(s), anesthesiologist, and nurses. As soon as the patient was unconscious the surgeon typically left the operating room but remained in the hospital building and was available to be contacted by beeper and telephone. When the operation ended the resident contacted the surgeon who came back to the operating room area and signed the completed operative report that the resident had written. The Operative Report listed all the people present during the operation and explicitly stated that the surgeon, not the resident, performed the operation.

Errors were committed by residents operating alone. Although no systematic comparison of surgeons' versus residents' errors was made, it appeared that patients operated on by residents fared somewhat worse than patients with similar operations conducted by attending surgeons. The residents stated to each other (but not to the surgeons) that they did not like the responsibility of operating alone. They stated that they often had questions for the surgeon during the operation, but they were reluctant to call the surgeon for advice or assistance after that surgeon left the operating room unless there was obvious danger. A number of instances were recorded when residents operated alone when they explicitly stated that they wished the surgeon were present, but because the situation was not one of "danger" they did not call the surgeon.[2] The absence of the surgeons at these times was one of the incentives that led the residents to complain to the surgeons that they were not spending enought time teaching them — which led to the present study (See Chapter 1, "Encounters with Surgeons").

The residents were reluctant to call the surgeons for several reasons. First, the surgeons had much power over the future careers of the residents (cf., Bosk 1979:148–165). Second, because it was important for the residents that the surgeons think them competent and confident (traits often confused by surgeons). Asking for help both betrayed their lack of confidence and brought their competence into question. Third, the few surgeons who engaged in the practice displayed unquestionable annoyance when a resident called them for advice or assistance during an operation they had left. Residents were well aware of the annoyance of the senior surgeons and did not wish to unnecessarily incur their disapproval.

A typical example occurred when Dr. White was in his office writing while his resident operated on his patient. When his receptionist informed him that the resident called from the operating room while he was operating on his patient, he cursed angrily and made remarks about being interrupted by children. Although by the time he spoke to the resident his voice was calmer, his irritation was nonetheless clear. He said in a manner which transmitted his wishes, "You don't need me there, do you?" The message to the resident was one which conveyed to the resident that he better be able to carry it out alone.

If the surgeons who practiced this form of substitution spoke of it at all, they said that it gave the residents experience and confidence that they were trusted to operate on their own. However, such direct substitution by the resident for the surgeon, in the absence of the surgeon, was done with the intent to deceive the patient, and it knowingly transgressed a hospital regulation.

A second kind of substitution was in some ways a more nefarious variation of the practice of using residents as spies to find out how other surgeons carried out procedures. A surgeon would agree to perform a surgical procedure which he had not previously performed and which was beyond his present competence. It worked like this: Many of the surgeons at Meadowbrook University Hospital were reluctant to refuse to operate on a patient because of their lack of experience or knowledge. For example, general surgeons were willing to admit that they did not do cardiac or urinary surgery. But they were unwilling to admit that they had no experience in any aspect of general surgery.

Those surgeons who agreed to carry out such procedures did so with the expectation that one of the residents who had experience in that procedures would carry it out for them. After a surgeon agreed to perform an operation for a patient, he began to inquire of the residents about their knowledge and/or experience of that operation. When they discovered that a resident had been present or assisted (such distinctions were rarely questioned) in that kind of an operation in the past the surgeon requested in typical indirect fashion for that resident to "assist" him in the surgery. Frequently the resident only learned of the surgeon's inexperience at the time of the operation, at which time the resident came to realize that their roles had been reversed. Instead of the surgeon teaching the resident, the resident was teaching the surgeon. Chapter 9, "The Natural History o Surgical Decisions and Their Consequences," discusses such a case in detail. All of the third and fourth-year residents stated that they performed this service a number of times for senior surgeons. The residents were willing to play these roles, because they were dependent upon the senior surgeons for their professional future and because the residents wanted to gain as much surgical experience as possible before they were independent.

CONCLUSION

Barriers to communication existed for many reasons. First, the surgeons were not only working together with colleagues, they were also competing with them. Having information about others and guarding information about oneself gave surgeons a competitive advantage. Competition contributed to their reluctance to admit even normal limitations in knowledge, technique, or experience. These barriers prevented accurate, effective evaluation of surgeons not only by each other but also by other medical professionals and patients.

Second, the cultural image of surgeons as confident, optimistic heroes, compelled them to hide situations which contradicted that image. They concealed their doubts, anxieties, mistakes, inexperience, and ignorance from their colleagues. The image of a decisive, powerful curer was not compatible with admitting weakness, incompetence, fear, or failure. Radiating optimism was not compatible with expressing uncertainty or asking for help. The heroic surgical role not only created barriers to substantive communication among surgeons, but it also intensified their sense of isolation.

The barriers to communication had serious consequences for the nature of their professional culture. Communication of information is essential for enhancing group interaction and functioning. It is also essential for transmitting contemporary empirical knowledge about innovations in research and technology.

Hage wrote that communication is the key to coordination of decisions in organizations (Hage 1983). That these barriers to communication among surgeons were likely to have deleterious effects upon their patients was illustrated in a nine-month experiment of cooperation and sharing information among a group of 23 surgeons in three New England states in which the surgeons observed each other in the operating room, shared information with each other, and cooperated intensively. Teams from each hospital visited other medical centers, observed operations, wrote reports comparing operations, and shared results with each other. They adopted changes based on their observations and cooperative behavior. The results indicated that the death rate declined 4.4 percent in the first year and 3.6 percent in the subsequent two and a half years (O'Connor et al. 1996).

NOTES

1. It was known that this was false because the author was present at many of the negotiations that Dr. White had with Provincial Hospital that preceded the communication with the Department of Surgery members reported in this chapter.

2. Data on operative morbidity and mortality suggest that the experience of the surgeon, particularly the number of similar operations performed by the surgeon, is a major factor in subsequent morbidity and mortality (although other data suggest that the volume of specific surgical procedures in a hospital is a more significant variable than the surgeon who performs the surgery) (cf., Kelly and Hellinger 1986).

Chapter 6

COMMUNICATION WITH PATIENTS

~

When a surgical procedure is being considered, it is helpful when a genuine bond of communication and personal responsibility is established between the surgeon and the patient.

(LeMaitre and Finnegan 1975:116)

Don't talk medical talk to me. Explain it in words I can understand!

(Surgical patient in Meadowbrook University Hospital)

INTRODUCTION

Problems in doctor-patient communication are described in numerous anecdotes, patients' accounts, polemics, and scholarly writings. Physicians, especially surgeons, are frequently described as inaccessible, callous, cold, uncaring, insensitive, preoccupied with technique, withholding, and frequently misleading in communicating with their patients and patients' families (cf., Atkinson 1988; Byrne and Long 1976; Fisher and Todd 1993:1–16; Fisher 1993:161-162; Golden and Johnston 1970; B. Good and M. Good 1981; D. Gordon 1994; Hauser 1981; Helman 1994:65–94, 142–144; Kleinman 1980; Martin 1992; Paget 1993; Plaja and Cohen 1968; Taylor 1988; West 1993). These writings place responsibility for

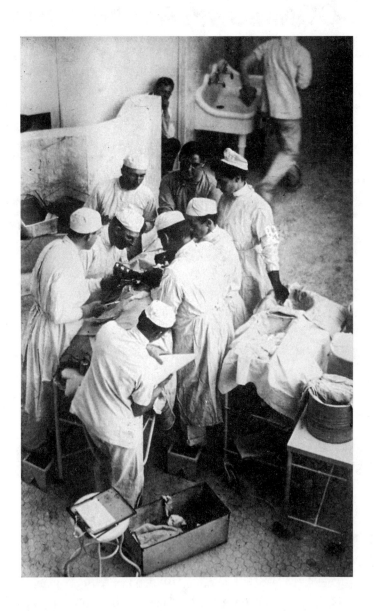

William Stewart Halsted operating.   Courtesy, Johns Hopkins Medicine.

understanding the patient upon the more powerful physician or surgeon. Medical anthropologists and sociologists attribute problems in doctor-patient communication to differences in the cultures of medical and lay persons (cf., B. Good 1994; D. Gordon 1994; Fisher and Todd 1993:1-6). Few of these accounts, however, attempt to understand the comprehensive cultural underpinnings of surgeon-patient encounters, including the historical background, the role of the hospital organization, or the role of the patient. The culture of the physician or surgeon, in particular, is likely to go unexamined. An exception to the latter is *The Silent World of Doctor and Patient*, in which the relationship of the historical origins of the doctor-patient relationship to the contemporary practice of medicine is examined (J. Katz 1984).

At Meadowbrook University Hospital surgeons' communication with their patients was more guarded, more withholding, and more misunderstood than was their communication with their surgical and other medical colleagues. The reasons for their difficulties in communicating with patients did not, however, lie in the surgeons' intentional lack of concern for the welfare of their patients. Their commitment to becoming a surgeon who treats and cures patients indicated that they had that concern. The reasons lie rather with some of the basic components comprising the culture of surgeons which have continued to be perpetuated in the contemporary organization of surgical practice.

This chapter discusses some ways in which the culture of surgery, including both the history of surgery and the contemporary organization of hospital surgical practice, structures patient-surgeon communication. It examines patient-surgeon communication as concurrently embedded in, reflecting, and shaping surgical culture.

PROBLEMS IN PATIENT-SURGEON COMMUNICATION

Communication between surgeons and patients has been influenced by: a) the historic fact that surgeons cause pain, injury, and risk of death to patients; b) the predominance of technology in surgical practice; c) hospitals' institutionalized arrangements for surgical practice; d) expectations (by surgeons and patients) for surgeons to be heroic and active; and e) surgeons' disinclination to admit doubts or failures, acknowledge the inevitability of death, or quietly listen to patients' concerns and fears.

The practice of surgery, whether on the battlefield or in the hospital, has historically been linked both to severe pain as well as to a very high rate of patient deaths. Surgeons have until recently been in the paradoxical position of causing significant pain and death to many of their patients, while their efforts were dedicated to saving them from pain, disease and death (cf., Fox 1993). Although surgeons "must have a kind of courage...that refuses to accept mastery by events" (Aird 1961:14), they frequently found themselves instead mastered by the effects of disease, infection, and terminal illness upon their patients.

Before the advent of antiseptics and antibiotics death was likely to result from many operations. Before the advent of anesthesia pain was inevitable. In order to perform effectively, surgeons found it necessary to shield themselves psychologically from identifying and empathizing with the terrors and fates of their patients. They had to ignore the patients' cries of pain. Instead they had to concentrate on believing that their operative skills would ultimately be effective in relieving the patient of pain. In order to continue to operate with skill and speed, surgeons had to distance themselves from those whose pain they inevitably caused and who frequently died under their hands.

Modern surgeons have a love affair with technology that may surpass that of other physicians (cf., Reiser 1978). The practice of surgery in general and advancements in surgery in particular have been more dependent upon technological advances, such as, for example, anesthesia, antisepsis, endoscopes, telesurgery, and computerized scans) than have other branches of medicine. (See Appendix C for a description of "cybersurgery" — the most recent and futuristic technologies.)

Surgeons' passion for technology had an effect of shielding them from communicating with their patients (cf., Hahn 1985:89). Machines can divert attention away from personal interaction. Technological language can also shield its speakers from experiencing undesirable emotions (cf., P. Katz 1990). Technologies, unlike patients, do not communicate fear, pain, dissatisfactions and distrust. Selzer wrote: "What is the difference between a surgeon and an internist? The surgeon, armed to the teeth, seeks to overwhelm and control the body; the medical man strives with pills and potions to cooperate with that body, even to the point of making concessions to disease. One is the stance of the warrior: the other, that of the statesman" (1982).

Surgeons use language that reflects their active use of technologies. For example, in describing operations to patients the surgeons at Meadowbrook spoke of their actions — stapling, removing, excising — rather than the effect on the patients. The surgeons seldom addressed patients' major concerns. Their patients, however, were not familiar with the technologies. They were likely to prefer a dialogue with the surgeon which addressed metaphors that reflected their concerns and expectations, such as how they were likely to function or to feel after the operation. Patients wanted the surgeons to say, for example, "When you first come in the operating room, you will be....".

When surgeons discussed diagnoses with patients they preferred to say that something was wrong with a diagnostic technique than with the patient. For example, Dr. Michael explained to a patient with a mass in his chest, "There is something wrong with the chest x-ray." He did not say: "There is something in your chest." Dr. Robinson told a patient with a possibly malignant breast mass after he biopsied its contents with an aspiration needle, "The needle tells me that I need to take out that lump" (cf., B. Good and M. Good 1981). To refer to the needle as being suspect rather than to the sample from the patient's body extracted by the needle was consistent with surgeons' language which reflected their reliance on technology. The surgeons were more comfortable using technological metaphors in communicating with their patients.

This perception that surgeons avoid direct communication with patients to distance themselves from their own emotions can be inferred from other research. For example, in a study of patient-physician communication in several medical and surgical services in a general hospital Golden and Johnston found that physicians' anxiety prevented them from recognizing the severe amounts of anxiety their patients experienced (1970). In studies with large samples of patients and physicians West found that male physicians manifested anxiety in dialogues by interrupting more than female physicians as well as all male and female patients (1993). In a similar vein, Konner writes that the clinical detachment of a physician is "not just objective but downright negative" and that this may actually require "a measure of dislike" (Konner 1987:373).

Some of the practices surgeons at Meadowbrook University Hospital used to shield themselves from their patients' distress were embedded in the organizational practices of the hospital. Compartmentalization of inpatient and outpatient care was developed for hospital efficiency. The isolation and ritualization in the operating room, including the isolation of the patient's head from the rest of the body, were developed for maintaining antisepsis and for efficiency. But both of these practices may have been retained and perpetuated, in part, because they also served to shield surgeons from empathizing with the distressing emotions of their patients.

The compartmentalization of inpatient surgical care results in patients being cared for by many different people. Nurses, technicians, social workers, residents, and other physicians, such as oncologists and radiologists, typically care for patients in the hospital. Each of these specialists cares for a specific aspect of the patient;

none consider the patient as a whole person. Although the specialists know what their task is vis-a-vis their patients, the patients were usually not clear about each of the specialists' roles.

The organization of surgical outpatient consultations shielded surgeons from experiencing the emotions of their patients. Different stages of the surgical experience, such as undressing, undergoing tests (e.g., blood pressure, x-rays, blood), and discussing complaints, diagnosis and recommendations for action, and paying, are undertaken in different rooms, different time periods, and with different personnel. The patient, who is unaware of the particular organization of the hospital, is often shunted from one room to another, from one task to another, often waiting for a person or procedure of which he has little or no knowledge. There is a predetermined structure, but no one tells the patient what that structure is. The arrangements enable the surgeon to see large numbers of patients in a day in different geographical locations, such as in multiple outpatient rooms, in the operating room, and on the inpatient surgical ward. The arrangements also enable the surgeon to see each patient for a specialized task, such as diagnosing, operating, or supervising post-operative recovery. The arrangements additionally facilitate separation of the surgeon's multiple roles (including those of financial entrepreneur, data-collector, diagnostician, confidant, and bearer of bad news). Such spatial, temporal, and role distinctions allow the surgeon to separate himself from the total observation, care, and identification with the patient. He has only a negligible opportunity to become acquainted with and follow a particular patient through his surgical illness.

The rituals that are enacted in the operating room also shield surgeons from the emotions of other patients and from their own emotions. Rituals shield them from confronting the emotional expressions accompanying their gruesome, injurious interventions upon living human beings. In addition to separating the head of the patient from the rest of his body, operating room rituals facilitate a mind-set which focuses on a specific body part rather than the whole person. They facilitate surgeons' existing penchant for action and to avoid responding to distressing emotions. But outside of the operating room surgeons are not so protected.

The protective effect of operating room rituals was illustrated in a situation in which surgeons were confronted outside of the operating room with a condition that was very familiar to all of them when they were operating inside of the operating room. In a lecture hall in Meadowbrook University Hospital they watched a movie which illustrated different techniques for draining and lancing pus-filled abscesses. The surgeons in the audience who were watching the film of the procedure squirmed uncomfortably in their seats and looked away from the screen. They uttered comments, noises, and jokes which indicated their disgust. They reacted in a manner which diverged significantly from their usual equanimity in the operating room and reacting to the same stimuli when they were the ones who drained and lanced pus-filled abscesses and were accompanied by the smells of putrid abscesses. Without the protection of the rituals, isolation, and action of the operating room, the surgeons experienced emotions that most other people would normally feel when viewing the lancing of a pus-filled abscess (cf., Sankar 1988).

Many of the problems in surgeon-patient communication at Meadowbrook University Hospital may be attributed to surgeons' identity as active heroes, who are strong, confident, certain, and optimistic. The heroic image and active posture discouraged them from admitting doubt, fears, worries, or from acknowledging the inevitability of death to their patients or to themselves. Their passion for activity deterred them from quietly listening to patients' concerns and fears. Maintaining their optimistic, active image discouraged surgeons' from communicating unfavorable news to their patients. It made them more likely to depersonalize their patients through humor and through references to their procedures or their organs.

COMMUNICATING NEGATIVE INFORMATION

The surgeons at Meadowbrook University Hospital had relatively few *overt* problems in communicating with patients because of two factors. First, they were skilled at avoiding direct communication. Second, the hospital's organizational structure reduced the likelihood that one person could or would communicate the total picture of a patient's medical condition to the patient.

Most of the surgeons at Meadowbrook University Hospital protected themselves from participation in their own and their patients' emotions by avoiding discussions of death with their patients (cf., D. Gordon 1994). They behaved as if death invalidated their active, heroic posture and optimistic attitude. Whereas such avoidance served to support their belief in the efficacy of their actions, it also served to obstruct communications with their patients. Whenever possible the surgeons avoided discussing bad news with their patients. When they were compelled to communicate pessimistic information they frequently used euphemism and indirection. These techniques usually served to obscure the information that they were attempting to transmit. Surgeons were particularly reluctant to communicate information about terminal conditions and the imminence of death to patients and families of patients (cf., M. Good et al. 1990; Taylor 1988). They spoke of the patient's pathologies as conditions exterior to the patient. However, the very subjects they avoided in communication with their patients were those which they appeared to enjoy talking about with their colleagues. They frequently joked with their colleagues about the most gruesome and apparently frightening aspects of their work, such as death and mutilation.

Surgeons transmitted their specific modes of communicating with patients to their residents explicitly and implicitly in the process of teaching them. An example of explicit training in positive communication was that of Dr. Jennifer. Dr. Jennifer was one of the more sensitive surgeons in the Meadowbrook University Hospital Department of Surgery. He prided himself upon his good communicative ability. Yet he made distinctions about how much to communicate to his patients according to the social class of the patient. He explicitly gave his residents the following advice about talking to terminal patients: "You tell a patient what he wants to know. If the patient asks you the prognosis, you tell him. If the guy is a laborer there is very little that he has to do. But if he is an executive he's got things to do. You have to level with him."

Although Dr. Jennifer advised his residents to be direct with patients, he did not address the feelings that either patients or his residents were likely to experience. Instead he transmitted to the residents the ways in which he protected himself from participating in those feelings. He particularly revealed insensitivity to concerns of lower-class patients, pointing out that it was only necessary to level with executives because they have "things to do." Dr. Jennifer, in common with the other surgeons in the Department, was unable to confront or to communicate to his residents the fear and isolation experienced by virtually all terminally ill people. The following case illustrates a surgeon's reluctance to communicate information about terminal illness and the imminent possibility of death to a patient. It contrasted with his ease in discussing her death with other surgeons:

> The patient was a 63-year-old woman who, according to Dr. Michael's estimation, was likely to die within 72 hours. However realistically Dr. Michael expressed to himself, to the resident, and to his colleagues about her life expectancy, he found it difficult to communicate the gravity of her condition to her and to her relatives. He appeared reluctant to admit his helplessness.

> Dr. Michael spoke to the patient's daughter on the phone: "She's about status quo. We're having a lot of problems with her lungs. Her right lung is not working, and she's just breathing with the left lung. She's got a little

pneumonia in it. She's very stable. She's now on a ventilator, and we want to get her off the ventilator..." "Yes, I'm pleased with the progress. Her stomach is healing. We drained an abscess in her abdomen, and the last thing was the tracheotomy. We had to get a tube in the windpipe. Instead of through her mouth, now it's through her neck. We had another problem where there was air under her skin and it puffed it all up. Her only problem is her left lung. And we'll wait until she gets rid of the infection and then we'll put her off the ventilator. I'd like to appear optimistic, but I do not want to appear overly optimistic."

Immediately after the phone conversation with the patient's daughter, Dr. Michael told the resident, "She'll never get off that ventilator. She probably won't live two more days."

However, when the patient's husband came in later that day, Dr. Michael also spoke to him optimistically. He emphasized action, "She still has her tumor. We went around the tumor. In another day she'll be able to drink."

When the patient's husband asked, "Will she have to take treatments?" Dr. Michael answered, "She's had her treatments, and they didn't work. She had a tube in her mouth. The only problem is her left lung. We have to wait until it starts working again."

However, when the patient's husband left, Dr. Michael said, "She needs some new lungs."

The patient began to decline quickly soon after the conversation with the patient's husband. The x-ray taken of her lungs at that time showed no lung — only white. Nothing was left to do. Dr. Michael told the resident, "Mrs. Eppstein is conking out. The x-rays show no lung. I expect something drastic."

Immediately following this statement, Dr. Michael spoke to the patient's husband, "Your wife does not look good. Her x-ray [not her lungs] is very bad, and I don't think it is going to get better. There is not much more we can do. We hoped it would reverse itself. But unfortunately, even though we gave her treatment, it didn't." The patient's husband asked, "I guess there's nothing we can do?" Dr. Michael replied, "We should know today." The patient's husband appeared to be accepting the inevitability of his wife's imminent death, and said, "There are some things you cannot do." However, Dr. Michael refused to accept this obvious statement, and replied, "We're doing everything we can."

When the patient's daughter entered the room, Dr. Michael explained to her, "Your Mum's not doing very well. She has very, very bad pneumonia. The problem is resistant to any form of therapy that we're giving her. She cannot deal with any type of infection. I don't think she's going to do well. Things are very bad with her. If something will happen, it will happen tonight."

The patient actually lived 24 hours beyond Dr. Michael's prediction. He commented wryly on his lack of control over the situation, "They never die when it's convenient to die."

The following case illustrates a process of deceptive surgeon-patient communication in which a surgeon withheld negative information from a patient. He focused instead upon his active posture and his optimism. Although the patient's condition was hopelessly inoperable and probably allowed him no more than eight months to live, Dr. Aranow deceptively communicated optimism about his condition.

The patient was a 52-year-old man with difficulty in breathing who came to Dr. Aranow on referral from his family doctor. After viewing the x-rays Dr. Aranow pointed to the patient's chest and told the patient, "We'll have to look into that area. It is a quick surgical procedure in which we cut a small hole here, [pointing to the base of his neck] and put a telescope through it to your chest to look at your chest."

Dr. Aranow was describing a mediastinoscopy (passing the scope through an incision in the neck to into the mediastinum — the area in the thorax, between the two pleural sacs) to examine the mediastinum, bronchial tubes, lungs, and lymph nodes and to collect nodes for biopsy. It was a limited procedure for the surgeon because very light (sometimes only local) anesthesia was used, and only a small incision was made. However, a mediastinoscopy was not a small, inconsequential procedure for the patient. Dr. Aranow represented an operative procedure which is intrusive, frightening, and uncomfortable for the patient as "quick," and involving cutting a "small hole."

In the operating room Dr. Aranow passed a bronchoscope through the mouth to look at the bronchial tubes and other air passages. He then then made an incision in the base of the neck and passed a mediastinoscope through the small hole at the base of the front part of the neck to explore the mediastinum, and he took biopsies of suspicious-looking lymph nodes in the area (lymph nodes in the mediastinum area are the first to be involved in lung cancer metastasis). He sent these specimens of the lymph nodes to the histology lab and requested a frozen section which required an immediate response.

Dr. Aranow waited while the pathologist examined the specimens. The pathologist reported that the specimen showed that it was large cell (oat cell) carcinoma of the lung, the fastest growing lung cancer. Although chemotherapy and radiotherapy might prolong his life for a few months, the diagnosis implied that the cancer was inoperable and that the patient was not likely to live beyond nine months, regardless of treatment.[1]

After the patient woke in his hospital bed and recovered from the small operation, Dr. Aranow "informed" him of his findings in an optimistic voice: There is a problem in that lung. But, because of its nature we are not doing anything surgical. You'll have some x-ray and drug treatments. Another specialist will see you."

Dr. Aranow gave the patient a misleading message. Although he acknowledged a "problem," he emphasized optimistically that the patient did not need surgery, that he only needed "treatments" by another specialist. As intended, the patient received the surgeons' message as a great relief from his fears of lung cancer. He replied, "Great news, doctor! Fine! I sure feel good today!"

Dr. Aranow visited the patient the following day and spoke in an optimistic tone of voice as he continued to deceive the patient. He told the patient,

"Your tests are pretty good. You'll see Dr. Lehrer tomorrow, and he'll start you on something." The patient replied, "Fine, doctor." Dr. Aranow did not tell the patient that Dr. Lehrer was an oncologist and that "something" was chemotherapy and radiotherapy for his inoperable cancer.

When Dr. Aranow spoke to the patient's wife he was only slightly more revealing about the severity of her husband's condition. He said, "The problem is that your husband has a tumor on his lung. I suspected this as soon as I saw his x-ray. It was a matter of determining what type of tumor it is. It is best treated by x-rays and drugs."

Dr. Aranow did not use the word "cancer" or "malignancy." He told her that they had to determine the type of tumor instead of informing her that it was an extremely fast-growing cancer and that he would probably live no longer than nine months. Even though little could be done to save the patient, Dr. Aranow nevertheless emphasized active treatment. By emphasizing what could be done, he failed to explain either the risk of treatment or the choice of not treating. Further, he denied how he, the surgeon, was reduced to passivity in fighting a disease which had no hope.

The wife asked, "Couldn't you operate?" Dr. Aranow replied, "Yes, we could operate, but he would be worse off with an operation." Dr. Aranow was unable to say "no," or to say, for example, "We cannot operate. There is essentially nothing we can do to save his life and little to prolong it."

The wife asked, "How bad is it?" Dr. Aranow answered a bit more accurately, "Very." He continued, "There is some local spread in the area. I'll speak to him tomorrow. Whatever he wants to know, I'll tell him. It's up to him to ask the question. The type of therapy we'll give him is x-rays and drugs. They do respond well initially. I will arrange it. The drugs are given by Dr. Lehrer. He needs the drug treatments first and then the x-ray treatments." Even in this pessimistic situation Dr. Aranow managed to convey optimism by offering treatment options, and he used many active words, such as "speak," "arrange," "tell," and "give."

When Dr. Aranow telephoned the family doctor who had referred that patient to him, he spoke completely differently, "He has an oat cell cancer, unfortunately. He has a protocol combining chemotherapy and x-rays. He'll respond quickly to the chemotherapy." Dr. Aranow said: "Eight months, if that."

The following case at Meadowbrook also illustrates the contrast between a surgeon's active posture expressed in doing something for the patient, on the one hand, and his passive posture in avoiding communicating bad news to that patient, on the other hand:

> Dr. Russell's patient was a 53-year-old woman who presented with a large, solid lump on her breast and a swollen armpit. After biopsying the lump in his office, Dr. Russell was convinced that the patient had breast cancer and that the axillary nodes were likely to be involved. He based his assumption not only upon his visual inspection but also upon the lab report of the biopsy which identified malignant cells. After receiving the result from the lab he telephoned the patient, "I'm calling you about the results of the lab investigation. The area you mentioned is a little bit suspicious. It's not very suspicious, but it's suspicious enough that we'll have a biopsy in that area. It's the kind of thing that we must do something about. We'll put you to sleep."

> He continued: "We'll make a small incision two centimeters long over the area of the breast where the *thickness* is and take it out and give it to the pathology lab. If it is a cancer, we'd have to take off more breast. I've discussed this with [your family doctor] and I suggest that you give him a call. It is likely not serious. But it is suspicious, and we want to do something about it. If you agree, I can get a bed for you."

> When Dr. Russell finished this conversation, he told his secretary, "Book a bed for her for Thursday. We'll take off her breast."

The surgeons' reluctance to communicate unfavorable or pessimistic information to their patients reflects both the American cultural value that emphasizes individual control and a belief that the will of the patient contributes to recovery (B. Good et al. 1980). Physicians' culture and training emphasize their ability to save people from disease. Such emphasis neglects to address how to confront failures to save a patient's life. The sense of despair and hopelessness that many physicians experience when interacting with a dying patient was described by an internist:

> *I still don't know what to say to a doomed patient. A visit to a terminal patient is very painful to me. As I approach the room, my muscles tighten and I feel anxious. I know that the patient will watch every movement and every expression. ... I can't wait to get out. I am relieved when I walk into the hallway.* (Rosenbaum 1988:114)

> *[When I go to a patient's funeral] I am convinced that everyone [is] saying, 'That's her doctor who goofed.'...that is the way I always feel when one of my patients dies...It doesn't make sense. I was engaged to prevent death and now I've lost.* (Rosenbaum 1988:212)

The surgeons at Meadowbrook University Hospital were highly reluctant to admit to their patients, as well as to their colleagues, that they had made mistakes. Admitting mistakes was at variance both with the image that they held of themselves as well as that which they expected others to hold of them. They attempted to maintain their image as competent, caring, courageous heroes. And admitting mistakes was perceived as risky in a competitive organizational culture.

If errors were likely to be detected surgeons gave brief explanations to patients. For example, during an operation for a cholecystectomy (gall bladder removal), Dr. Jennifer accidentally tore a gastric vein. As a consequence he had to remove the spleen.[2] After the operation Dr. Jennifer told the patient, "We had to take out your spleen." When the patient's family doctor received the report he called the surgeon and asked him why the spleen was removed. The surgeon replied, "He presented with symptoms of cholelithiasis (gallstones). Unfortunately during the operation the top short gastric vein ruptured, and I removed his spleen." In this discourse Dr. Jennifer used the active voice, with himself as the actor, in describing the operative procedure to the patient. However, he used the passive voice, with the gastric vein as the object and himself as the subject, in describing the error to the family doctor. It was as if the gastric vein, not himself, were responsible for the error, and he actively remedied that error by excising the spleen.

In another case, the surgeon also had to remove the spleen during a hiatal hernia operation. Three and a half weeks post-operatively the patient visited the surgeon and asked, "Why did you take my spleen out?" The surgeon responded, "In fixing the hiatal hernia the tip of the spleen sits against the esophagus. From time to time, in fixing a hiatal hernia, there are a couple of small blood vessels that might get ruptured." Here too the surgeon described his activity by using active words (such as fixing the hiatal hernia), but described the error of severing the spleen using passive words (e.g., "might get ruptured"). He also used objective words (e.g., "the" [not "your"] hiatal hernia; "there are" [not "you had"] a couple of small blood vessels.)

In the course of teaching surgical residents surgeons sometimes mentioned mistakes that other surgeons had made or they mentioned mistakes that they had made in the distant past. But only infrequently did they refer to their own recent mistakes. As an example of referring to another surgeon's mistake, Dr. Michael accidently perforated the common bile duct during an operation for cholecystectomy. In that operation the gall bladder was acutely inflamed, and he had to remove it retrograde. He detected the perforation by putting a saline solution in and checking for leakage and was, therefore, able to repair it. Because he was teaching a resident at the time, he spoke about a similar error by Dr. Ofir that was undetected and that resulted in the death of a patient. Dr. Michael told the resident, as part of his teaching, "Remember the Death Rounds [i.e., Mortality Rounds] a few months ago when Dr. Ofir's patient died, because he didn't realize that he perforated the common bile duct."

Communication, Decision Making, and the Active Posture

The active posture of surgeons contributed to problems in their communication with patients in three ways: 1) It predisposed surgeons to present information which justifies action; 2) It encouraged surgeons to assume decision-making authority for their patients; and 3) It tempted surgeons to expose their patients to greater risk or greater discomfort than their patients would be likely to prefer if they were to make an informed decision. These influences of the active posture on surgeon-patient communication are illustrated in the following case:

> The active posture was manifest in a situation in which Dr. White attempt-ed to make decisions for a patient. Dr. White's patient was an 88-year-old woman who was accompanied by her 59-year-old son and his wife. The patient was diagnosed with stones in her bile duct which caused two recent episodes of acute cholescystitis (gall bladder inflammation). While the patient was getting dressed in another room after being examined, Dr.

White discussed the patient's options with her son and daughter-in-law. He said, "Your mother is almost ninety, and she's still bright and active. The chances of a stone contributing to her demise is very high. If she is operated on, the risk to her life is on the order of five to ten percent. The risk of not operating on her is probably greater than that. It's not an easy decision. We're talking about a fairly significant risk in making it. If you want to leave the decision to me, I'll make it."

The son responded, "I don't think that you, me, or my wife has a right to make that decision for her. It's not proper for anyone to make that decision. Whatever needs to be discussed should be discussed with her and decided by her. She's sound enough to make her own decision. We'll wait until she's home where she's comfortable to make a final decision."

Having the decision-making authority unexpectedly taken away from him, Dr. White recommended a speedy decision and reformulated the problem by encouraging the patient to make a quick, active decision. He said, "I think the decision should be made in a few days. Delaying a decision is like making a negative decision."

The son, reasserting his mother's autonomy, said to Dr. White, "We'd like you to discuss this with her by herself, without us present." Dr. White did talk to the patient alone. In doing so he presented the options to her as he did to her family — in a way which encouraged an active, quick decision. The 88-year-old patient made the decision and decided to undergo the operation. She had the operation, and she recovered successfully. However, the surgeon's predisposition to an active posture led him to present information in a way which encouraged the family and the patient to make an active decision.

Communication of Risk and the Active Posture

The active posture of the surgeon influences the ways in which surgeons perceived risk and in which they communicated risk to their patients. Their communication of risk reflected a lack of awareness that the patients may have a very different perception of risk than they do. Typically, the surgeons at

Meadowbrook University Hospital represented operative procedures that were routine for them as also routine and non-risky for their patients.

> Similar to the incident described earlier in this chapter in which Dr. Aranow minimized the bronchoscopy and mediastinoscopy procedures to his patient by representing them as "making a little hole," Dr. Robinson told a 54-year-old female patient with shortness of breath and pain in the chest and an indication on her x-ray that there was a mass in her chest: "Mrs. Briggs, do you know why you are in the hospital?" She replied, "No." The surgeon continued, "There is something wrong with the *chest x-ray* [the x-ray is the problem, not the patient's lungs]. We want to look down your lungs with a telescope. It is about this long and this wide. You will not be asleep. *The whole thing is simple and only takes fifteen minutes,* and we'll try to find out what the problem is."

In another case a patient of Dr. White clarified the differences in the patient-surgeon perceptions of surgery when he asked, "Is it going to hurt? I'm scared." Dr. White responded, "I'm not scared." The patient replied, "Because you are the doctor."

THE PATIENT'S ROLE IN COMMUNICATION BARRIERS

The patient also plays a role in the barriers to communication with the surgeon. The heroic image of the surgeon is a belief shared by the patients as well as by the surgeons. Their shared belief serves to perpetuate and confirm that image. Patients expect surgeons to be heroic, omnipotent, and optimistic so that they too can retain the belief that they will be saved or cured by the surgeon. Patients' hopes usually act together with the surgeons' optimism to solicit optimistic prognoses from their surgeons (cf., Margalit and Shapiro 1997). (See note about the frontispiece etching in which the artist could not sell his etching when he called it "Indecision;" he only sold it when it was renamed, "The Surgeon.")

Surgeons are not alone in circumventing pessimistic information about patients. Patients frequently act inconsistently and ambiguously about receiving pessimistic information about themselves. For example, after a male patient returned to the surgical ward following his operation, Dr. Russell attempted to explain to the patient about the operation. He asked, "Do you know why you had the operation?" The patient answered, "No." Dr. Russell continued, "Would you like to know why you had the operation?" The patient answered, "No. I'm sure you did your best."

An example illustrating the patient's role in misinterpreting communication with the surgeon occurred with Dr. Jennifer, who visited Mr. and Mrs. Ferguson, a 62-year-old patient and his wife, on his daily Rounds. They asked Dr. Jennifer about the results of the diagnostic tests. Dr. Jennifer told them that a "growth" was found in his bowels. When Mrs. Ferguson persisted in asking for more details, Dr. Jennifer responded to each of her subsequent questions, even asking if they wanted to hear "that much."

When they insisted that they wanted answers to everything, he carefully responded to each of their subsequent questions. He explained about the cancer, what they had done about it, and what the literature said was the treatment-of-choice. Both asked specifically how long Mr. Ferguson had to live. Dr. Jennifer explained the statistical chances of surviving three years, five years, and ten years. Dr. Jennifer spoke to the Fergusons for 45 minutes, an unusually long time for him. And he spoke in a highly sensitive manner.

It was therefore a surprise when three days later the hospital administrator called Dr. Jennifer to come to his office. He told Dr. Jennifer that Mr. and Mrs. Ferguson had complained to him that Dr. Jennifer had been cold, insensitive, and rude to them and gave them unsolicited information. That report of the Fergusons was so disparate to what actually occurred that it could only be attributed to the tragic nature of the news that he had conveyed to them.

A similar incongruity between the actual encounter and the patient's and family's report of that encounter was described by a contemporary internist in his autobiography (Rosenbaum 1988), who tried to follow the sensible dictum, "Listen to the patient. Tell them what they want to know and only what they can handle." However, a patient of his told him, "When I wake up, tell me the truth. If it's cancer, I need to know. Don't hide anything from me." When the patient woke up the surgeon told her that she had inoperable, untreatable lung cancer. When the internist visited her soon afterwards she told him, "[The surgeon] is wonderful, so honest and direct. I love him." However, when the internist visited her later, she asked him, "How good is [the surgeon]? What are his credentials? I don't want him to come and see me anymore. I can't stand him" (Rosenbaum 1988:116).

These incidents suggest that patients and their families may reinterpret communicative events differently when the emotional weight of the encounter is very high, such as when they receive information about terminal illness. The fear, helplessness, and rage elicited after the meaning of an unfortunate condition is digested may be directed against the messenger.

CONCLUSION

The dominant themes of surgical culture — action, heroism, certainty, and optimism — are not compatible with identification with, or communication with, helpless, hopeless patients. It appears that surgeons are selected for, and trained to select, those characteristics that facilitate their immunity to responding emotionally to the personal events to which they expose their patients and themselves.

Communicative distance from patients protects surgeons from being overwhelmed by the emotion-laden sights, sounds, and smells that they regularly encounter. Distance shields them from the intrusive acts that they perform upon patients. It protects them from their own confrontations with mortality. Surgeons typically shield themselves from the personalities, sexuality, fears, pains, and losses of their patients to avoid evoking their own identification with the patients. They can thus avoid arousing the fears, pains, sexual feelings, and losses within themselves. If surgeons empathized with each of the large numbers of fearful, suffering, sick, and dying patients that they treat, their efficacy as effective surgeons would be compromised.

The content of surgical practice involves injurious intrusions into the most intimate depths of peoples' bodies. Surgeons see numerous naked, sick bodies daily. They regularly cut into those bodies, exposing blood, organs, excreta, dismembered limbs, organs, and other body parts. Although the patient is usually anesthetized and a curtain usually hides the patient's face from the surgeon's view, a conscious mental exercise is necessary to remind oneself that the person who is being injured and mutilated does not feel and that the surgery helps, not harms, the patient. The process of repressing normal feelings of empathy is necessary during surgery. This requires the surgeon to continually protect themselves. Otherwise they would be forced to experience intolerable feelings of disgust, horror, fear, or excitement, and their own confrontations with death.

Generations of surgeons have created, elaborated, and perpetuated these communicative modes in their culture to serve specific and essential purposes. The culture of surgeons protected them from empathizing with their patients' fear and pain. It protected them from being aware of their own ultimate helplessness in the presence of human mortality and occasionally from guilt over their mistakes.

Surgery, while supported by scientific advances and sophisticated technology, nevertheless remains dependent on human skill and judgment. Inevitably some surgical procedures will fail. Sometimes patients will die, even though the operations were successful. Although research has shown that patients are likely to benefit from improved communication with their surgeons about their surgery (Reading 1981), the communication barriers that have been embedded in surgical culture may nevertheless contribute to surgeons' overall efficacy. It is questionable whether surgeons' technical efficacy would change if they were to empathize more with their patients and confront their own limitations, their ultimate helplessness, and the tragic implications of their occasional mistakes.

NOTES

1. At the present time patients who are aggressively treated for oat cell carcinoma are likely to live more than nine months.

2. Accidental injuries to the spleen during surgery were not uncommon in surgical practice, and its incidence has not decreased in recent years. Accidental splenectomies were found in cholecystectomies, and in surgeries involving the esophageal hiatus, stomach, kidney, and the aorta (Coon 1990).

Chapter 7

HOW SURGEONS MAKE DECISIONS: INFLUENCE OF THE ACTIVE POSTURE ON DECISION MAKING

~

It is ... important to study how it is that those who make decisions will arrive at such decisions and how they differ from those who habitually make judgments less well.

(B. Williams 1981:1)

Because speed was all important, the surgeon had no time to pause and consider his next step...Unexpected difficulties,...demanded lightning decision and immediate action.

(Cartwright 1968:13-14)

INTRODUCTION

Decision-making is at the heart of surgery. It is the primary metaphor for surgeons' definition of themselves. A leading surgery textbook states that surgery is where the "art of decision is best nurtured" (Gius 1972:1). Speed, accuracy, and

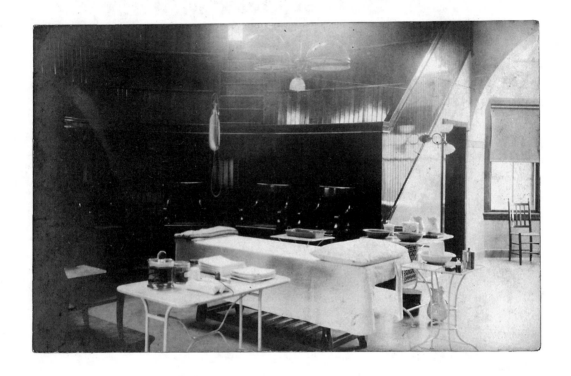

Courtesy, Mary L. Martin, Ltd.

confidence in decision-making are principal criteria by which surgeons critically evaluate themselves and other surgeons. They evaluate and select surgical residents primarily upon their ability to make decisions under stress. This criterion for selection perpetuates a surgical culture which places greater value upon quick, confident decision making than upon analysis of alternative actions and upon the long-term consequences of each alternative.

Although surgeons make large numbers of decisions in the course of a working day and place high value upon quick, accurate, confident decision making, their perspective on surgical decision making is limited. It is particularly limited to those decisions which are considered to be major, because they are consistent with their heroic image and active posture. Most of the surgical literature on decision making only refers to major decisions, such as determining diagnoses, deciding whether to operate, and to those decisions made in the operating room. For example, Spencer wrote: "A major portion of decision making occurs in the operating room" (1978:9). Most of the surgeons at Meadowbrook University Hospital appeared to concur with Spencer.

Although the surgical literature and the surgeons' perspective of themselves restricted decision making to major dramatic choices, in reality surgeons make numerous little decisions outside of the operating room in the course of their daily work. Not only was the majority of their working time spent outside of the operating room (See Figure 1, page 36), but most of the important decisions made about the operation were made long before the operation. Surgeons (in common with most other people) rarely recognize that the little decisions that they are constantly making are in fact decisions. Nor do they recognize that these little decisions frequently become major decisions. Few realize the profound extent to which non-medical criteria influence their surgical decision making. Indeed, medical criteria often comprise only a proportion of the actual bases for making their decision.

Many surgeons obscure the processes by which they make decisions, with the result that they remain unaware of the number of options that exist for making their decisions (P. Katz 1985). Ways in which surgeons conceptualized decisions and in which they obscured many of their decision-making processes are the subjects of this chapter, of Chapter 8, "Surgical Decision Making, Referrals, and 'Keeping' Patients," and of Chapter 9, "The Natural History of Surgical Decisions and Their Consequences."

The number of publications on surgical decision making has increased dramatically in the last decade (Birkmeyer and Birkmeyer 1996).[1] The contemporary literature on decision making in surgery and medicine clarifies only a limited range of the actual, real-life decisions that physicians and surgeons make. Most of that literature examines quantitative, objective, logical decision making models which are solely based on medical criteria. Some of the literature examines the ethical bases of major medical decisions, such as termination of life support or informed consent for experimental treatments. Rarely, however, does the surgical or medical literature examine the little decisions that physicians continuously make in the course of their working day. These are decisions which are usually considered minor and are intimately woven into the warp of their professional activities. The literature on medical or surgical decision making rarely explicitly includes the influences of the culture of the patients, physicians, hospitals and medical systems upon their decisions.

These three chapters on decision making examine the cultural variables that influence surgical decision making. Some of these influences include:

- *The culture of surgery in general.* This includes surgeons' predisposition to the active posture, their communication barriers with colleagues and patients, their financial needs, and their unacknowledged competitiveness with other surgeons.

- *The culture of the hospital and its environment.* This includes the social relations between surgeons and other physicians, the social organization of the hospital, the policies of the hospital board (cf., Rhee 1977; Maynard et al. 1986), and the ways in which fees are determined (cf., Wolfe and Badgley 1974).

- *The culture of the patient.* This includes marital status (cf., Greenberg et al.1988), medical payment plan or insurance coverage (cf., Greenberg et al.1988; LoGerfo 1977; Posner et al. 1995), financial status, social class, race, or ethnicity (cf., Braveman et al. 1995; Egbert and Rothman 1977; Hauser 1981; Pernick 1985; C. Rosenberg 1987:27; Routh and King 1972).

- *The specific cultural background of the surgeon.* This includes their educational, subcultural, financial, and psychological background (cf., Eisenberg 1979; P. Katz 1985).

- *The culture of the region.* This refers to the geographical location of the hospital (cf., Bunker 1970; Greenberg et al.1988; Lewis 1969; Vayda 1976; 1984; Wennberg and Gittelsohn 1973).

Although most surgeons would acknowledge that their decisions can be influenced by their cultural environment, they discount the power of that influence. They retain a belief in their own objectivity and continue to strive for objective certainty. They regard cultural influences as undesirable interferences which limit their individual professional autonomy. They do not accept the inevitable presence of these influences, nor do they include consideration of them in their decision-making processes.

These three chapters on decision making analyze three major topics and illustrate them with case studies:

- How cultural factors influence surgical decision making.

- How surgeons obscure their own decision-making processes.

- How both cultural factors and obscuring of decision making contribute to causing little decisions to expand into major decisions, which result in major consequences for surgeons and especially for patients.

Most of the examples of decision making in these chapters describe decisions that were compromised by the surgeons' lack of awareness of, or concern for, the influences, processes, and implications of their own decision processes.

However, the focus upon compromised decision making does not imply that most of the Meadowbrook University Hospital surgeons' decisions were flawed. The opposite was the case: Emphatically, the majority of the myriad decisions made by the surgeons at Meadowbrook University Hospital appeared to be sensitive, ethical, and, as far as could be determined, medically optimal.[2] The emphasis here upon the suboptimal decisions, like the emphasis upon the pathological over the healthy in the fields of surgery and medicine, is for the purposes of increasing the understanding of the details of decision making, the variables that influence the processes, as well as the implications and outcomes of the decisions.

THE INFLUENCE OF THE ACTIVE POSTURE UPON DECISION MAKING

Surgical decision making is influenced more by the active posture of surgeons than by any other aspect of surgical culture. Decision-making is an active noun or verb. The active posture is so embedded in the culture of surgery and is so unquestioningly accepted as an inherent characteristic of surgeons that most surgeons ignore its profound influence upon their decision making.

Spencer defined surgical decision making as "the rapidity with which observations can be made and formulated into a hypothesis, so that a decision is made and an appropriate action taken" (Spencer 1978:9). He estimated that "a skillfully performed operation is about 75 percent decision making and 25 percent dexterity" (1979:16). In articles on surgical education and surgical competence, Spencer additionally emphasized three basic skills for surgeons, all of which involve active decision making: 1) "capacity for deductive reasoning and decision making," 2) "emotional characteristics," and 3) "dexterity." Foremost under the criterion of emotional characteristics Spencer emphasized that "a surgeon must have the capacity to make consecutive decisions under stress" (1978:9).

In the course of their internships and residencies surgeons are explicitly taught the advantages of the active posture and the dangers of not acting. They are implicitly taught to prefer action through jokes and banter which compare themselves favorably to endlessly temporizing physicians. The most common means of explicit teaching was to present cases in which not acting or delaying action resulted in mortality or increased morbidity for a patient. Appendicitis is frequently used as an example of the advantage of quick, active decision making for surgeons (even though it is much less commonly found in practice than other less dramatic examples of decision making). Deciding to operate when appendicitis is suspected can save a life. Moreover, there is comparatively little risk of operating if the diagnosis is wrong.

Surgeons vs. Internists

Surgeons have learned over the centuries that it is better to act than to wait. As a result, surgeons are more likely to weigh errors of omission more gravely than errors of commission (cf., Salem-Schatz et al. 1990:477; Ortiz de Montellano 1980). Cassell wrote: "They are tempted to do something, anything" (1991:15).

Surgeons' active posture is reflected in their perceptions of risk which differ from those of patients and internists. Surgeons' perceptions of risk are influenced by a mode of teaching and learning that emphasizes categorical risks and by their clinical experiences and those of their teachers and colleagues more than by their interpretation of statistics (cf., Timmermans et al. 1996).

An example of the difference between surgeons' and patients' perceptions of the meaning of risk was illustrated in the case of a 70-year-old woman who was in the Intensive Care Unit (ICU) in the terminal stages of lung cancer. Her end-stage condition was discussed in the previous chapter. Dr. Robinson did not expect her to live longer than 10 days. She had eight tubes in several parts of her body. Dr. Robinson, the thoracic surgeon, remarked that he had rarely seen so many tubes on one patient. She appeared to be in considerable distress. One of her tubes was connected from a ventilator through her mouth to her trachea and enabled her to breathe.

Dr. Robinson believed that she might be more comfortable with one less tube. He wanted to give her a tracheotomy so that she could breathe through her trachea instead of being ventilated through her mouth. However, he did not question the patient to determine her perception of her condition. The operation would not prolong her life, nor would it enable her to speak. As a surgeon who had performed numerous tracheotomies, he considered such an operation to be simple and not risky (because she was close to death with or without the intervention). For a post-operative patient near death and in considerable distress, it was by no means clear that an operation which cut into her trachea would not cause additional distress. Nevertheless, without asking her perception of her situation or her opinion of the intervention, Dr. Robinson explained to the patient: "You've had this tube in you for two weeks now, and it's not comfortable. We will put a little tube in you and put a windpipe in your neck. It's called a tracheotomy. *It's not a big operation.*" In this incident not only did Dr. Robinson perceive the effect on the patient differently from that which she was likely to perceive it, but most notably, he did not bother to ask her opinion.

Surgeons' cultural bias toward valuing action reflects a relatively high tolerance for the undesirable consequences of therapy (Brett 1981:1150). Their tolerance is likely to differ significantly from that of a patient who is the one who experiences the undesirable consequences of the decisions. The differences in perspectives about action versus non-action and about risk between surgeons and internists were at least as great as the differences between surgeons and patients. At Meadowbrook University Hospital the surgeons frequently criticized residents for spending too much time thinking about decisions. They believed that too much thinking was of little use. For them thinking involved "standing around," "worrying,", "putting hands in pockets," "wringing hands," or "doing nothing." Acting was most highly valued. For surgeons, uncertainty was an undesirable condition which they tolerated poorly and which they quickly attempted to eliminate (cf., Harvard Medical Practice Study 1990:51).

The high value placed upon the active posture in decision making by surgeons compared with decision making by internists was illustrated in the negotiation and consequent expectations for managing a patient who was comatose due to an unknown etiology. This case was presented to Dr. White for consultation by Meadowbrook's Chief of Medicine, Dr. Carpenter. The patient was a 51-year-old male who suddenly became comatose while undergoing standard diagnostic tests in the medical unit. No disease process had been found from the results of the numerous tests. Yet the relatively young patient remained mysteriously comatose. Further laboratory tests to determine the cause of the comatose condition continued to yield no information. The patient's condition had remained the same for more than two weeks while in the care of the internist, Dr. Carpenter. His EEG was normal, and he was considered to be neurologically salvageable. Dr. Carpenter and the other internists in the Department of Internal Medicine were distressed and puzzled by this patient's condition. They requested a surgical consult with Dr. White because they had exhausted their medical repertoire.

Dr. Carpenter presented the data of the case to Dr. White. Dr. Carpenter said: "I wonder what he has — encephalopathy, septic shock, catheter sepsis, staph? There are no stones found in his gall bladder. My conception is that he probably had acute pancreatitis. He is deteriorating badly, and we have no idea why." He posed questions of doubt ("I wonder what he has?"), emphasized the negative findings (i.e., that no cause was evident), and used sentences in the passive voice: "Everything was examined," "The etiology is unknown." Dr. Carpenter ended with words of uncertainty, failure and helplessness: "He is deteriorating badly and we have no idea why."

Dr. White, the surgeon, responded by using action words and the active voice. He asked, for example, "Have you done anything to rule out obstructive uropathy?" First he suggested several etiologies, each of which required a surgical intervention to confirm. Then Dr. White concluded, "It looks like he's not getting better, and it probably wouldn't harm him more if we took a look around. I suggest a laparotomy (exploratory abdominal surgery). It wouldn't hurt him very much. I think the family should understand that it is a fishing expedition — a last ditch effort. It will allow us to biopsy his liver and maybe his kidney. He may have some septic stuff inside."

Dr. White used action language. He explained what he wanted to do — to operate, to biopsy, to take a look. In contrast, Dr. Carpenter, the internist, responded introspectively, passively, and negatively, emphasizing doubt about surgical action and fear of such action upon the outcome. At one point in which Dr. Carpenter expressed doubts and fears in the consultation, Dr. White strategically asked him to repeat how long the man had been in the coma. He knew the answer, but he chose this technique to remind Dr. Carpenter of his failure to diagnose or cure the patient.

When Dr. White assessed the disadvantages of not acting he used many negative words, including double negatives in some instances: "*Not* going to the operating room *won't* help him. His chances of doing any good are small. He could have an intrabdominal infection. If we drain his abscess, he may wake up. If we *don't* drain his abscess, he'll probably *not* wake up."

Dr. Carpenter reiterated his doubts and concerns using negative words. He asked Dr. White, "What is the mortality rate for laparotomies?" He said, "I *don't* see what you'll do in his abdomen that will make him wake up. But, he's going to die anyway. But I'm not sure you can do *no* wrong. You can decide."

Dr. White responded actively, "I'm inclined to operate."

Dr. Carpenter again initiated doubts and negativity and used interrogative sentences: "Frankly, I *wouldn't*. Do you think that there is strong enough evidence for it? Do you have anything that may lead you to believe that there is something wrong in the belly?"

Dr. White answered positively, "The sequence of events as I understand them has been...[he repeated the history of the illness]. I've never been sorry for doing a laparotomy on someone who's critically ill."

Dr. Carpenter replied again with doubts, negativity, and hopelessness: "I *cannot* visualize that you would find anything that will make a difference."

Dr. White responded by evoking an optimistic argument for action. He said positively, "What would you say if Pathology called you and said, 'This guy's got an abscess'? There's nothing in this man that is irreversible [i.e., his brain is okay]. He's young, and there is a possibility of saving him."

Dr. Carpenter said pessimistically, "I hope you find something. I'd like to be wrong once."

Dr. White optimistically replied, "I think he may not make it, but I wouldn't be surprised if he wakes up after the surgery."

Dr. Carpenter responded, "Wouldn't that be lovely!"

In this case the decision was made by the fact that the surgeon was the only one who offered an active, positive possibility, however remote, of rescuing the man from death. It is of considerable interest that Dr. Carpenter, the internist, never admitted to having participated in the decision to operate, although, in fact, as the physician in charge of the patient, he was the only physician with authority to make such a treatment decision. The surgeon's role was that of a consultant who could only recommend treatment to the internist. However, Dr. White acted as if he took the responsibility for the decision to operate. The active posture was comfortable and familiar to him. Dr. White did perform both a laparotomy and a tracheotomy on the patient. No pathology was found. A week after the operation, the patient died. The autopsy (which did not include the head) revealed no pathology and no evidence for the cause of death.

The surgeon's active decision making was expressed in the language of the active voice, positive approach, and optimistic outlook. The internist's reluctance to act was expressed in the language of passive voice, negative approach, doubt, and pessimistic outlook. Observations of decision making in several different cultural contexts, including medical ones involving pediatricians, psychiatrists, surgeons, and family practitioners, and non-medical committees including those in military, government, and academic contexts, suggest that in situations of uncertainty when decisions have to be made, and most participants are hesitant or reluctant to make a decision, a suggestion for an active decision is usually accepted (P. Katz 1991; P. Katz 1984; cf., Dawes 1988, 1989:55-56). In the hospital setting, as in the case described above, in situations of uncertainty when surgeons and internists collaborated in decision making, the active and optimistic posture of the surgeon was more likely to be accepted and implemented.

"We are Surgeons. We Have to Know!"

During one of their weekly Surgical Rounds the surgeons at Meadowbrook University Hospital discussed a patient with suspected pancreatic cancer who had for two weeks been in the prior care of an internist. Dr. Sund, the surgeon conducting the Rounds, commented on the slowness of the internists, "Most of the investigations [determining the patient's diagnosis] should have been done in 48 hours, not two weeks. These procedures shouldn't have been delayed."

Dr. Sund continued, "With biliary obstruction, time is important. You'll be wrong occasionally. But as surgeons we are not interested in something that is 90 percent. We're interested in a protective situation. We're not internists. We don't sit around and stroke our beard and say it is *likely* to be cancer of the pancreas. We are surgeons. We have to know. That is why a laparotomy is essential to get a better look at the pancreas. The man at the [operating room] table knows more what should be done."

Dr. Sund posed a question to the surgeons present which was designed to elicit support for an active posture in diagnosing surgical conditions. He asked, "How many people here have operated on a patient with a history of extra-hepatic biliary obstruction and found that they made a mistake?" Dr. Sund correctly estimated that few surgeons in Rounds were willing to admit mistakes in this context (cf., Millman 1976), and could therefore use the surgeons' silence to support his active, interventionist surgical decision over medical ones.

The following case of a terminally ill patient illustrates a different situation in which an internist and surgeon made decisions: Mrs. Hess, a 78-year-old patient in the (ICU) Intensive Care Unitwho was terminally ill with adenocarcinoma of the right lung, causing pleural effusion, a huge hilar mass, and bronchial obstruction. The internist in charge of the ICU, Dr. Blair, and the surgeon, Dr. McCullars, perceived their options as: a) whether to exchange the patient's temporary pacemaker for a permanent one, and b) whether to drain her pleural effusion. They defined the options as actions — whether to prolong her life by carrying out major invasive interventions and/or minor invasive interventions. However, neither the internist nor the surgeon explicitly stated the salient third option — whether to not intervene at all and permit her to die. Even though the patient's imminent death was the overriding reality determining their decision making, they did not explicitly state the option of non-action.

They avoided the non-active decision (doing nothing) and decided, according to Dr. McCullars' suggestion, to undertake what they considered to be a minor intervention in order to determine the seriousness of the effusion. Dr. McCullars decided to do a surgical procedure to drain the pleural effusion. However, the surgeon's and internist's perception that this intervention was minor contrasted with the patient's most likely perception that this intervention was major, because it caused her considerable discomfort. They did not discuss these decisions with the patient, even though she was alert. And they did not discuss the decision with the family.

Dr. McCullars made two holes between her ribs at the third intercostalspace to drain the fluid. He determined that the effusion was due to the cancer, which indicated a grim prognosis. Their decision at this stage was that of either taking out the chest tube which would lead to a more natural "death" or leaving it in to let the patient die a more agonizing death.

Dr. Blair, the ICU internist, did not want to make the decision, even though he was the one responsible for making a decision, because he was officially in charge of the patient. Dr. Blair also did not acknowledge that even no explicit decision constitutes a decision in fact. He again asked Dr. McCullars, the surgeon, to make the decision. Dr. McCullars first replied, "What the hell are you talking about? It's a decision you'll have to make!" Then Dr. McCullars gently recommended an active decision to the internist, "It will be more comfortable if the chest tube is out now [causing death for the patient]. Maybe we should take the tube out." Dr. Blair responded, "It hurts. I want to make it as gentle as possible. I am playing God. I'm not comfortable about this decision. I want to talk to the family."

The literature supports the observations in Meadowbrook University Hospital that surgeons make more active decisions than internists. For example, in a study eliciting recommendations from surgeons and internists (gastroenterologists) on a hypothetical duodenal ulcer, Elashoff et al. found that "surgeons consistently recommended surgery more often than did gastroenterologists" (1980:750). Some studies comparing characteristics of surgeons, indicated, however, that older surgeons were more likely to recommend surgery than younger surgeons (Vayda et al. 1981).

The case of Dr. Blair's consultation with Dr. McCullars in the ICU illustrates that: a) The surgeon had a more active posture toward the patient than the internist (the internist called the surgeon in the hope that the active posture would save the patient); b) The ways in which decisions are framed determined the options considered available (cf., Marteau 1989). For example, because the surgeons did not consider the option of doing nothing, the only decisions he expressed were those of doing something; c) Not making an explicit decision constitutes decision making, without acknowledging that it is decision making. For example, by not say-ing, "Let's let the patient die," only decisions of intervention were considered. The result was that the patient suffered greater discomfort; and d) Such a major decision about the patient's quality and length of life was made *without* consulting the patient and *before* consulting with the family. The internist, not the surgeon, suggested that the family be consulted (even though in this case the surgeon also knew the family). The case also illustrates difficulties in making decisions about terminally ill patients for which no cure, heroism, or even palliation is possible.

SURGEONS' AND PATIENTS' PERSPECTIVES ON DECISION MAKING

Surgeons' decisions are affected by the culture of patients. The medical literature has documented ways in which the sex, marital status, social class, or medical insurance of patients affected the kinds of care provided (cf., Greenberg et al. 1988; Hauser 1981; LoGerfo 1977; Egbert and Rothman 1977; Pernick 1985; Rosenberg 1987:27). Most contemporary North American medical schools teach potential physicians to be sensitive to patients' cultures, as well as to engage the patient in taking joint responsibility with the physician for decision making. Physicians who explicitly consider their patients' cultures and collaborate with the patient in making decisions are likely to serve them better medically. However, optimal decision making is compromised when the physician, knowingly or unknowingly, gives differential and inferior treatment to patients with less prestigious social characteristics than to those with more prestigious ones. Decision making is also compromised when a physician is unaware of being influenced by the patients' culture. Many physicians, if not most, believe that they utilize entirely medical considerations in their decision making.

The provincial health systems in Canada pay fixed reimbursement so that all surgeons received the same fee for each specific procedure, regardless of the economic status of the patient. Yet, class, ethnicity, and other markers of patients' status influenced some of the responses of surgeons to their patients. For example, the following case illustrates how surgical decision making was differentially influenced by the culture of two patients who presented with similar symptoms. However, the differential treatment in this case study fell to the disadvantage of both of the patients.

Same Symptom, Different Treatment

Within a period of six weeks two male patients in their fifties presented to Dr. White with stomach pains of several months duration. For both of these patients their pains intensified in the two weeks prior to their first consultation. The medical symptoms of both patients most likely indicated diagnoses of gastric ulcer. But a smaller possibility existed for their symptoms to indicate diagnoses of stomach cancer. Their condition was a difficult one to diagnose definitively. Nevertheless, Dr. White treated each of these patients significantly differently.

The first patient was a 58-year-old man who was a wealthy and prestigious presence in Meadowbrook City. He was also the brother of a member of the Board of Trustees of Meadowbrook University Hospital. The second patient was a 55-year-old immigrant blue-collar worker. Dr. White decided to treat the symptoms of the first man aggressively. He examined the patient's stomach with a gastroscope, and, fearing, without substantial evidence, that the patient might have stomach cancer, he decided to perform a partial gastrectomy (removal of part of the stomach). This was an extremely aggressive treatment which was described by Dr. Nordberg, who was familiar with the case, as "overkill."

Dr. White treated the patient aggressively in order to protect himself from malpractice by missing the small probability that the diagnosis was cancer. After the operative procedure the patient was eventually diagnosed as having gastric ulcers. As a result of the partial gastrectomy, the patient no longer had problems with his ulcers, but he had unnecessarily lost part of his stomach. He appeared to remain unaware that his ulcers could have been treated successfully with far less aggressive intervention.

When the second patient came to Dr. White with stomach pains which appeared equal in severity to those of the first patient, Dr. White suggested that he take Maalox, an over-the-counter stomach drug. When after four weeks the patient returned with no improvement in symptoms, Dr. White wrote him a prescription to relieve his pain, and instructed him to continue taking Maalox. After four more weeks the patient returned because his symptoms still had not been alleviated. It was only after eight weeks that Dr. White finally examined the patient's stomach with a gastroscope — the procedure he conducted immediately upon the first patient — and discovered that he had stomach cancer. If the cancer had been discovered early and treated immediately and aggressively there may have been a possibility that the patient's outcome would have been more favorable. However, by the time of the operation, eight weeks after originally coming to the surgeon, the cancer had metastasized. The patient died eight months after surgery.

Resisting Decision Changes

Once surgeons made a decision they often attempted to legitimize that decision, and they were extremely reluctant to revoke it. The active posture which encourages surgeons to make decisions rather than wait or think, and the heroic image of the surgeon which discourages doubt or admission of errors deter surgeons from reexamining a decision.

The following case illustrates that once a surgeon makes a decision, he is extremely reluctant to revoke that decision, even when the clinical evidence suggests that it is wrong:

> A male surgery patient was in the surgery ward of Meadowbrook University Hospital for rectal bleeding. Dr. Roddy thought that the bleeding was due to "nothing more than hemorrhoids." Nevertheless, to protect himself from malpractice, he ordered a large series of diagnostic tests, most of which were invasive and uncomfortable for the patient. The patient complained about the discomfort that the tests caused him. He told the nurse that he wanted no more testing. The nurse, resident, and patient communicated the patient's wishes to Dr. Roddy.

> Despite Dr. Roddy's belief — which he did not express to the patient — that the tests were probably unnecessary and despite the patient's request to forego the rest of the tests, Dr. Roddy was unwilling to make a decision to forego subsequent testing. The patient overheard some of the discussions of the disagreement between the nurse and Dr. Roddy about the necessity for undergoing tests. Shortly after overhearing the nurses' reservations the patient said to Dr. Roddy in an upbeat tone, "I have a funeral of my mother. Can I go out today?"

> Dr. Roddy realized that the patient was lying in order to leave the hospital. Nevertheless, he agreed to let him out for one day, but he still refused to rescind the orders for the subsequent tests. Dr. Roddy understood the reasons for the patient's sudden recollection of his mother's death. He predicted that the patient would not return. He was nonetheless relieved because the patient made the

decision that he was unwilling to make. The patient was listed as leaving the hospital "Against Medical Advice" (AMA), a status which protected Dr. Roddy from being accused of negligence, if the patient's rectal bleeding were to subsequently worsen.

In this case, the surgeon's active posture in which he made a decision and was not willing to rescind the decision was actually a process of passing the decision making onto the patient. The patient had even fewer options than the surgeon for rescinding that decision. The process of sticking to a decision may be conceived as making yet another decision. Or it may be conceived as not making a decision or retaining an inactive posture.

THE ACTIVE POSTURE AND HOSPITAL CULTURE

The following cases describe ways in which surgeons made active decisions to utilize their knowledge of the culture of the hospital. The culture of the hospital includes knowledge about the statuses, roles, and abilities of specialists. Knowledge of hospital culture is essential for efficaciously mobilizing resources for patient care. It is not enough to know that a pathologist performs laboratory tests or an anesthesiologist anesthetizes patients. It is also important to know the format, protocols, or rules for requesting their service. And it is important to distinguish differences between specific professionals' behaviors, such as their accessibility, reliability, or competence. An active posture facilitates both gathering knowledge about the hospital as well as utilizing its facilities effectively.

For example, Dr. Michael had a patient with a huge retroperitoneal mass. He sent a specimen of that tumor to the pathology department. The diagnosis from the pathology lab came back as adenocarcinoma. Dr. Michael did not believe that it could be adenocarcinoma because of the size of the tumor. When he discovered that the pathologist who made the diagnosis was a junior person, he suggested that they send it back to the senior pathologist. He knew and trusted the senior pathologist. After the second pathologist examined the specimen he received another diagnosis which he considered to be accurate.

Similarly, when Dr. Nordberg wanted to know about the progression of the metastasis of his patient after he had died (described in Chapter 4, "Styles of Surgeons"), he actively sought out the pathologist whom he most respected to do the autopsy. He presented the specific problem of the origin and pathway of the metastasis to that pathologist. The pathologist was able to examine the body specifically to assess the metastatic pathways.

In another example of the importance of knowing the hospital culture, including its personnel, Dr. Nordberg specifically acted to choose an anesthesiologist whom he knew he could trust to carry out a particular anesthesiological procedure. On the previous day when Dr. Robinson had operated on a patient for a lobectomy (removal of a lobe from the lung) the assigned anesthesiologist had tried and failed three times to pass a double lumen tube (which would pass oxygen and the anesthesia to only one lung), and another anesthesiologist had to be called. A day after the operation the patient leaked pleural and blood fluids through a gap in the chest wall (which was caused because the resident had not secured the knot tightly enough when he had sewed the patient up). That patient had to be rushed again to surgery. Dr. Nordberg knew that an anesthesiologist who could successfully pass a double lumen tube was again needed. He did not wait until the anesthesiology department assigned an anesthesiologist to him. He forcefully decided, utilizing his active posture and knowledge, to demand that Dr. Greenberg, the most talented anesthesiologist in the department, be present.

CONCLUSION

The active posture of the surgeons at Meadowbrook University Hospital influenced the ways in which they made decisions, the ways in which they perceived the options available to them, and the ways in which they perceived risks. Surgical decision analysis with its claims of objectivity has become increasingly popular among surgeons. It is based upon probabilistic theory assessing explicit symptoms using Bayesian logic. This way of reasoning differs from the ways in which surgeons (and other physicians) are taught to think in clinical situations. Surgeons making clinical decisions usually depend upon categorical, schematic reasoning which, in turn, relies upon tacit knowledge (cf., Eli 1996; Bergus et al. 1995; Malterud 1995).

Although decision analyses may appear to minimize some biases in decision making, they contain their own biases. Douglas and Wildavsky, social scientists who examined the cultural components of risk behavior in decision making, pointed out that risk assessors cannot give objective analyses when they are dealing with uncertainties:

They slide their personal bias into the calculations unobserved ...
judgments of risk and safety must be selected as much on the basis
of what is valued as on the basis of what is known... Serious risk
analysis should also focus on the institutional framework of
*decision making (*Douglas and Wildavsky 1982:80-81).

According to Douglas and Wildavsky, even the statistics upon which a decision is made cannot be objective: "Objectivity means preventing subjective values from interfering with the analysis... There is the delusion that assigning probability is a value-free exercise" (1982:71).

One of the major deficiencies of surgical decision analysis is that it assumes decisions are made in the absence of context. Douglas and Wildavsky claim that: "Specialized risk analysis impoverishes the statement of a human problem by taking it out of context. The notion of risk is.. essentially decontextualized and desocialized. Thinking about how to choose between risks, subjective values must take priority. It is a travesty of rational thought to pretend that it is best to take value-free decisions in matters of life and death" (Douglas and Wildavsky 1982:71)..

Decision analysis encourages decontextualization of problems. Taking the context of problems into consideration is essential in coming to an optimal decision about diagnosis or treatment (cf., Sankar 1988; Atkinson 1988). These contexts may include the presentation of the symptoms in light of the culture of the patient, or the characteristics of the surgeon, hospital, or type of reimbursement for fees. Extensive research exists which illustrates how decisions or risks are evaluated differently when they are presented in different ways or in different contexts (cf., Jou et al. 1996; Kordes de Vaal 1996; Mazur and Hickam 1996; Redelmeier et al. 1995; Salem-Schatz et al. 1990; Tversky and Kahneman 1984).

The biases that surgeons have toward taking risks influence the decisions they make. They also influence the ways in which they present information to the patient when they encourage the patient to make decisions. Brett wrote: "The ultimate concrete reality of a medical event derives from its interaction with individuals rather than statistically manipulated populations...medical decisions involve human beings — both doctors and patients — with unique attitudes and values" (1981:1152).

"Objective" surgical decision trees which ignore non-medical influences on decision making serve to reinforce surgeons' illusions that non-medical variables do not influence their decisions. However, if surgeons acknowledge that cultural criteria inevitably enter into decision making, they would be able to incorporate them into their decision-making models, making these models closer to reality. They can prevent undesirable criteria from unduly influencing their decision making.

The following two chapters present case studies which illustrate the influences of the hospital and the medical and surgical culture upon decision making (Chapter 8), and the ways in which small decisions expand into large decisions (Chapter 9). These chapters examine the influence of referrals, money, and competition upon decision making, the natural history of decision making, and the implications of surgical decision making for patients.

NOTES

1. Of 86 studies of surgical decision analysis only six were published before 1980, and 44 appeared between 1990 and 1994, but only 13 percent of publications of surgical decision analysis were published in surgical journals (Birkmeyer and Birkmeyer 1996).

2. This statement is written to counter the impression that such troublesome decisions that are described in these chapters are more prevalent than non-troublesome ones. Although an ideal anthropological posture is one of suspension of judgment, the ethnographic researcher can never be completely neutral in studying behavior (cf., Devereux 1967). Therefore, this departs from the more customary neutral stance by making an evaluative statement. The assessment of the author, as a non-physician, of the medical competence of surgeons is limited (cf., M. Good 1995). At the time of the field work she relied upon the surgeons' and surgical residents' assessments of specific incidences discussed in these chapters.

Chapter 8

SURGICAL DECISION MAKING, REFERRALS, AND "KEEPING" PATIENTS

~

Money, unfortunately, is one factor that occasionally prevents doctors from doing their best for their patients.

(Nolen 1970:183)

INTRODUCTION

Surgeons receive a larger percentage of their patients through referrals from physicians than do many other medical specialists (Crile 1978:122; Shortell and Anderson 1971:40). They are financially dependent upon their ability to obtain referrals. They solicit referrals from other physicians, and they compete with other surgeons for patients. The surgeons at Meadowbrook University Hospital paid a great deal of attention to activities which they believed would increase referrals. Chapter 4, "Styles of Surgeons," described how Dr. White spent more time communicating with physicians to cultivate referrals than he did in communicating with, or caring for, his patients. Dr. Nolen, whose books candidly described his experiences as a surgeon, admitted to the influence of competition when he wrote, "Money, unfortunately, is one factor that occasionally prevents doctors from doing their best for their patients" (1970:183).

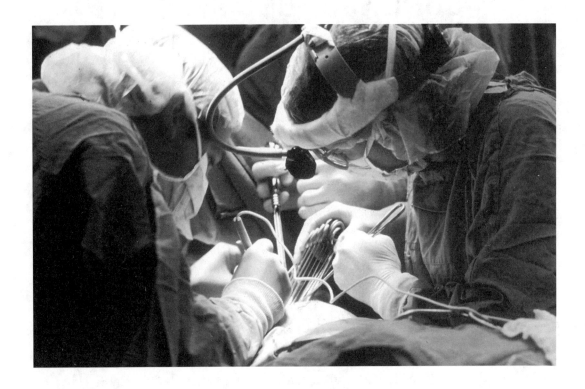

Courtesy, Johns Hopkins Medicine.

Decisions that physicians make about referrals to surgeons are also frequently based upon factors other than medical (P. Katz 1985; Shortell and Anderson 1971; Shortell 1974). Obtaining referrals, recruiting patients, keeping patients, and other aspects of making money enter inextricably into surgeons' decision-making processes. Nevertheless, surgeons inevitably proffer medical reasons for their decisions. Even when non-medical factors influence decision making, they express their decisions in medical language. Admitting other reasons for surgical decisions would be unacceptable to them and their patients. They frequently believed that their decisions were really based on medical reasons.

Decisions may be influenced by the hospital organization, by the culture of the surgical specialty, or by the network of social relationships and the personal preferences of the referring physician. Decisions about referral, however unimportant they may appear, carry significant implications for the care of the patient. When referral decisions are governed by non-medical criteria, and these criteria are not acknowledged and communicated, the results may be detrimental to the patient. George Crile, a surgeon, wrote:

> *In order to have a constant stream of referrals, the surgeon must please the referring physicians. Sometimes this is best accomplished by doing what those physicians approve of or want done. When these desires run contrary to the best judgment of the surgeon, conflicts of interest again appear. If the surgeon does what he thinks his colleagues expect, he may not be doing what he believes is in the best interests of his patient.* (1978:122).

Studies of referral behavior indicate that many decisions about referral are not related to patients' medical conditions (Shortell and Anderson 1971). They may be governed by the physicians' status, role, or income. In a fee-for-service system a surgeon who refers a patient to another physician or surgeon loses the income he would have earned by treating the patient himself. Referral entails the psychological cost of acknowledging (to himself, to the patient, and to the referred physician) the inability of the one who refers to treat the illness (cf., Shortell and Anderson 1971:46).

Reciprocity is one factor that can influence referral decisions. A surgeon may refer patients to a physician after the surgeon has completed his treatment, or a surgeon might invite a physician to "assist" at an operation (for which he receives a fee). Nolen wrote that referrals are important for maintaining social relationships with peers: "If you're a specialist...and count on other doctors to send patients to you, then it's imperative that you be nice not only to patients but to the doctor that sends them to you. As a result, a lot of butt-kissing goes on in the medical world" (1970:155).

When physicians refer patients to a particular surgeon (or if they decide not to refer the patient to another) they typically use language which suggests that it is entirely on the basis of the best medical care for the patient. It is highly unlikely that a physician would tell a patient that he is referred because "we belong to the same club," or that "he usually invites me to assist in the operation." Neither would a surgeon tell a colleague that he is not referring a patient to him even though he knows how to do the operation better or because needs the income more.

REFERRAL DECISIONS BASED ON NON-MEDICAL FACTORS

At Meadowbrook University Hospital an example of a referral decision that was based upon the organizational structure of the hospital and a surgeon's personal interest rather than upon a patient's medical condition was illustrated by a former patient of Dr. Michael. This 39-year-old woman had been a surgical patient of Dr. Michael 10 years previously for removal of a polynidal cyst (a hair follicle embedded in a cyst). On this occasion the patient came to the emergency room with a condition which was completely unrelated to the previous surgical condition. She had pancreatitis, a condition usually requiring medical (gastroenterological), not surgical, expertise. However, hospital policy permitted a surgeon who had once treated a patient to claim subsequent responsibility for that patient. Although this patient had a medical problem which indicated that she should be referred to an internist in the Department of Medicine, she was instead referred to Dr. Michael, a surgeon.

Even though Dr. Michael was aware that the patient with pancreatitis should be under the care of an internist, he did not refer the patient to an internist. Instead he kept the patient and requested a consultation from an internist. This decision did not deprive the patient of internal medicine's expertise. But because Dr. Michael remained in charge of her case he made all the decisions. He decided not only *if* an internist were to be consulted but also *which* internist to consult, how to interpret the results, and, most important, how to use the internist's advice about how to treat the case. His right to claim the patient, and the revenue, as his own because his previous treatment of her superseded the medical conditions which would have mandated that an internist — a gastroenterologist — manage her case. Johnson reported a physician saying, "I don't mind sending my patient to a specialist, but I want that specialist to let me manage the patient" (1995b:461).

Referral decisions are often influenced by the surgeon's personal networks of social relationship. For example, Shortell found that from 96 to 98 percent of internists' referral selections included physicians who were on the same hospital staff (Shortell 1974). Such a pattern appeared to be the norm at Meadowbrook University Hospital. Dr. Russell referred a patient to Dr. Turunen, one of the two urological surgeons in the surgery department. When questioned as to why he referred the patient to Dr. Turunen and not to Dr.Gottlieb, the other urologist, he replied: "Dr. Turunen is my friend. There is no question that Dr. Gottlieb is the best, but I don't like him."

Another mechanism that surgeons at Meadowbrook University Hospital used to hold onto their patients when they did not have the required expertise to treat them was by using residents as substitutes for surgeons. (Some of the implications for practice using residents were described in Chapter 5, "Communication with Colleagues.")

The following case describes how a surgeon held onto a patient and avoided referring that patient to specialists by utilizing a resident's skill: A 57-year-old male was referred by his family practitioner to Dr. Aranow, a general surgeon at Meadowbrook University Hospital, for surgery for cancer of the rectum. This kind of surgery for this specific rectal cancer was usually performed by the only proctological surgeon at Meadowbrook, Dr. Sund. When the patient came to Dr. Aranow he accepted him under his care. He did not tell the patient that there was a proctological surgeon in the department who had considerable experience in that kind of surgery, whereas he had little experience. He did not tell the patient that he had neither performed that particular kind of surgery, nor seen it performed.

Dr. Aranow knew that the chief resident had assisted Dr. Sund, the proctological surgeon, during the past year and therefore had familiarity with this kind of operation. On this basis he made a decision to accept the patient and to have the resident perform the surgery for him in his presence in the operating room. There was nothing illegal about this decision: Dr. Aranow's license and general surgery specialty legally entitled him to perform this kind of surgery, despite his lack of experience. And the resident was legally permitted to operate if the surgeon were present.

The chief resident performed the operation as Dr. Aranow watched. In a reversal of roles of teacher and student, the resident explained to Dr. Aranow the cutting and stitching techniques that Dr. Sund, the proctological surgeon, typically used. The operation was successful. The patient never discovered that Dr. Aranow had no experience whatsoever in that kind of operation. He never knew that Dr. Sund was the only surgeon in the hospital with that specific expertise, and he never discovered that the chief resident, and not Dr. Aranow, performed the operation. Dr. Aranow, of course, received the fee for performing the procedure.

However, decisions to use residents as substitutes for, or to teach, attending surgeons frequently resulted in surgical errors. Most of these errors were small. Most often the residents did not recognize many of the small errors they made, because they were the most knowledgeable person in the operating room (either when they were left alone in the operating room or when they taught their teachers). If such errors were detected at all it was either because of disastrous results or because of subsequent good supervision.

Ideally residents spent their five years of surgical training learning from the senior surgeons who supervised them as they learned. In these ideal situations senior surgeons systematically corrected residents' mistakes as they made them. They scrutinized and advised residents about the decisions they made. However, when senior surgeons made decisions based on non-medical factors, such as allowing a resident to perform an operation that the senior surgeon could not perform in order to retain the patient, they abrogated their surgical decision-making responsibility and compromised the care of the patient.

An example of the detection of an error because a resident subsequently received good supervision from a senior surgeon occurred when Dr. Nordberg, a careful, conservative surgeon who never left his resident alone in the operating room, allowed that resident to perform a hiatal hernia operation while he, Dr. Nordberg, only supervised. He allowed the resident that autonomy because he knew that the resident had done four previous hiatal hernia operations alone, unsupervised under the auspices of Dr. Roddy.

However, during the operation, Dr. Nordberg noticed that the resident erroneously began to attach the esophagus to a portion of the stomach posteriorly, instead of the correct way, which involved employing a 270° wrap-around. Dr. Nordberg showed him the correct way. Then he carefully inquired if that were the way he usually did that operation. The resident explained that he always did it that way. But he added that he had always performed that operation without supervision. In the past no one had been present to correct him. If he had not had the supervision of Dr. Nordberg in this last year of his residency, he probably would have performed all his subsequent operations erroneously.

THE EFFECT OF NEW TECHNOLOGIES UPON SURGEON'S REFERRALS

The introduction of new technologies in Meadowbrook University Hospital contributed to increasing competition among different specialists, particularly between surgeons and internists. Competition was increased because internists were able to perform diagnostic tasks that had traditionally been the exclusive domain of surgeons. For example, flexible, fiber-optic endoscopes permitted observations of, and entry into, the living body which had only previously been observable when the body had been cut open by surgeons.

Endoscopic procedures, including, for example, bronchoscopy (of the bronchial tubes and lungs), gastroscopy (of the stomach and esophagus), and cystoscopy (of the bladder), replaced those surgical operations which examined and biopsied those areas for diagnoses. Laparoscopic surgery also depends upon the observations and instruments within an endoscope and is carried out through very small incisions. Beginning in the 1970s many specialists, such as internists, gynecologists, and radiologists, as well as surgeons, learned these endoscopic procedures. Using endoscopy requires special training and greater hand-eye coordination than most surgery (cf., Ballie and Ravitch 1993; Escarce et al. 1997). One of the results was that physicians in different specialties vied with surgeons for patients who required such examinations (cf., Gamradt and Brandt 1993). Surgeons no longer had exclusive expertise to examine and biopsy the internal organs of patients. Such competition resulted in major reductions in patient loads for surgeons.

When the endoscopes were first introduced at Meadowbrook University Hospital several of the internists in the hospital learned how to use them before any of the surgeons did. The immediate effect was to reduce the numbers of operations requiring examinations, such as laparotomies, or minor biopsies, such as mediastinoscopies. When a few of the surgeons began to learn how to use the endoscopes, the internists tried to get the hospital to prevent the surgeons from having hospital authority to use them. They claimed that performing endoscopies constituted diagnostic internal medicine procedures and should be performed by internists, whereas operating constituted surgical procedures and should only be performed by surgeons. Although the internists did not succeed in preventing the surgeons from learning the new technologies, they had hoped that by having a monopoly over the endoscopes they could prevent the surgeons from using them.

The internists wanted to increase their own patient load at the expense of the surgeons' patient load.

REFERRAL DECISION FOR PROFIT

The following case illustrates how the decisions of two surgeons were influenced more by competition for the management of a patient than they were by the medical condition of the patient.

The patient was Mr. Bowman, a 58-year-old male who came to Dr. Russell, a general surgeon in the Department of Surgery at Meadowbrook, with symptoms of gastric reflux and heartburn of many years standing. Mr. Bowman had first gone to his family physician, who subsequently referred him to Dr. Russell after his symptoms worsened. Clinical and radiological (x-ray) examination of Mr. Bowman indicated that he suffered from a large hiatal hernia. (A hiatal hernia is a condition in which part of the stomach which is normally exclusively in the abdominal cavity extends through a gap through the diaphragm into the thoracic cavity.) It is rarely a life-threatening disorder. Most hiatal hernia repairs can be performed equally successfully by either a general surgeon, who operates through the abdominal cavity, or a thoracic surgeon, who operates through the thoracic cavity. In a small minority of cases, however, (such as an unusual stomach angle or a previously unsuccessful repair) a hiatal hernia performed thoracically was more likely to be successful (Mustard 1970).

In many instances the type of surgery to be performed is determined by the surgeon who is in charge of the case. The surgeon in charge can be selected in several possible ways. He may be chosen because he had previously performed surgery on that patient, even if the previous surgery was unrelated to the present symptoms (such as occurred with the patient of Dr. Michael who had pancreatitis, mentioned earlier in this chapter). He may be chosen because the patient came through the emergency room and that surgeon, or the resident of the surgeon, was on duty when the patient was brought in. Some of the surgeons at Meadowbrook volunteered for emergency room duty when their patient loads were low in order to "recruit" more patients. Most commonly, however, the surgeon is selected by referral from the primary or referring physician, who is most likely to be a family practitioner, internist, pediatrician, or gynecologist.

These methods for referral do not necessarily assure that the surgical specialist best qualified to treat the patient's condition is put in charge of the case. Many physicians who refer patients to surgeons are unaware of the specifics of a surgeon's expertise. Nolen wrote, "Often the G.P.'s who refer the cases don't know much about the technical aspects of the surgery" (Nolen 1970:158). However, patients usually remain unaware of the differences in expertise (as was the case when Dr. Aranow's resident performed the proctological surgery that only Dr. Sund was qualified to perform). Most patients assume that the referring physician has chosen a surgeon who is well qualified to treat their specific medical condition.

In many cases, such as that of a hiatal hernia, the pattern of referral to a surgeon usually determines the kind of operation to be performed. If the family physician or internist refers the patient to a general surgeon, the hiatal hernia will most likely be repaired abdominally. If the referral is made to a thoracic surgeon, it will most likely be repaired thoracically. However, most physicians who are not surgeons are unaware of the conditions that may be favorable for either thoracic or abdominal surgery of hiatal hernias.

Mr. Bowman's hiatal hernia was one which called for a thoracic repair. It may be unsuccessful if it were performed abdominally. Neither the family physician nor Mr. Bowman knew this. Dr. Russell knew how it should be optimally repaired. However, Dr. Russell's referrals in recent years had not increased as fast as those of some of his colleagues. In recent months his referrals had particularly fallen off. He complained that the proliferation of surgical specialists took away much of the business that had previously been the exclusive domain of the general surgeon. Dr. Russell was especially concerned about losing patients, because he was struggling to finance a new summer house.

Dr. Russell was a general surgeon without specialty training in thoracic surgery. He only knew how to repair a hiatal hernia abdominally. The referral of Mr. Bowman's hiatal hernia presented him with a dilemma. He knew that the operation should be performed thoracically to increase the possibility of success, and that there was about an 85 percent chance of failure if it were performed abdominally. He also knew, however, that failure of a hiatal hernia repair was rarely life-threatening. It was not likely to be detected by the patient immediately after surgery (and thus could not be easily attributed to the type of surgery). Instead, the hernia would probably reappear within a period of months. He was faced with a decision about whether to perform the surgery himself through the abdomen, or whether he should refer the patient to a thoracic surgeon.

Dr. Russell avoided making a decision by consulting with, not referring the patient to, a thoracic surgeon in his department, Dr. McCullars. Dr. McCullars was his personal friend. Dr. Russell did not *refer* the patient to the thoracic surgeon as would have been medically appropriate. If he referred that patient, he would have had to relinquish him. By asking Dr. McCullars for a *consultation* he kept his patient. (Consultation is different from referral: When a surgeon asks for a consultation, the surgeon remains in charge of the patient, and the consulting physician gives the surgeon advice about the surgeon's patient. When a surgeon refers the patient to a physician the physician takes charge of the patient, and the patient is no longer under the care of the surgeon.) By making a decision for a consultation rather than a referral, Dr. Russell did not decide appropriately for his patient's welfare. Instead, he turned the decision — but not the patient — over to Dr. McCullars.

Dr. McCullars knew about his friend's worries about his decreasing referrals and about his difficulties in financing his summer house. When Dr. McCullars received the request for consultation he examined the clinical and radiological data on Mr. Bowman's hiatal hernia. He verbalized the details of his decision-making process (while alone with the author):

"This hernia will probably not hold if Harry [Dr. Russell] does it. If he's lucky, it may hold until the patient goes home. It's clear that it should definitely be done thoracically. But Harry is terribly worried about his income. That summer house means a lot to him. But it's above his head. He needs money now. He is my friend. It's a tough decision. But if I take it from him (i.e., decide that it be done thoracically by me), he'll think twice about consulting me again, knowing I'll take his patients. He's a friend who's in financial trouble. I'll let him do it."

Throughout this decision-making process neither surgeon explicitly discussed his reasons for his decisions. Both knew what was best for the patient — to refer the patient to Dr. McCullars, the thoracic surgeon, so that the patient would be operated on thoracically. Both knew that this decision was not beneficial for the patient. However, the entire discussion about the operation between the two surgeons and with the patient used only medical language; it obviously did not use the language of finances or friendship.

Dr. Russell performed the hiatal hernia repair abdominally on Mr. Bowman. During the surgery it became evident that the hiatal hernia repair was unlikely to "hold" and that the patient would have to return for another hiatal hernia operation, done thoracically, within a year. The evidence about its failure to "hold" became more glaringly apparent while Dr. Russell was operating, and the patient was open, and the repair was in process. But Dr. Russell did not reverse his decision.

After the surgery Dr. Russell met Dr. McCullars in the surgeons' lounge and said, "Whew, that was tough! I don't know how long it will last!" With that comment Dr. Russell expressed hope that the surgical repair would last beyond the immediate post-operative period, so that he could avoid being blamed for the failure of the operation. But it also expressed his awareness that the operation he had just performed was inadequate.

This example of decision making illustrates how responsibility for decision making was passed from one person to another. Neither person overtly defined the options, the implications of the decision, or the basis for the decision. Dr. Russell refused to make a decision, even though he was aware of which decision would have been in the patient's best interest. Dr. McCullars decided to "return the patient" to Dr. Russell not for medical reasons but rather on the grounds of friendship and on encouraging subsequent referrals to him by his colleague. Notwithstanding both of their awareness of what was the best decision to make for the patient, both surgeons discussed the decision and the options solely in the language of medicine.

REFERRALS FOR CANCER PATIENTS

Cancer patients typically consult with a number of specialists for the diagnosis and treatment of their disease. Most cancer patients have little or no knowledge of the range of specialists available, the appropriateness of the specialists' expertise for their cancer, or the limits of the expertise of the specialists. For example, in a study conducted by Princeton Survey Research Associates 76 percent of Americans surveyed said that they would choose a surgeon who has treated their family for a long time without a problem over one with much higher ratings but with whom they are not familiar (Auerbach 1996:16-17).

Most cancer patients are simply referred by the first doctor who suspects or diagnoses their cancer. This is usually a family doctor, internist, or gynecologist. That doctor may refer the patient to a surgeon, a surgical oncologist, a medical oncologist, a radiation oncologist, or to an internist who specializes in the area where the cancer is located. The referral is the result of the decision of the first doctor, and he usually bases that decision upon his knowledge of the disease and of specialists. The referral depends entirely upon the knowledge of the referring physician. The specialist to whom the patient is referred is the one who determines the type and quality of treatment and care of the cancer patient. However, not all primary care doctors and very few patients are aware of the most appropriate specialist to treat a specific malignancy.

Cancer patients comprised a large proportion of patients for the surgeons at Meadowbrook University Hospital (and most general hospitals) (cf., Rosenberg

1984). Cancer patients, therefore, contributed to a substantial proportion of surgeons' and hospitals' income. Most of the surgeons, however, had limited knowledge and training about cancer (S. Rosenberg 1984; Tobias et al. 1981).[1] Their expertise in treating cancer patients lay in diagnosis, specific surgical interventions, and immediate post-operative care. Their knowledge of chemotherapeutic options was limited (Tobias et al. 1981).

In contrast, oncologists have a very wide range of knowledge about cancer and treatment of cancer patients. Their knowledge includes that of different kinds of chemotherapy and radiotherapy. They have knowledge of a much wider range of options for the care of cancer patients. In common with other specialists, oncologists are likely to provide treatments with better outcomes than are non-specialists (cf., Jollis et al. 1996).

Some of the surgeons at Meadowbrook University Hospital were faced with decisions about whether to "keep" their cancer patients and treat them post-operatively themselves or to "lose" them by referring them to medical oncologists. Some surgeons were reluctant to refer their patients to cancer specialists, because through the process of referral they would "lose" their patients, including the emotional bond with, the control and management of, and the income from their patients.

The surgeons' decisions about referring patients to oncologists were based more upon their wish to keep their patients than upon the welfare of their patients. However, those surgeons who made decisions to keep their patients did not explicitly acknowledge either to themselves or to their patients that they were making decisions on any basis but the medical welfare of their patients.

The Chief of Surgery, Dr. White, devised a number of strategies to keep cancer patients in the Department of Surgery and to avoid referring them "out" to physicians in other departments. One of his strategies was that of initiating clinical (research) trials for the follow-up treatments of specific kinds of cancer patients. For example, Dr. White's motivation for initiating one of the breast cancer trials was to retain the breast cancer patients under his department. He encouraged the general surgeons to "keep" their breast cancer patients by recruiting them into one of the breast cancer trials. Recruiting the breast cancer patients into a trial which included post-operative treatment meant that the surgeons, not the oncologists, remained in charge of the decisions for their care.

Similarly the surgeons at Meadowbrook University Hospital were able to keep most of their colon and rectal cancer patients by recruiting them into a colo-rectal clinical trial which was also initiated and run by the surgeons. To be sure, they consulted with the oncologist on staff, and referred some patients for treatment by the oncologist or radiologist. But they retained control over those patients and made the final decision on their post-operative treatments.

Most of the surgeons at Meadowbrook agreed to participate in these clinical trials. These surgeons were, however, aware that the patients would be likely to receive more expert care if an oncologist were in charge of them. They kept these patients because they did not want to lose them, because they were helping their department, complying with their chief, and participating in research. Many appeared to convince themselves that if their chief and the hospital committee approved their research trials, they were probably helping their patients by recruiting them for these trials.

Dr. White wanted to retain the lung cancer patients in the surgery department and not lose them to the oncologist. He tried to encourage the two thoracic surgeons to initiate a lung cancer trial. Whereas he easily persuaded Dr. McCullars to participate in a clinical trial, he needed the participation of both thoracic surgeons. Dr. Robinson, the senior thoracic surgeon, refused. He instead decided to refer all his lung cancer patients post-operatively to the hospital's medical oncologist, Dr. Lehrer, because he knew that Dr. Lehrer was the best informed physician to make decisions about and manage treatment for the patients with lung cancer. Dr. Robinson also knew that his own knowledge of oncology, except for surgical oncology of the thoracic region, was significantly less than that of the medical oncologists. Any clinical trial that Dr. White might initiate would not necessarily promote the best treatment for all of his lung cancer patients. In spite of the pressure upon him to treat his own cancer patients post-operatively by entering them in the lung trial, and in spite of his strong wish to increase his income by participating in a clinical trial, Dr. Robinson made an explicit decision to refuse to participate in the clinical trial and instead to refer his patients to the oncologists.

Dr. Roddy made a different decision about clinical trials for surgical patients who had colon or rectal cancer. In this trial half of the patients received a drug having some immunological properties, and one-half of the patients received a placebo. Neither the patients nor the surgeon knew which group the patients were in (called a double-blind prospective placebo clinical trial). Like Dr. Robinson, Dr. Roddy was aware of the fact that he knew less about the treatment, care, and management of colo-rectal cancers than the medical oncologists, and he also knew that his patient load would increase by participating in the trial. However, unlike Dr. Robinson, Dr. Roddy decided to participate in the cancer trial.

Dr. Roddy agreed to the Chief's urging to initiate a clinical trial for the colo-rectal cancer patients. As a result, most of the hospital's surgical colo-rectal cancer patients were referred to him post-operatively. In this way, Dr. Roddy was not only able to "keep" his own patients, but he was also able to obtain the colo-rectal patients of the other general surgeons for treatment. When Dr. Roddy made his decision to conduct the colo-rectal clinical trial, he did not think about the implications for the patients. He did not discuss his decision with his friend, Dr. Robinson, or with anyone else. In this way he made a decision without acknowledging that he was making a decision. He perceived it not as decision making but rather as agreeing to a legitimate request by the Chief of Surgery to engage in research for the good of the department. After Dr. Roddy decided to participate in the clinical trial Dr. White submitted a research protocol to the Hospital's research committee, and obtained their approval.

Dr. Roddy was not completely at ease about his decision to participate in the colo-rectal oncology trial and thus deprive those patients of the expertise of the medical oncologist. After several weeks of participation in the clinical trial he discussed his decision with his friend, Dr. Robinson, whom he knew to have refused the Chief's request to keep the lung cancer patients in the surgery department's clinical trial.

Dr. Roddy began a conversation with Dr. Robinson while they were sitting alone in the surgeon's lounge: "You know the Chief asked me to be in charge of the whole colo-rectal program."

Dr. Robinson responded by asking him, "What's in it for you?" Dr. Roddy answered, "I'm involved in research. But I have a problem. A patient of Dr. Sund [a colo-rectal or proctological surgeon] with colo-rectal cancer, who comes to me for oncology [i.e., the clinical trial] called me several times this weekend. He was admitted to Emergency. He's in bad condition — liver metastasises, ulcerated mouth, pain. I asked him, 'Why call me? Why don't you call Dr. Sund, your surgeon? I'm just the oncologist.' [He referred to himself as an oncologist even though he has no special training or certification in that specialty.] The patient told me that when he called Dr. Sund, Dr. Sund told him to call me."

"What I want to know is," Dr. Roddy said to Dr. Robinson, "should I take him? Should I be the oncologist for colo-rectal? Why didn't Dr. Sund take him?"

Dr. Robinson responded, "Sund wants a clean practice — hemorrhoids and taking colons out. That's all. No messy end-stage cancer!" He continued, "You have to decide whether you want to continue oncology. What's in it for you that you are the colo-rectal cancer expert? You know that the Chief suggested it because he's worried that we're losing patients to Internal Medicine. He wants oncology for Surgery. You know we have an excellent medical oncologist on staff, Dr. Lehrer. He's good. But he's got no practice because of what Surgery is doing with these trials. You're taking his colons and rectums. [Drs.] Russell and Deborah are taking all his breasts. All he's got are some lymphomas and my lungs. He may leave."

Dr. Roddy said, "I'll have to think about that." After a moment he continued, "I figure I've got four options — one, leave this region for the East. Two, go to a small town. Three, stay here at Meadowbrook and fight. Or, four, stay here at Meadowbrook and join the system."

The day after their conversation Dr. Roddy met Dr. Robinson in the cafeteria and said, "I've been thinking about our discussion. I didn't realize that Lehrer [the oncologist] had so little practice that he may leave. I've decided to share some of my patients with him, especially the ones who need palliative care, like Dr. Sund's [messy, end-stage] patient last weekend."

Dr. Roddy had made another decision as a result of his conversation with Dr. Robinson. His decision was, at best, a compromise. He would share some of his patients with the oncologist, particularly the difficult, complaining, "messy end-stage" patients. That decision, however, did not tackle the major questions that Dr. Robinson had presented to him — whether he was qualified to treat oncology patients, whether the patients would be receiving better care from an oncologist, and whether he was ethical in keeping patients from being treated by, or from knowing that they had the choice to be treated by, the medical oncologist. By making this compromise decision, Dr. Roddy failed to explicitly examine the substantive medical issues regarding the range of treatment choices that a medical oncologist, but not he, was able to give to patients.

Even though both Dr. Robinson and Dr. Roddy had the same access to information, and both wished to increase their patient load and their income, they made completely different decisions about the problem of how to treat cancer patients post-operatively. Their decision-making process differed in how they defined the problem, the components they considered or ignored, and their willingness to confront hard questions. They stated their options differently. Most significantly, they arrived at different decisions.

Dr. Robinson made himself aware of the components of the possible decisions and clarified his options. He considered the consequences of the decisions for himself, his Chief, surgical colleagues and his patients. In contrast, Dr. Roddy confused the decision-making process and the options in several ways. He did not recognize or acknowledge that he was faced with a decision. Instead of defining it as a decision, he defined it as agreeing to the Chief's request to participate in research. When he finally acknowledged that he had made a decision, he obscured the subject of the decision. For example, he introduced the subject matter indirectly, i.e., "You know the Chief asked me to be in charge of the whole colo-rectal program?" He thus presented himself as the passive object of someone else's decision, as if the decision were not his. Dr. Roddy did not acknowledge that his behavior had consequences for his patients. He did not clarify the options available for making the decision.

He ignored the substantive medical issue — whether he was qualified to make treatment decisions about salvageable cancer patients. Instead he stated the issues to be professional loyalty — helping the Department of Surgery rather than the Department of Medicine — or personal concern for a colleague — the oncologist who was losing so many patients to surgeons that he might be forced to leave — or convenience — treating a patient with "messy end-stage cancer."

Finally, Dr. Roddy deprived his patients of their decision-making power by not informing them about options that were available to them. He did not appear to be concerned about the implications for the patients and the patients' families. The patients remained unaware of the decisions which had been made for them, even though these decisions had serious consequences for the quality and duration of their lives.

CONCLUSION

For the surgeons at Meadowbrook University Hospital obtaining referrals, keeping patients, and other economic considerations influenced their decision-making processes. It is probable that these influences are inherent in a system in which surgeons' income and hospitals' viability is dependent upon such decisions. Crile supports this assumption:

> *Training, practice, and economic pressures can push the surgeons'*
> *thinking in the direction of more frequent, more radical, and more*

remunerative surgery. It is not that the surgeon consciously decides to do an operation for economic reasons. The decision is more subtle, and is based on training and on habits of practice which through the years have been influenced by economic pressures, always in the same direction. If there is a question between operating or not operating, it is economically sound to operate. If it is a question of a big operation or a little one, it is better economically to do the big one. If it is a question of surgery versus radiation, it is surgery that gives the advantage to the surgeon. Finally, if it is a question of doing the operation oneself or referring the patient to a better qualified specialist, it is obvious that there is little profit to be derived from referral. (Crile 1978:115)

Although surgeons at Meadowbrook University Hospital made decisions based on increasing referrals and retaining patients, few surgeons appeared to recognize that such concerns influenced their decisions.

Further, few surgeons recognized that they were making decisions until after they had made them. The results of decisions were affected by their recognition, or lack of recognition, that they were making decisions.

In most of the cases described in this chapter surgeons made surgical decisions which had serious and predictably detrimental consequences for the patient. Yet these decisions had profitable consequences for the surgeons financially and professionally in the Department of Surgery. These surgeons choose not to make the criteria for their decision making explicit to themselves, to each other, or to their patients. They passed decision-making responsibility to others and acted as if, and often convinced themselves that, their decision-making criteria were medical.

NOTES

1. An exception were those surgeons whose specialty was oncology and were certified surgical oncologists. Meadowbrook University Hospital had no surgical oncologists on its staff. S. Rosenberg stated: "modern oncologic management involves levels of expertise in chemotherapy, radiation therapy, and specialized surgical techniques that are not common to most general surgeons" (1984:632).

Chapter 9

THE NATURAL HISTORY OF
SURGICAL DECISIONS AND
THEIR CONSEQUENCES

~

*Surgical decisions would be clear and easy if medical science had
progressed to the point that all agreed which treatment is the best. Since
this utopia is not yet here, economic considerations sometimes motivate
the physician to accept that part of the scientific evidence that best
supports the method that gives him the most money.*

(Crile 1978:121)

*He is continually operating in secret as a matter of necessity; the most
sensible give the decision up to him.*

(Bell 1821)

INTRODUCTION

Surgical decisions that can make the difference between life and death and between
health and illness usually begin as small, simple, trivial ones which subsequently
evolve into major decisions. Surgeons tend to focus on the small incremental stages

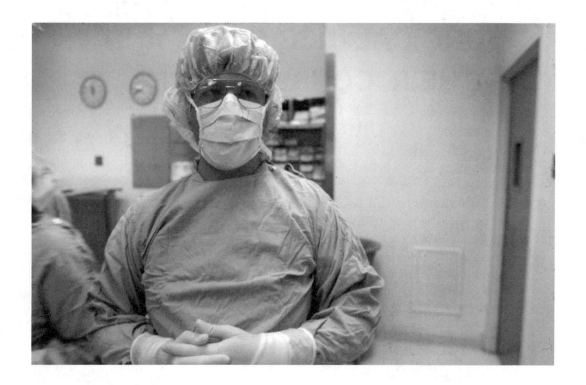

as if they were isolated, minor decisions with insignificant consequences, instead of visualizing the final outcomes (cf., Kahneman and Tverksy 1979). This chapter presents a natural history of how a few apparently trivial, inconsequential decisions evolved into complex, major decisions which had significant consequences for patients.

Most surgeons are insufficiently aware of most of the decision-making options that are available to them. They are not aware of the ways in which their decisions are dependent on their awareness of those very options. These options remain obscure not only for surgeons, but also for most medical professionals as well as for most lay persons. The difference is that knowledge of surgical options is a professional responsibility for surgeons. Whereas the consequences of most of the everyday decisions made by lay persons do not affect the mortality or morbidity of others, surgeons' decisions do. The following case illustrates how surgeons obscured the decision-making process so that they did not know that they were making decisions. Their lack of awareness led them into additional, unanticipated, and significant decisions.

DECISION ABOUT A CLINICAL TRIAL

Informing the Surgeons

Dr. White, the Chief of Surgery at Meadowbrook University Hospital, decided to initiate a research project in his department. In order to implement the research and integrate it into his surgeons' routines, he needed their support and active participation. Since Meadowbrook University Hospital was a university-affiliated teaching hospital the surgeons were encouraged to participate in research. But because of Meadowbrook's origins as a community hospital, few of the surgeons had training or experience in research. Research would confer prestige upon the department and all its members. It offered the possibility of increasing their referrals and gave greater justification to their identities as scientists.

Dr. White's research project involved a prospective clinical trial of breast cancer patients who were to undergo mastectomies. The project compared the results of radiological procedures (x-rays) with those of histological procedures (microscopic examination of cells) for determining the cancerous involvement of internal mammary lymph node — the nodes on the primary route for metastatic progression of breast cancer. It thereby compared two different methods for evaluating the stage of a patient's breast cancer.

Dr. White first mentioned the idea of participation in the clinical trial to each of the general surgeons individually. For two days as he met them informally in the hallway, cafeteria, or elevator, he said to each of them, "How'd you like to participate in research on your breast patients?" He described the research to each of them in extremely non-specific terms: "We'll see if histological involvement of internal mammary nodes gives us another indication of stages." He asked each surgeon a general question in a highly informal manner, in an informal place, and in an informal context, such as when they were walking, eating, or riding the elevator. He offered no details. Dr. White behaved as he had done when arranging the amalgamation with Provincial Hospital (described in Chapter 4, "Styles of Surgeons"). The informality and generality of the presentation encouraged the other surgeons to give informal, positive general responses. They said: "Yes, it sounds okay." "Tell me about it when we've got time." "Well, I get a lot of breasts."

Because Dr. White mentioned the research in such a casual manner, it appeared to the other surgeons that he was merely asking their opinion about whether they were interested in that research. He implied that he merely wanted the surgeons' tacit approval before proceeding farther. It also implied that serious questions belonged in a less informal context and would be dealt with subsequently. He did not say that he wanted them to make a decision at that time.

The surgeons responded in the same casual manner. They did not ask questions. None made more specific inquiries about the research, such as whether the research was invasive, how the patients would be selected, or how they would obtain informed consent. None of the surgeons realized that at that moment they were making a decision.

Each of the surgeons to whom Dr. White mentioned the research responded in a positive manner. They knew that Dr. White wanted the department members to become more involved in research, and they all wanted to enhance their scientific identities. They all knew that participating in clinical trials constituted not only a way for them to be researchers, but also that it probably would help them retain their breast cancer patients post-operatively. They expected that their research involvement would be minimal and that Dr. White would write up the protocol, get it approved, and at the most, inform them of a few extra procedures they would have to follow.

During the following days Dr. White wrote a protocol for the research. It included the description of the procedures for first obtaining the radiological diagnoses (for example, having the patient check into the hospital earlier than usual for injections and x-ray through the Department of Nuclear Medicine). It also included general descriptions of the surgical procedures for excising the lymph nodes and the histological procedures for evaluating the samples. The protocol also outlined provisions for blind histological and radiological examinations, patients' informed consent, and a starting date for the clinical trial.

Dr. White did not consider or anticipate difficulties in surgically locating and excising the lymph nodes, recruiting patients, or getting their informed consent. He submitted the protocol to the Hospital Human Research Committee, and it was approved at their next meeting.[1] After approval Dr. White sent a copy to each of the general surgeons on the staff, accompanied by a memo which stated: "Enclosed is the protocol for the Internal Mammary Node Biopsy Trial. We will begin on March 12. I'll be glad to offer every assistance in this research." Neither the protocol nor the memo asked for the formal approval of the participating surgeons. Their informal approval had already been obtained in the hallways.

The clinical trial involved a number of procedures in addition to the usual ones for suspected breast cancer. These included: 1) obtaining patients' informed consent about participating in the research days before the surgery was to begin; 2) having the patient sign into the hospital earlier than she would otherwise have had to enter in order for her to be tested by the Nuclear Medicine Department; 3) having the patient injected with radioactive dye and exposed to radiation; and 4) removing additional lymph nodes from a less accessible area than normally (i.e., internal mammary nodes rather than axial nodes). None of these procedures, including the removal of additional lymph nodes, had any therapeutic value for the patient. They had only diagnostic value for the research. Most significantly, the trial involved invasive cutting of pectoral muscles and other internal tissues which would not ordinarily take place without the research trial.

Informing the Patients

From the moment the surgeons began to recruit patients into the trial they discovered that they were faced with a number of unanticipated problems that required decisions. The first decision was that of how they should inform the patient about the trial. It was a particularly crucial decision because the only time the surgeons considered that they had for informing the patient was during the initial visit when she was informed about the likelihood of cancer and of a mastectomy. At this moment the surgeon had the obligation to offer her the options of entering, or refusing to enter, the clinical trial, and to explain to her the consequences of participating — an additional day in the hospital, injection with dye, subjection to radiation, and additional lymphatic excisions. He had the obligation to inform her that these research options would not help her; they would only contribute to medical knowledge.

Dr. Deborah, who worked part-time at Meadowbrook, conducted the hospital's breast clinic. He depended upon the Chief of Surgery for his operating privileges, the weekly use of the examining room and receptionist, and most of his referrals to the clinic. Dr. Deborah, in common with the other surgeons who were initially asked about the research in a casual encounter with Dr. White in the hallway, had never realized that this informal encounter constituted a decision to participate actively in the clinical trial.

In the Breast Clinic Dr. Deborah examined 15 to 20 women a day who had been referred to him by their primary physicians for suspected breast cancer. On the day in which recruitment for the clinical trial was to begin Dr. Deborah encountered difficulties in persuading his breast cancer patients to agree to undergo the additional procedures and to sign the informed consent form that entered them in the clinical trial. Most surgeons find it difficult in any circumstance to inform their patients that they probably have breast cancer. The surgeons at Meadowbrook developed a variety of ways to inform them. Many of their techniques were indirect (see Chapter 6, "Communication with Patients"). However, such indirect ways of communicating did not work with the patients that Dr. Deborah wanted to recruit for the research trial.

The exchange between Dr. Deborah and Dr. White about such concern is described in the following paragraph. It illustrates how avoiding making a decision is passed down from one person to another. Dr. Deborah did not initially realize that he had made a decision to participate in the research trial. He then avoided making a decision about informing his patients about the research. He turned that decision over to Dr. White. Dr. Deborah acted as if he were communicating to Dr. White that, because he had no say in the original research decision, Dr. White should carry out the decision:

When Dr. White was confronted with Dr. Deborah's dilemma about how to inform his patients about the research trial, he responded by making a further decision — that Dr. Deborah's patients need not be fully informed. But Dr. White avoided the immediate implications of that decision by not facing those patients himself. He told Dr. Deborah to carry out the decision that he, Dr. White, had made. Dr. Deborah, who was dependent upon Dr. White for his patient referrals and part-time appointment, carried out Dr. White's decision not to inform his patients fully. Dr. Deborah had the option of either fully informing his patients himself or persuading Dr. White to inform those patients more thoroughly, or of withdrawing from the research. He did not exercise any of these decisions. He let Dr. White decide for him. By such a division of labor between Dr. Deborah and Dr. White, the decisions were compartmentalized. Although two people were making two decisions, no one person took responsibility for making any decision.

As a result of Dr. White's suggestion that Dr. Deborah need not fully inform his patients, Dr. Deborah proceeded to inform each of his breast cancer patients of the research trial as if it were a routine part of the customary operation for treating the cancer. First, he explained to each breast cancer patient that, although he did not think that her breast lump was malignant, it may be malignant, and she might have a mastectomy. Then, before the patient could adequately comprehend the gravity of the information, Dr. Deborah continued to explain that it would be necessary for her to have a biopsy under general anesthetic, a nuclear medicine diagnostic test, and a histological examination of the internal mammary lymph node to determine her status. Dr. Deborah continued to pile on information to the overwhelmed patient. He informed her when she should go to the hospital, where she should go, and what she should bring. Immediately after overloading her with the litany of information, he presented the informed consent form for her to sign for participating in the research. As he gave the form to the patient, he stated that the form explained all these procedures he had just mentioned.

Dr. Deborah explained the information about the clinical trial to each patient at the same time that he gave the highly distressing news to that patient that she may have breast cancer, but without telling her that part of the "treatment" was not, in fact, for her, but for a research program. The explanation of the research procedure was included in the general explanation of the hospital procedure, such as when to check in, where to go, and when the tests would begin, as if they were the normal treatment procedures. The patient's distress at learning that she might have cancer was likely to preclude her paying close attention to the subsequent information. The fact that the information about the research procedure was presented as an inevitable and usual component of the treatment at the same time as she received the emotional impact of the news of possible cancer made it likely that the patient would have no inkling that options were available to her.

Embedding information about the research trial as inseparable from the mastectomy procedure, the routine hospital procedure, and the information about her disease status assured that the consent was not truly informed. The patient's stress obscured the boundaries between the decisions about the necessary and the optimal procedures. There was no way in which the patient could distinguish that each required separate decisions which required her consent based on adequately understood information. Dr. Deborah's actions ensured that his patients were not aware of their actual decision-making options, including refusing to participate in the research trial.

The Procedure

The implications of the original decision that Dr. White presented to the surgeons in the hallway continued to affect the surgeons and patients. On the day the first research patient booked into the hospital the surgeons unexpectedly became aware that none of them had ever seen or carried out the procedure of removing internal mammary nodes before. Moreover, none of the surgeons were certain that they would be able to recognize the internal mammary lymph nodes for biopsy.

Although Dr. White initiated the research, wrote the protocol, presented it to the hospital committee, and arranged the organizational details for carrying out the clinical trial, he did not know how to identify or to excise the internal mammary lymph nodes. He did not admit in his protocol that he did not know. He did not inquire which surgeons in the Department of Surgery had such knowledge or experience. Although he had described the procedures technically in the proposal for the Hospital's Research Committee, he had given no thought to carrying out the details of the operative procedure. He did not consider the ability of the surgical staff to perform the procedure. He did not consider the risks that the procedure entailed for the patients.

When, as the day approached of the first patient's operation, Dr. White realized that none of the surgeons on his staff knew how to excise an internal mammary node, he began to make discreet inquiries of the residents about their experience with internal node biopsies. Through this means he discovered that one of the senior residents had seen the procedure performed a year earlier at another hospital when he had been a junior resident. Although the resident had never performed that operation, and the extent of his knowledge was unclear, Dr. White nevertheless asked him, "Do you want to show Lou [Dr. Deborah] how to do it?"
 The resident agreed to perform that part of the operation and to teach Dr. Deborah, who was a senior surgeon, how to do it.

Three surgeons were present in the operating room for the first internal mammary node biopsy and mastectomy in order to learn the technique from the resident. Dr. Deborah performed the mastectomy (and the original breast biopsy to ascertain if there were a malignancy). Dr. White and Dr. Roddy observed the operation. The resident identified and excised the internal mammary lymph nodes and taught the three observing senior surgeons how to identify and excise the nodes.

The resident, however, had difficulty in locating the nodes while operating. He explained to the surgeons that he was looking for the internal mammary artery which indicated where the internal mammary lymph nodes would be. None of the surgeons had been aware either of the difficulty in locating the nodes nor, significantly, of the depth of the nodes within the thoracic tissues. They became aware of the injury to those tissues which resulted from this operative procedure. They had not considered that this procedure was so invasive that it would likely increase the probability of post-operative infection, post-operative recovery time, and additional morbidity to the patients.

During the operation Dr. Deborah exclaimed, "I wouldn't want my mother to go through this!" Dr. White commented, "We're going to have an increase in post-operative infections with these patients. If we get too many, we'll have to look into it. " The surgeons only became aware of the increased risks to the patients after they made the decision to operate and after they performed the first operation. None of them had previously questioned the risks. When they became aware of the risks they did not decide to stop the clinical trial. They only considered stopping after "too many" post-operative infections would appear.

Decision-making was obscured and distorted at several points: First, surgeons made decisions without realizing at the time that they were making decisions. They were not aware that they were making a decision because the information was presented to them in a way that did not communicate that a decision was being asked of them. Dr. White's authority as Chief of Surgery discouraged questioning and led them to conclude that he had considered the options, values and consequences of the research (cf., Holm 1995).

By his informal approach Dr. White deprived his surgeons of their options to decide whether or not to participate in the research. They then proceeded, at Dr. White's instigation, to deprive their patients of their option to decide about whether or not to be subjects in the research. They did not let the patients know that the research trial consisted of additional procedures which were distinct from the mastectomy and that were not therapeutic. They obscured the options for their patients in the same way in which Dr. White obscured the options for the surgeons.

By obscuring, avoiding, and staying unaware of decisions, Dr. White and the other surgeons also remained unaware of the nature and consequences of what they were undertaking. In doing so the surgeons deprived themselves of the knowledge both of how to do the operation as well as of the considerable risk for increased post-operative infections for the patients.

The case of the Breast Clinical Trial illustrates the way in which large decisions can become the result of several smaller ones, many of which typically are not recognized as decisions. By unwittingly giving tacit informal approval of the research that Dr. White described, the surgeons made small decisions which did not even appear to be decisions. Dr. White transformed their small decisions into a much larger one. Only after he got the research officially approved did the other surgeons realize that their tacit, informal approval had been transformed into a major commitment. Through this incremental process, the surgeons made a decision which had serious implications for themselves and even more drastic consequences for their patients.

WAYS OF OBSCURING DECISIONS

The clinical cases that have been presented in these last three chapters have illustrated ways in which the culture of the surgeons entered into the decision-making processes. These processes were ubiquitous in the surgeons' daily lives as they enacted their multiple roles as clinicians, researchers, teachers, colleagues, income earners, and human beings.

The data in these chapters suggest a variety of ways in which surgeons obscured their decision-making processes. These processes often resulted in non-medical criteria exerting influence over the decision-making process, with important consequences for the patients. These cases indicated the ways in which cultural variables, such as social relationships, hospital organizational structure, competition for referrals, and increased departmental and hospital prestige played significant roles in decision-making among surgeons.

One of the ways in which surgeons obscured their decision-making processes was by not acknowledging that they were making a decision. Yet, they took decisive action without realizing that they were making a decision. For example, in the Breast Research Trial the information was presented so casually that the surgeons did not know that they were making a decision about participating in that research trial.

Because of the way in which some surgeons obscured the decision-making options available to them, they transmitted restricted options onto their patients. The surgeons communicated to the patients that they had no decision-making option available to them. For example, the patients in the Colo-Rectal Trial were not made aware that they had the option of being treated by a medical oncologist rather than a surgeon. The surgeon, Dr. Roddy, did not let the patients know they had the option of being treated by a medical oncologist who could present them with more options based on the latest contemporary knowledge.

In the case of the hiatal hernia, when the family practitioner referred the patient to a general surgeon who could not do the operation thoracically, neither the patient nor the family physician were aware of making a decision about the kind of hiatal hernia operation the patient would receive. They were not aware that there was a choice. And they were not aware of the serious consequences of that choice. The two surgeons who were aware of the implications of that decision obscured their decision making by colluding in their refusal to take responsibility for making the medically optimal decision. Similarly, in the Breast Cancer Trial the surgeons did not communicate to their patients that the trial was separate from the usual procedure for the mastectomy or that they had the option of refusing to participate.

A second way that surgeons obscured their decision-making process was by embedding the decision in irrelevant or distracting information. The surgeons in the Breast Cancer Trial, fearing that if their patients knew about the research they might not agree to participate, made decisions to obscure information about the research by embedding it in the emotionally-laden announcement to the patient about cancer and the mastectomy and the details of entering the hospital. As a result, the patients did not know they were making a decision about research that had implications for their well being.

In the case of the Colo-Rectal Trial and in the Breast Cancer Trial surgeons did not know that there was a decision to be made. When Dr. Roddy said to Dr. Robinson, "You know Dr. White asked me to be in charge of the whole colo-rectal problem at the hospital," he embedded the decision in a context of adherence to the Chief's wishes. He implied that he had no choice and that he did not make the decision. Similarly, when Dr. White presented the idea of research to the surgeons in the hallway he embedded the decision about research in the distracting context of informality in place of a formal presentation. The result was that the surgeons approving the research idea did not know they were making a decision.

A third way that surgeons obscured the decision-making process was by making a series of small decisions which led to major decisions. The original decision about the Breast Cancer Trial appeared to the surgeons in the hallway to be small, simple, and limited. However, it led to a series of other decisions that had major implications for the surgeons involved and for their patients. Those include the decision to withhold full information from potential subjects, to operate without really knowing how, and to subject patients to unnecessary discomfort and increased risk. In the hiatal hernia decision, a small decision to consult rather than refer the patient led to serious consequences.

A fourth way that surgeons obscured the decision-making process was by passing the decision-making buck. The surgeons in the Breast Cancer Trial who found that they would not get patients to participate in the Breast Cancer Trial if they told them the truth passed the decision on what to do to Dr. White, who decided to confuse the patient in order to bypass their reluctance. In the case of the Hiatal hernia, Dr. Russell passed the decision regarding the kind of hiatal hernia operation onto Dr. McCullars, by asking for a consultation instead of referring the patient to him. In the Colo-Rectal Trial Dr. Robinson passed the decision-making buck by referring only his "messy, end-stage" patients to the oncologist.

A fifth way that surgeons obscured the decision-making process was by representing complex decisions as simple ones. The decision to participate in the Breast Cancer Trial was presented to the surgeons as a simple decision whose increasingly complex implications required additional decisions.

A sixth way that surgeons obscured the decision-making process was by representing simple decisions as complex ones. In the Colo-Rectal Trial when Dr. Roddy was making a decision about continuing to participate in those trials, he did not admit that he had a simple decision to refuse to participate, as Dr. Robinson did, or to continue. Instead he obscured the options by saying that he had four choices, one of which was to leave Meadowbrook University Hospital. He did not clarify the actual simple options about a simple decision — of referring the colo-rectal cancer patients to a trained medical oncologist.

SURGICAL CULTURE AND SURGICAL DECISIONS

Surgeons make a large number of decisions in the course of their working day. Some of these decisions are clearly defined and recognized as major surgical decisions. They included whether to operate, when to operate, which diagnosis to make, which interpretation of clinical data is preferable, and how much risk to expose patients to by operating or by not operating. Those decisions that are discussed in the surgical literature, surgical rounds, teaching seminars, and among colleagues, are commonly acknowledged to be the legitimate major surgical decisions. These decisions usually result in explicit guidelines for surgical behavior.

However, the majority of decisions that are actually practiced in surgery are smaller ones and appear to be minor. Some are not even recognized as decisions, because surgeons perceive them to be irrelevant, unimportant, or unacceptable to the practice of surgery. These include decisions such as, "Am I treating this patient differently because I don't want to lose patients or because I'm afraid of a lawsuit?" "Is my patient getting the same care when I leave my resident alone to operate?" "Would I have referred this patient if I weren't in such financial difficulty at this time?" "Shouldn't I have reported Dr. X's drinking problem?" "Should I refer my urological patients to the urological surgeon who is my friend or to the better urological surgeon?" "What and how much should I tell patients and their families about their conditions?" "How should surgical residents be selected?" "What are the best ways to teach the surgical residents?" And, "How much autonomy should residents be allowed?"

Because such non-surgical decisions are less likely to be acknowledged as real decisions than the major surgical decisions, they do not receive appropriate consideration as decisions. Though they are not surgical decisions, the action taken is described in surgical terms and as having a surgical basis. They are also seldom explicitly discussed among surgeons. These decision processes tend to be excluded from the surgical literature, medical decision-making literature, surgical rounds, and teaching seminars. rgical colleagues. Because they are unlikely to be incorporated into departmental protocols or guidelines, they encourage surgeons to act in highly individualistic ways when they make these kinds of decisions — that is, if they acknowledge that they are making decisions at all. The autonomy of action on which surgeons place such a high value results in reduced accountability to other surgeons and to their patients.

Because small, non-surgical decisions are not considered as decisions-to be-made, they often inadvertently lead to situations that require major decisions. They are often embedded in contexts in which their identities as decisions are not recognized. Yet it is precisely *because* they are not recognized as decisions by the people making the decisions, that they can lead to behavior and policy that result in *de facto* major decisions having already been made (cf., P. Katz 1984).

Many, perhaps most, surgical decisions are made in situations in which multiple cultural variables combine with medical variables to influence the decision-making process. However, medical decision-making literature, medical and surgical rounds, and surgeons themselves neglect to acknowledge the ways that cultural, including organizational, contexts influence medical decision making. Surgeons typically recognize exclusively medical criteria for medical decision making, and consequently confuse the ideal with the real. However, the cultural contexts of decision-making influence biomedical decisions and have medical consequences for the patients that can be significant.

CONCLUSION

Non-medical criteria are likely to enter into medical decision making in situations in which there are no clear-cut guidelines, and where obscurity prevails. These include those in which there are no formal protocols for making specific decisions and in which accountability in the department, hospital and larger political entity (such as State or Province) is lax. When the parameters for decision making are not well defined the chances increase that non-medical criteria, such as surgeons' competition, desire for referrals and increased prestige, enter into the decision-making process (cf., Knafl and Burkett 1975).

One way in which surgical decisions can be made to be responsive and accountable to standards set by the surgical profession or the locale or hospital where surgeons practice is to construct surgical guidelines or policies. Guidelines or policies make "an unambiguous recommendation about the management of a specific clinical problem in a specific class of patients" (Eddy 1982a:343). The analyses of the outcomes of these policies, according to Eddy, should not only include the consequences for an individual patient but should also estimate the costs and effects that would ensue if the policy were adopted by others and applied broadly to all similar patients. As much as possible, the outcomes examined should be the outcomes of interest rather than immediate measures of these outcomes (1982a:347).

However, physicians traditionally have "resisted standards of practice that prescribe specific details of their day-to-day conduct of medical care" (Eichorn 1990:76). They do not want their freedom compromised. Indeed, American physicians have been weak in policing their own members (Douglas 1994:35). They do not understand that guidelines actually would increase their freedom by providing a structure for routine matters so they could devote their attention to the specifics of each case. Guidelines can help define those situations that do and do not require individualized decisions, and the criteria for telling the difference.

The cases presented illustrated how surgeons' decisions were highly influenced by cultural variables, such as their active posture and competition. However, the surgeons used exclusively medical terms for discussing their decisions with patients and with each other. They only acknowledged the criteria of medicine in the use of the language of medicine for their decision making. They ignored the embedded cultural variables which influenced their decisions and utilized the terminology of the medical variables to conceal the cultural ones. For example, in the case of the hiatal hernia the criteria for decision-making was virtually entirely non-medical, (e.g., potential for continued referrals, maintenance of colleagueship and friendship, increasing the income of a financially burdened surgeon/friend, not admitting limitations). Yet, the entire written and verbal communication between the two surgeons and the referring physician used the language of the medical indications for performing that particular surgery.

Making medical decisions using exclusively medical terminology and hiding the cultural influences upon those decisions have implications for perpetuating the culture of medicine and the culture of surgery. They not only perpetuate the belief that biomedical criteria are the only ones that are actually considered in surgical decision making but also that they are the only ones that *should* be considered. Ignoring the influence of the non-medical cultural criteria in medical decision making has the effect of increasing the non-medical influence upon decision making, precisely because it further obscures awareness of the actual decision-making process.

Decisions depend upon the past history and experience of the surgeon, his posture or style, and his conscience. According to Kahneman and Tverksy, decisions are influenced not only by probability and the value of possible outcomes but also by the manner in which these probabilities are presented (1979). The consequences of these decisions for the patients, the hospital surgery department, the surgeon, surgical education, and the surgical profession are indeed significant. However, if guidelines for specific conditions exist in a department, surgeons are likely to be reasonably consistent in their decisions, and the surgeons are freed from extraneous considerations to make decisions exclusively on the basis of the medical condition of the patient.

The solution for improving medical decision-making is not to increase knowledge about medical events. It is rather *to make explicit how decisions are actually made and what they involve, including their evolution and results. It is to make protocols, guidelines, or rules explicit.*

Understanding the dynamics and principles of the *actual* decision-making process among medical practitioners is important because decisions affect medical outcomes and the quality and cost of medical care. Eddy suggests that a "better description of clinical decision-making might assign a prominent role to clinical policies — guidelines..." (Eddy 1982a). Indeed, guidelines, policies and protocols must be based upon substantive knowledge of the way that medical practitioners *actually* make decisions. Such procedures can increase the autonomy for all of the participants, including the physician and surgeon, their colleagues, and patients.

NOTES

1. At the present time hospital review boards, including that of Meadowbrook University Hospital, would not be likely to approve such a protocol without an informed assessment of the risks involved and the assurance, including informed consent forms, that such information would be communicated to the patient.

Chapter 10

OPERATING ROOM RITUALS

~

The success [of the operation] depends not only on the skill but also upon the care exercised by the surgeon in the ritual of the operation...success may well depend upon the scrupulous, exacting, and unceasing supervision and close scrutiny of every smallest incident of procedure.

(Moynihan 1920b:45; 65)

INTRODUCTION

The activity that was of central importance to all of the surgeons at Meadowbrook University Hospital was operating in the operating room. Each surgeon unequivocally stated that he preferred the drama, tension, and spotlight on his skills that performing in the operating theater afforded, regardless of his style, specialty, or full-time or part-time status. This chapter is about the action that takes place in the operating room and the rituals that are performed there. It illustrates the excitement, mystique, and awe that operating evokes for all its participants. And it examines some of the functions of the surgical rituals for the practice of surgical science. It illustrates how artistic and scientific roles are expressed in their ritual behavior, and how these roles influence surgeons' thinking and practice.

The first part of the chapter describes the rituals in detail. The second part discusses the rationale for calling these behaviors "rituals" and the scientific

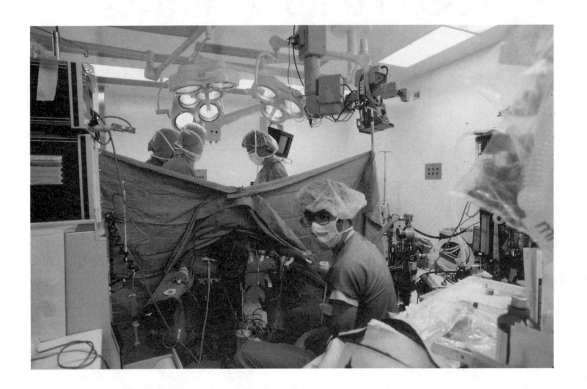

functions of the rituals. It discusses some ways in which the rituals enhance the autonomy of the participants.

INITIAL OBSERVATIONS

At first glance a naive observer who peered through a window in the secluded, restricted room, called the operating room would assume the activities inside to be sacred rites usually found in traditional cultures. He would see six masked people (the surgeon, surgical resident, anesthesiologist, scrub nurse, and circulating nurse) in green and white costumes which cover all parts of their bodies except their eyes. These six people orchestrate a slow, quiet, synchronized dance around a naked person who is lying motionless on a raised platform. The performers make exaggerated movements, such as passing in a stylistic manner shiny pointed objects to one another In one of the movements of the silent dance, for example, one of the performers lifts both hands above his head, makes a graceful 360° turn around the back of the person next to him, and assumes a place on the other side of that person.

Entrance to that innermost isolated room is permitted only to those people who have specialized, restricted knowledge — those who know the language, have undergone the cleansing ritual, and have the appropriate costumes and masks (with the exception of the prostrate one). The carefully orchestrated rhythm and timing are accompanied by hushed awe, as in the most sanctified rituals in any society. The silence is interrupted at set times by loud talking and laughter. Moreover, the people carrying out these rituals believe that their dance wards off dangers from invisible organisms.

One of the performers is clearly in charge. He is almost always a male, and he initiates beginnings and endings of movements. He signals others to hand him specific objects. He is the person who is entrusted with the most dangerous movements. He cuts into the prostrate person and exposes his innermost organs. He decides the beginning and the end of the silences, the timing of the movements, and the joking in the chamber. He is the surgeon.

Richardson described it as: "...green-gowned students gathering in awe-in-spired reverence round the master. In his hands he holds the balance between life and death" (1968:3). Moynihan wrote: "In the ritual of a surgical operation the mysteries are imposed not only upon the high priest and upon the acolytes, but upon the congregation also" (1920b:50).

These rituals are not primitive. They are essential components of one of the most scientifically advanced and technologically complex medical fields — that of surgery. The ritual leaders have had the most advanced training in medical science and technology available. Indeed, these rituals facilitate a scientific process by increasing the autonomy of the scientist participants.

THE OPERATING ROOM

In Meadowbrook University Hospital, as in most modern hospitals, the surgical area is isolated from the rest of the hospital. The operating room is, in turn, further isolated from other parts of the surgical area. Loewenthal wrote: "The patient undergoing an operation is peculiarly vulnerable to infection. It is desirable, therefore, that the theatre suite should be physically separated from the rest of the hospital" (1968:3).

The surgical area may include dressing rooms, lounges, storage rooms, offices, and laboratories, as well as the operating room. Entrance to the surgical area is restricted to those people who are properly costumed and who are familiar with the rituals (cf., Wilson 1954:13-14; Fisher and Peterson 1993). These include surgeons, anesthesiologists, pathologists, radiologists, operating room and recovery room nurses, students, doctors, nurses and ward orderlies who work in that area.[1] All of the people in the surgery area wear uniforms which indicate the specific areas within the surgical area that they may enter. The only uninitiated person to enter the surgical area is the surgical patient who, although costumed, is unfamiliar with the rituals. The restrictive entrance procedures and costume requirements contribute to the maintenance of cleanliness and prevention of contamination. Identification and separation of cleanliness and dirt into sterile and non-sterile categories are the most important concepts in the operating room. These concepts govern the organization of the activities in surgery, the spatial organization of rooms and objects, and the costumes worn. They also govern most of the rituals performed.

The surgical area of Meadowbrook University Hospital has four parts, the periphery, outer, middle, and inner areas (see Figure 2). Physical barriers separate these four areas. From outside to inside these areas are differentiated according to increasing degrees of cleanliness. They function to prevent contamination from dirtier areas to cleaner ones. The periphery, the least clean area, includes the offices of the anesthesiologists, a small pathology laboratory for quick (stat) analyses of specimens, dressing rooms for men and women, and lounges for nurses

Figure 2

Surgical Areas in Meadowbrook University Hospital

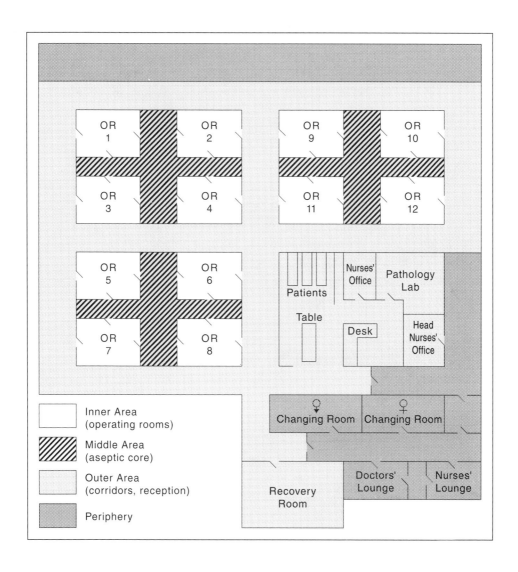

and doctors. To enter the periphery area a person must wear a white jacket for identification as a member of the medical staff.

The outer area is separated from the periphery by a sliding door. Within the outer area, a nurse at the main desk can prevent the door from opening if an unauthorized person tries to enter. Entrance to the outer area is restricted to patients and to those medical personnel who wear blue or green costumes. The largest and most populated part of the outer area consists of an open corridor with a bulletin board on which the daily operating schedule is posted and a blackboard which indicates the current use of operating rooms.

Patients awaiting surgery lie on narrow gurneys which are lined in a single row along one wall of the open corridor. A nurse who is in charge of coordinating the timing and activities in each operating room sits at an exposed desk in the outer area, and is in continual intercom communication with each operating room. The outer area also contains a large recovery room which houses patients immediately after their surgery is completed.

The middle area consists of three separate areas called "aseptic cores." Each aseptic core contains five doors, one of which links to the outer area. Each of the other doors leads to an operating room. Each aseptic core contains a long sink, three sterilizing machines (autoclaves), and many carts and shelves containing surgical equipment, sheets, and towels. In order to enter an aseptic core a person must wear a mask which covers the mouth and nose, coverings for shoes and for hair, and a blue or green outfit.

The innermost area contains the operating rooms and small laundry rooms. In each aseptic core there are four operating rooms and two laundry rooms. Each operating room contains three doors. One door adjoins the outer area and is used exclusively for the patient to enter and leave the operating room. The second leads to the aseptic core and is used by the operating room staff. The third door leads to the laundry room which serves as a depository for contaminated clothing and instruments.

Preoperative Rituals

In the 1920s, Sir Berkeley Moynihan wrote: "the ritual of an operation commences before, sometimes long before, the incision is made, and may continue for a long period after the wound is healed" (1928:45).

One of the more important operating room rituals, scrubbing, takes place in the aseptic core before each operation begins. It is a procedure by which selected personnel wash their hands and lower arms according to rigidly prescribed timing and movements. The purpose of scrubbing is to remove as many bacteria as possible from the fingers, nails, hands, and arms to the elbows. The people who scrub are those who actually carry out, or directly assist in, the surgery. Not everyone in the operating room scrubs. The surgeon, assistant surgeon(s), and the scrub nurse, participate in the scrubbing ritual. The anesthesiologist and the circulating nurse do not scrub. Medical students and other surgical assistants, including referring physicians, consider an invitation to scrub an honor.

Scrubbing, Gloving and Gowning Rituals

At Meadowbrook University Hospital the procedure for scrubbing was formalized in the series of highly detailed instructions which operating room nurses communicated to novices. Before a person begins to scrub he checks the clock in order to time the seven-minute procedure. He turns on the water by pushing a button with his hip and reaches for a package which contains a nail file, brush, and sponge which are saturated with an antiseptic solution. For two minutes he cleans under each of his nails with the nail file. For two-and-a-half minutes he scrubs one entire arm, fingers, hand, and forearm, while intermittently wetting the sponge and brushing with running water. Using a circular motion he scrubs all of the surfaces of his fingers on one hand, his hand, and, finally, his arm to the elbow. After rinsing that arm thoroughly under running water, he repeats the procedure for two-and-a-half minutes on his second hand. After scrubbing for seven minutes he discards the sponge, brush, file, and paper and turns off the tap water by pressing a button on the sink with his hip.

After the scrubbing ritual has finished — a ritual which does not yet place him in the category of "sterile" — the surgeon and his assistants entered the operating room by pushing the door with their hips. They hold their lower arms and hands in an upright position, away from the rest of their bodies. They are forbidden to allow their scrubbed hands and arms to come into contact with any object or person, because they are not yet completely sterile. As such, they are able to contaminate a sterile object and become contaminated by contact with a non-sterile object.

The scrub nurse (who is considered sterile) hands them a sterile towel to dry their hands. They dry each finger separately and throw the towel into a container on the floor. The scrub nurse holds the outside, sterile part of a green gown for the surgeon and his assistants to wear. They insert their hands through the sleeves, without allowing their hands to touch the outside of the gown. At this point their hands, although scrubbed and clean, are not sterile, but the outside of the gown is sterile. After their arms pass through the sleeves, the scrub nurse holds their sterile gloves in place with the open side facing their hands.

The surgeon, followed by his assistants, thrusts one hand at a time into each glove. They accomplish this in one quick movement, whereby a hand is brought down from its upward position, thrust forward inside the glove, and the glove is snapped in place over the sleeve of the gown. When only one (sterile) glove is on the surgeon is not permitted to adjust it with the other (unsterile) hand. However, when the second glove is on, both hands are sterile, and he can adjust his gloves.

At this stage the gown is not completely fastened, and in order to fasten his gown the surgeon unties a tie of his gown at waist level. Although this tie had been sterile, he hands it to the circulating nurse, who has not scrubbed (and is therefore non-sterile), and she brings the tie to the back of his gown. The back is a non-sterile area of the gown. The surgeon helps her reach the back by making a 360° turn while she holds the tie and secures this and two more ties to the back of the gown.

Principles of Sterility and Contamination

The rituals of scrubbing, gowning and gloving reflect basic principles based on the scientific studies of contamination which underlie most of the rituals in the operating room:

1) In the operating room, objects, or parts of objects and people, are classified either as sterile or non-sterile. These are designated here as S or NS
    a) Non-sterile objects are further classified as clean, dirty, or contaminated.
    b) No part of the circulating nurse or the anesthesiologist is sterile.
    c) Parts (the front from the waist to the armpits) of the surgeon and the scrub nurse are sterile.
2) To remain (or become, symbolized by >) sterile, sterile objects may only come into contact (c = contact) with other objects that are sterile. (S c S > S)
3) To remain sterile, sterile objects may not come into contact with anything that is not sterile.

4) Non-sterile objects may come into contact with other non-sterile objects, and both remain non-sterile. (NS c NS > NS)

5) Sterile objects may be transformed into non-sterile objects by contact with objects which are non-sterile. (S c NS > NS) or (NS c S > NS) This process is called contamination.

6) Contaminated objects can only be restored to sterility by either placing them in an autoclave for a specified period of time, or, in the case of a person's clothes, by discarding the contaminated clothes and replacing them with sterile clothes. If gloves become contaminated, it is required to rescrub the hand for three minutes before replacing the gloves and the gown.

Before the operation begins most objects that are sterile are either symbolized by the color green, or are in contact with an object which is colored green. Sterile instruments, for example, are placed upon a green towel which lies on a non-sterile tray. Although the green towel has been sterilized, it becomes contaminated at the bottom through contact with the non-sterile tray. However, the towel remains sterile at the top. And the sterile instruments lying on the top also remain sterile. The surgeon, his assistant(s), and the scrub nurse wear sterile gloves and a green or blue gown which is sterile in the front from the waist to the armpits and is designated as non-sterile in the back.

The potentials for manipulating the overhead light in the center of the operating room illustrate some principles of sterility and contamination. Parts of the light are considered to be sterile and parts non-sterile. Before the operation begins the scrub nurse places a sterile handle on the huge, movable, overhead light. This permits the light to be adjusted by the surgeon, his assistant(s), and the scrub nurse through contact with the sterile handle. The circulating nurse and anesthesiologist, however, are also able to manipulate the light by touching the non-sterile frame of the light. They cannot touch the sterile handle because they would contaminate the handle.

In order for a person to move to the other side of the person next to him, as the scrubbed members of the operating team stand next to the patient's table, a ritual must be enacted (described in the first section of the chapter): The person making the move turns 360° in the direction of his move, allowing his back to face the back of his neighbor. This movement prevents his sterile front from coming into contact with his neighbor's nonsterile back. Instead, his nonsterile back only comes into contact with his neighbor's nonsterile back.

Before the operation begins each member of the operating team is busily engaged in activities that are essentially similar for each operation. The surgeon and his assistant(s) gown and glove and check last-minute details about the forthcoming operation. The anesthesiologist checks his tools, his gas supply, and his respirator, prepares the instruments for monitoring the patient's vital functions, and prepares the patient for receiving anesthesia. In the outer area a nurse checks to insure that the patient is properly identified and that the operative site is verified. She independently checks the preoperative instructions written by the surgeon with the administrative order written when the surgery was booked. She also asks the surgeon to identify the proposed operation and the precise site of the operation. Finally, she asks the patient to identify his name and the site of the operation.

Within the operating room, the words, "clean," "dirty," "sterile," and "contaminated" assume different meanings according to different stages of the operation (See Figure 3). Before the operation begins, the operating room is considered to be clean. Dirty objects have been removed or cleaned. Instruments and clothes which have been contaminated by the previous operation have been removed. Floors, walls, permanent fixtures, and furniture have been cleaned with antiseptic solution. The air in the operation room is continually cleaned during, and between, operations by a laminar air filter system.

Fields of sterility and non-sterility within the operating room are mapped out, and everyone in the operating room, with the exception of the patient, is knowledgeable about these fields. Some of the fields, such as that surrounding the patient, are invisible. These fields are distinguished by the use of sterile paper sheets colored green. They provide only a minimal material barrier against airborne bacteria, although they serve as a symbolic shield separating fields of sterility and nonsterility. They are also used to isolate the operative area of the body from the rest of the patient's body (cf., Collins 1994; Fox 1992; 1994; Hirschauer 1991; 1994; Lynch 1994).[2] The sheets cover the entire body of the patient, leaving only a small opening for the operative area. Or they separate the head end of the patient from the rest of his body. The head end is considered non-sterile (unless the operative site includes the head) and is accessible to the anesthesiologist and his equipment, which are also nonsterile.

After the patient is rendered unconscious by the anesthesiologist the scrub nurse liberally applies an orange-brown antiseptic solution onto the patient's skin. She distributes this solution with a sterile sponge on a long holder using circular movements radiating outward from the center of the operative site. She discards and replaces the sponge with each action because the sponges become contaminated through contact with the patient's nonsterile skin. This action which transforms the

Figure 3

Discontinuity of Body Categories

Body Category	Outside Operating Room	First Stage (Incision)	Second Stage (Excision)	Third Stage (Closure)
Patient's Washed Skin	C	D	D	C
Patient's Gall Bladder (in gall bladder excision)	D	C	C	D
Patient's Colon (in colon resection)	D	C-Outside D-Inside	C-Outside D-Inside	D
Patient's Feces (in colon resection)	D	D	D	D
Patient's Blood	D	C	C	D
Surgeon's Blood	D	D	D	D

C Clean

D Dirty

▨ Discontinuity In Category

sterile sponge into a contaminated sponge also transforms the dirty body area of the patient into a clean, but not sterile, area. When this act is completed the sterile green paper towels are placed on the patient's body, exposing only the aseptic, painted, operative site.

Before the operation begins both the scrub nurse (sterile) and the circulating nurse (non-sterile) lay out and count all of the sterile instruments and sponges that are likely to be used in the operation. The circulating nurse obtains articles from their nonsterile storage place. When the outside of sealed packages is nonsterile and contains sterile objects inside, the circulating nurse holds the outside of the package. She either thrusts the objects onto a green sterile towel or asks the scrub nurse to grasp the sterile object by reaching down into the package and lifting the object upwards with a straight, quick movement.

These procedures are followed for each sterile needle, thread, or vial that is wrapped in a nonsterile wrapping. They are followed in order to prevent contamination of sterile parts of the instrument by the nonsterile parts of the package. The two nurses also simultaneously orally count items that are laid out for use during surgery, and the circulating nurse records the numbers of each item. Each item must be accounted for before the operation is completed. The last count must concur with the previous counts before the patient's operative site is closed.

The Operation

Although extensive variation exists among types of operations as well as among the medical conditions of patients, there is nevertheless considerable similarity in the structure of all operations. Operations comprise three distinct stages. Specific rituals are performed between and during each of the stages. Stage One consists of the incision or opening; Stage Two consists of the excision and/or repair; and Stage Three consists of the closure.

The operation begins after the anesthetized patient is draped, all sterilized instruments are counted and placed in orderly rows upon trays, and the nurses and doctors, wearing their appropriate costumes, are standing in their specified places. The anesthesiologist stands behind the green curtain at the head of the patient, outside of the sterile field. The surgeon stands next to the operative site on one side of the patient. If an assistant is present, he usually stands on the opposite side of the patient from that of the surgeon. The scrub nurse stands next to the surgeon with the pole of an instrument tray between them. The instrument tray is suspended over the patient's body. The circulating nurse stands outside of the sterile field, toward the outer part of the operating room.

Silence and tension prevail as the first stage of the operation begins. With a sterile scalpel the surgeon makes the first incision through the layers of the patient's skin. He then discards the scalpel in a sterile basin. By this action he transforms both the scalpel and the basin from the original category of sterile (S) to that of nonsterile (NS). The transformation takes place because the sterile scalpel (S) touches (c) the patient's nonsterile skin (NS) (The patient's skin, although cleaned with an antiseptic, is not sterile). The scalpel, which by this action has become nonsterile (S c NS > NS), touches the sterile basin and contaminates the basin (NS c S > NS). The surgeon uses another sterile scalpel to cut through the remaining layers of fat, fascia, muscle, and, in an abdominal operation, the peritoneum. The same scalpel may be used for all the layers that underlie the skin, because, unlike the contaminated skin, which is considered to be non-sterile, these layers are considered to be sterile.

As the surgeon cuts he or his assistant cauterizes or ties the severed blood vessels. The patient's blood is considered sterile once the operation has begun. However, before the operation, the patient's blood is considered to be nonsterile. This categorization was illustrated graphically at Meadowbrook University Hospital before a particular emergency operation in which a patient was bleeding externally from an internal hemorrhage. The nurses complained about "the man who is dirtying our clean room!" However, once the operation on this man began his blood was considered to be sterile. Sterile instruments which touched his blood during the operation remained sterile (S c S > S) until it then became contaminated by touching something nonsterile (See Figure 3).

The rituals reinforce the segregation of sterile and nonsterile objects while the initial incisions are being made. The surgeon typically utters terse commands, usually stating the specific names of the instrument he needs. The scrub nurse immediately places the requested instrument securely in the palm of the surgeon's hand. Sometimes she anticipates his request, and there are few words spoken. If the instrument remains sterile, the surgeon returns it to the scrub nurse, and the scrub nurse places it upon the sterile tray. If it becomes contaminated, as occurs, for example, with the skin scalpel after the first incision, the surgeon places it into a container holding non-sterile items and which, therefore, can only be handled by the circulating nurse.

The first stage of the operation ends when the first incision has been completed and the organs are exposed. Once the technical tasks of that first stage become routinized, joking usually begins. Most of the joking at this stage revolves around the operative procedures which are to be carried out during the next stage: "I can't wait to get my hands on your gallbladder, Mr. Van!" "Okay sports fans, we're going to have some action!" The joking abruptly ends just as the second stage of the operation is about to begin.

The second stage of the operation consists either of repair, implantation, or the isolation and excision of an organ, and the anastomosis (connection of two parts of the body which are not normally connected). This is the time of greatest danger and tension in the operation. Adherence to the rituals, including silence, is strictly enforced during this stage.

The second stage begins with the identification and isolation of structures surrounding the organ to be excised. The surgeon identifies (silently, or if residents are present, orally) vessels, nerves, ducts, and connective tissues, carefully pulling them aside and preserving, clamping, severing, or tying them. The surgeon utters abrupt, abbreviated commands for instruments to be passed to him by the scrub nurse, structures to be cut by the assistant(s), basins and materials to be readied by the circulating nurse, and adjustments of the operating table to be made by the anesthesiologist. These people respond to the surgeon's commands quickly, quietly, and efficiently. A delayed or incorrect response may be met with noticeable disapproval from the others.

During the second stage of the operation many of the classifications of sterility differ from those of the first stage. In a cholecystectomy, for example, the gallbladder is considered to be nonsterile before the operation begins. Yet during the first and second stages before the gallbladder is severed it is considered to be sterile. Once it is severed, however, it is transformed to a nonsterile category (See Figure 3), although it is considered to be clean. It is placed in a sterile container. But the sterile container becomes contaminated by its contact with the nonsterile gallbladder (S c NS > NS). Because it is nonsterile after it has been removed, it can only be handled by a person who is considered nonsterile, such as the circulating nurse. However, since the gallbladder is clean (but not sterile) and must be examined, it must not be further contaminated from sources outside of the patient.

To prevent further contamination of the gallbladder the circulating nurse wears a sterile glove over her nonsterile hand to examine the gallbladder and its contents. Although the outside of the gallbladder is not sterile, it is not grossly contaminated; it is clean but non-sterile. It is avoided by the sterile members of the team, yet only touched by the nonsterile members if they wear sterile gloves. Because of its intermediate and ambiguous category (clean but nonsterile), the ritual surrounding its removal and examination is complex, and the removed organ is avoided by most members of the operating team.

Although unexpected events may occur at any stage of the operation, they are more likely to occur at the second stage, because this stage has the potential for the greatest trauma to the patient's body. If a sudden hemorrhage or a cardiac arrest occurs, the rituals segregating sterile from nonsterile may be held in abeyance, and new rituals designed to control the unanticipated event take over. If, for example, hemorrhaging occurs, all efforts are dedicated to locating and stopping the source of the hemorrhage and replacing the blood that is lost.

However, even though immediate replacement of blood may be required, in such an emergency rituals are enacted which may ensure accurate matching, but which may also delay that replacement. The anesthesiologist and the circulating nurse independently check, recheck, record, and orally announce the blood type, the number and date of the blood bank supply, and the operating room request. At certain points in the ritual they glue stickers onto the patient's record and onto the blood blank record. This complex ritual involves repetition, separation, and matching records before the blood is transfused into the hemorrhaging patient.

If a patient's heart ceases beating, a prescribed ritual is enacted by a cardiac arrest team whose members enter the operating room with a mobile cart and enact prescribed procedures to resuscitate the patient. Considerations of preserving the separation of sterility and nonsterility are ignored while this emergency ritual is enacted.

Tension remains high throughout the second stage of the operation. Joking or small talk is rare. As the remaining internal structures become repaired and are restored in place some of the tension is lifted. The second stage of the operation ends when all the adjustments to the internal organs are finished and only the suturing of the protective layers, the third stage, remains.

The third stage of the operation begins with the final counting of the materials used in surgery. Both nurses engage in this ritual of counting by simultaneously orally counting all the remaining materials, including tools, needles, and sponges. The circulating nurse checks the oral count with her written tally of materials that she recorded at the beginning of the operation. When the circulating nurse has accounted for each item, she informs the surgeon so that he may begin the closing. The surgeon is not permitted to close without the circulating nurse's authority.

The rituals enacted during this stage of the operation are similar to those enacted during the first stage. The surgeon, or his assistant(s), requests specific needles and sutures from the scrub nurse, and they sew the patient closed, layer by layer, beginning with the inside layer. Although careful suturing is an essential part of the operation, this stage is enacted in a comparatively casual manner. There is considerably less tension than there was during the second stage and greater toleration for deviations from the rituals. Questions about the procedures are acknowledged and answered, and minor mistakes may be overlooked. If the surgeon touched his nonsterile mask with his sterile glove during this part of the operation, he would be less likely to reglove and regown than he would if the same incident had occurred during the second stage.

The silence of the second stage is replaced in the third stage by considerable talking, including joking and small talk. Most of the jokes revolve around events which had just occurred during the second stage. References are frequently made to actual and potential danger during this stage. "I thought he'd never stop bleeding!" "You almost choperated [sic] his spleen by mistake!" "Well, I hope he has good term life insurance!" "Don't buy any long-playing records, Mrs. Ross!" Much of the small talk revolves around future activities of the medical staff. The subject of small talk is less likely to be related to concerns about the patient. It may involve the next operation, lunch plans, or sports results.

When the closure has been completed the surgeon signals to the anesthesiologist to awaken the patient. The staff members finish recording information, transport the patient to the recovery room, and prepare for the next case. The operation is finished.

OPERATING ROOM RITUALS AND SCIENCE

How do surgical rituals coexist with biomedical scientific thinking and behavior in a scientifically and technologically advanced clinical field such as surgery? Although these rituals appear to be anomalous to surgeons who have advanced scientific, clinical and technological training, they are actually adaptive and necessary for the performance of scientific and clinical roles in general, including surgery, specifically.

Rituals are defined as "repeated, standardized, stylized, stereotyped behavior that is usually serious and dramatic, and often accompanied by awe and reverence" (Goody 1961; Leach 1968). Most ritual performers believe that their rituals are necessary and efficacious in achieving their goals. Rituals have multiple functions. They help people understand and control uncertainty in their world. They maintain order, stability, and predictability in situations where potentials for disorder, instability, uncertainty, and unpredictability exist. Rituals help to resolve social conflicts through masking and preventing conflicts. They have communication functions by encouraging group identity, social bonding, cohesion and solidarity through shared symbols and sometimes through neurobiological synchrony and tuning (cf., d'Aquili 1975; Gluckman 1970; Lex 1979).

Rituals are useful when boundaries between categories are indistinct or confused. For example, in many cultures rituals define the beginning and end of rainy and dry seasons, in marriage define kinship groups when they are not clear, mark the moment when children attain adulthood, and in sacred situations distinguish the holy from the profane. Rituals define categories by creating exaggerated boundaries between them. Most significantly, rituals increase autonomy for the participants (P. Katz 1981; 1984; 1988). When there is potential confusion about the appropriate behavior expected in a particular situation, people have little autonomy to act. Rituals, by defining categories and prescribing behavior permitted within each category, give the participants freedom to choose how to act. These functions of ritual, particularly those of increasing independence, are harnessed in clinical sciences, such as surgery, to enhance the scientific character of surgery.

Although the rituals performed by surgeons in the operating room, as well as some of those performed during surgical Rounds, inpatient and outpatient consultations and teaching, share similarities with all other rituals, they also possess an important difference. Rituals in surgery and in other modern, scientifically-based clinical medical specialties (cf., Bosk 1980; Barley 1988; Finkler 1994; Helman 1994 Koenig 1988) differ from rituals found in traditional societies in that they are grounded in systematic empirical science, and not in superstition, magic, religion, or habit.

Rituals and Boundaries

Rituals are used when boundaries between categories are indistinct and when there is potential confusion about the appropriate behavior expected, such as periods of transition. For example, surgical rituals mark transitions between sterile and nonsterile (P. Katz 1981). When there is confusion about which category is in effect, people are uncertain about how to act. They lose autonomy because they must direct their attention to figuring how they should respond. For example when a surgeon has only scrubbed but has not yet gowned and gloved he is neither fully sterile nor nonsterile; he has no autonomy to handle either sterile or nonsterile objects for fear of contaminating or being further contaminated.

In the operating room rituals occur in four different kinds of situations. In each of these situations there exist indistinct categories and, without exaggerated rituals, appropriate behavior would be confused. The description of the operating room rituals indicates that the situations in which rituals occur include: a) separating sterile from nonsterile objects; b) passing through the three stages of surgery (one, incision; two, excision or repair; and three, closure); c) managing unanticipated events, such as cardiac arrest or sudden hemorrhaging; and, d) matching information, such as blood types, operative sites, or instrument counts. In each of these situations there exists a potential confusion about the appropriate classification of events — confusion about the location of the boundaries between one category or stage, or in situations in which there is danger of contact of forbidden categories. For example, blood may not be properly matched or non-sterile objects may touch (i.e., contaminate) sterile ones. The major rituals that occurred in the operating room took place during these transitions to make it completely clear to everyone what kind of behavior was required, such as transitions from non-sterile to sterile, such as in scrubbing, or during changes in the phases of the operation.

Rituals create boundaries by making salient and exaggerating where one category begins and another one ends. Like the process of classification in science (where species are somewhat arbitrarily distinguished from other similar species), rituals function to separate and distinguish between categories which otherwise are indistinguishable. In surgery for example, the back area and below the knees and above the armpits in the front are ritually designated as non-sterile. Rituals demarcate in an exaggerated way which categories are in effect. Rituals designate, for example, "I have scrubbed, gloved, and gowned, and may therefore touch everything sterile." "We no longer enact behavior for the excision (stage 2) and can begin counting instruments to get ready for closure (stage 3)." By defining categories between formerly indistinct categories, rituals facilitate clarification of roles and behavior. People don't have to worry about how to act, because they are clear about the behavior that is expected of them. Ironically, by rigidly prescribing and coordinating behavior, ritual increases the individual's autonomy.

The rigid, ritually prescribed tasks of the scrub nurse, who must respond to the precise commands of the surgeon, may first appear to deny her autonomy. However, most operating room nurses stated that they enjoyed the role of scrub nurse at least as much as they enjoy the role of circulating nurse, because the role behavior is so ritually prescribed that it bestows considerable freedom. For example, an operating room nurse described the large degree of autonomy the operating room rituals afford her (cf., Wilson 1954:12):

The only place I feel in control in my job is in the OR. The autonomy I get is what makes me love the OR. Rituals give us control, give us power. If we don't have rituals the nurse would not have power. When we are the ones in charge of sterile technique we are in a peer relationship with the surgeon.

We need ritual in order to feel secure in a tense environment. We know the sterile techniques as long as we know the ritual.

I feel the scrub nurse has power; I don't feel it's subordinate. You have tremendous power in your ability to influence what's going on — lots of control. I control the instruments; I control the atmosphere in the room, the tension in the room. I control a careless surgeon. If the scrub nurse is a bitch the whole room is affected. Even if you have a surgeon who throws things, the demeanor of the nurse affects what's happening in the room.

She doesn't just follow the surgeon's orders. She gets things ready ahead. The instrument is in his hand before he thinks about it. The more we know the more we can anticipate. We know the sequence of what he picks up. (Mary Sweeny, personal communication 1984)

Increased autonomy for the participants occurs because rituals facilitate transitions. They facilitate transitions, for example, among the operative stages, or when the scrub nurse moves to the other side of the surgeon. Rituals increase autonomy by controlling motor action so that cognitive functions, such as making decisions, or mentally preparing for unexpected events, or even fantasizing, can flourish. The communicative and stress-reducing and conflict-preventing functions of rituals also contribute to increasing the freedom of the participants. Rituals in the operating room give surgeons increased autonomy to make decisions during the operative procedure to use time efficiently, and to coordinate the team's actions. All of these function to minimize trauma to the patient.

Jokes and small talk are examples of autonomy in the operating room. They take place after the rituals have ordered the sequence of behavior. Indeed, jokes, small talk, and questions take place only after the ritual transitions have occurred. Autonomy was restricted when danger, silence and awe prevailed during the transitions between the stages of the ritual. No questions and no jokes were entertained at those times. After the rituals marking the transitions were completed there was a great deal of autonomy — to joke, ask questions, and engage in small talk. However, jokes about the excised or repaired organs, or questions about the excision or repair do not occur during the excision or repair, the most dangerous part of the operation. Instead they occurred after the excision or repair were completed. It was only after the rituals ending that stage had already been performed that such autonomy could be realized.

Rituals, such as those in surgical settings can be highly adaptive for assuring positive clinical outcomes. They help to limit the access of pathological micro-organisms to the vulnerable patient. They control the anxieties of the surgical staff. They link them by a common set of symbols and predictable actions, thus giving them a sense of order (cf., Felker 1983; Koenig 1988). Rituals eliminate the need for thought and decision on vital but routine functions, They increase the freedom for participants to carry out their scientific roles more efficaciously.[3]

Rituals and Science

The major distinction between rituals in traditional settings and rituals in surgery is that most surgical rituals are grounded in systematic empirical science, and not in superstition, magic, religion, or habit. This means that most of the ritualized, (i.e., routinized, repetitive, and standardized) behavior of surgeons, surgical nurses, and residents are embedded in the tradition of empiricism and based upon principles of systematic empirical science. The surgeon and surgical nurses have strong links to the biomedical science traditions whose theories are continuously subjected to empirical investigation. Most of the scientific principles of surgery have been systematically empirically tested and verified to be efficacious for healing and curing.

In contrast, in most traditional/nonliterate medical systems, systematic empiricism is not practiced. In those medical systems categories such as clean and polluted are not so reliably verifiable. They are based to a larger degree upon beliefs which are not founded upon systematic empirical testing. The traditional clinician, although searching for causes of illness, does not subject his practices to systematic empirical investigation. He is more dedicated than the modern clinician to the perpetuation of tradition.

In scientific settings, such as surgery, categories, such as areas of sterility and nonsterility, can be empirically distinguished by observing, counting and comparing the numbers and types of micro-organisms in specified areas of each category. These tests can be replicated over large populations in order to validate the measurement instruments and verify the results. Such tests are facilitated because many of the underlying causes of infections are empirically known, as are some of the principles by which surgery heals, palliates, cures, or fails.

However, rituals are still necessary because degrees of uncertainty still exist when scientific empiricism is used. Despite scientific advances, post-operative infections still affect more than two million patients annually. The number of contributing causes of post-operative infection is so large that they include those related to the characteristics of the microorganisms, the operating room, staff-to-patient ratios, the operation, the surgical staff, the patient, and even subjective factors in the patients, such as psychological motivation (P. Katz and Kirkland 1988).

Empirical tests do not specify with certainty why a particular patient becomes infected, or why nosocomial infections (i.e., infections originating from a hospital) appear at a particular time. They can only suggest possible causes. The uncertainty of clinical medicine, therefore, presents surgical clinicians with only approximate guidelines for behavior. Rituals, when based upon principles of contemporary empirical science, can serve to reduce the uncertainty by prescribing definitive action that has proved to be effective. However, in order to enhance science, they must be subject to revisions as new knowledge becomes available.

Chapter 3, "Are Surgeons Scientists?" which discussed surgery's link to science, suggested a particular posture toward thinking and behaving. The empirical mode involves a posture of thinking and acting which includes skepticism, questioning of theories and hypotheses, and further questioning of anomalies and exceptions. The systematic empirical mode is one in which data are gathered, and subjected to rigid and systematic examination and analysis. In traditional societies the systematic empirical mode is much less likely to be found. Theories are usually accepted as statements of undisputed fact without verification. Veneration of tradition is likely to be more highly valued than questioning or changing practices based upon new knowledge.

Surgical rituals risk the danger of becoming non-scientific if the empirical posture of critical questioning and willingness to accept new practices based upon new knowledge is not routinely applied to them. Surgical rituals may become non-scientific when they are based upon outdated empirical scientific evidence that has been superseded by more recent studies. To stay scientific, surgical rituals should be continuously regarded from a posture of skepticism, and, if necessary, to systematic empirical testing to determine the efficacy of continuing the practice. The efficacy, however, does not only depend upon specific evidence that a particular ritual reduces the number or potency of micro-organisms. It may also include considerations of evidence that a particular ritual increases the coordination, communication, and morale of the staff.

CONCLUSION

Surgical rituals are not only adaptive and necessary for the performance of the science of surgery. They maintain order, stability, and predictability in situations in surgical practice where potentials for disorder, instability, uncertainty, and unpredictability exist. Surgical rituals based upon scientific principles increase the autonomy of the surgical staff to perform their clinical roles. They continue to exist in a scientifically and technologically advanced clinical field such as surgery because they are based upon the empirical scientific culture of modern medicine which values critical questioning and empirically tested knowledge. Surgeons should be continuously prepared to question, test, and abandon outdated practices, and they should accept new practices based upon new empirical knowledge. Only when a systematic, empirically grounded scientific posture is applied to surgical rituals can these rituals continue to facilitate the science of surgery.

NOTES

1. The improvement of communication and efficiency of the surgical "team" has been (since 1979) the subject of a biannual symposium which is sponsored by the American College of Surgeons' Committee on the Operating Room Environment (CORE) in collaboration with the Association of Operating Room Nurses, Inc. (AORN) and the American Society of Anesthesiologists (ASA) (Regnier 1995).

2. The significance of the operating room team's regarding the body as an object is not examined here. The meaning of the body and embodiment, however, is a subject of contemporary interest in medical anthropology (cf., Csordas 1994; K. Young 1989).

3. Rituals occur in other medical specialties during periods of the greatest uncertainty, such as for example, in psychiatry where rituals take place when making diagnoses (a process in all medicine of defining unclear symptoms), in dispensing medications, in group therapy sessions, and in formulating individual treatment plans among multi-disciplinary

team members (P. Katz 1988). In psychoanalysis, for example, the patient and the psychoanalyst are involved in a series of rituals, such as lying on the couch and sitting, respectively, all of which are designed to increase the autonomy of both the clinician and patient (P. Katz 1984).

Chapter 11

IMPLICATIONS OF THE
CULTURE OF SURGEONS
FOR MODERN MEDICINE

~

It is less important to invent new operations and new techniques of operating than to find ways and means to avoid surgery.
(Langenbeck, quoted in Schwartz 1983:13)

INTRODUCTION

The culture of surgeons includes an orientation toward active intervention; a proclivity toward taking risks; a propensity toward definitive assured decision making; an unwillingness to admit doubt or errors; a proclivity for using technology; an inclination to perpetuate the mystique of the confident, lone, heroic male; and thinking styles that are more categorical than probabalistic and tend toward certainty rather than inquiry (See Table 1, page 208). Surgical culture reflects surgeons' concurrent identities as both artists and scientists.

The culture described in this book is based on surgeons in a particular hospital at a particular time and place. This study and other studies of surgeons, both past and present, suggest that a basic culture of surgeons persists, despite the variations that exist in types of hospitals, particular surgeons, and specific places and times.

Courtesy, Johns Hopkins Medicine.

Most of the basic components of the culture of surgeons have continued to be transmitted from generation to generation of surgeons, even though surgery has been at the forefront of each technological era and has embraced the most sophisticated technology available (See Appendix C, "Cybersurgery: The New Surgical Technologies").

TRANSMISSION AND PERPETUATION OF SURGICAL CULTURE

Surgical culture perpetuates itself by the recruitment and training of residents through a long apprenticeship process. Residents are often attracted to surgery by the image of the surgeon, with its prestige, power, and heroic mystique that is shared by most people in North American culture. When medical students encounter their first rotation in surgery they are most likely not only to have this image of a surgeon but also to have some knowledge of the work that surgeons do. The medical students who want to be surgeons are usually those who find the excitement, action, powerful surgical image, and the considerable skills required to practice surgery to be compatible with their personalities and professional goals.

The surgeons in each university-affiliated hospital select from the original self-selecting pool of medical student applicants who seek to become surgeons. An important criterion for selection is that the candidate resembles the image of an ideal surgeon. Dr. White explained that his primary criterion was to ask: "Is this the kind of guy who[m] you want to work with?" Deaver and Reimann wrote: "It may well be counted among the joys of the surgeon to train worthy successors in the work he loves so well" (1923:105).

The ways in which the surgeons at Meadowbrook University Hospital selected future surgeons and evaluated potential surgical residents reflected their perceptions of the characteristics of a good surgeon. First, they tested the residents orally on their knowledge of diagnoses, treatment, and prognoses of those patients which they were asked to examine. The potential recruits varied in their actual knowledge bases, and they varied in their styles of answering the test questions. They particularly varied in the speed, decisiveness, and confidence they displayed (cf., M. Good 1995:7).

One candidate for surgical residency at Meadowbrook exhibited knowledge which was superior to that of the other candidates about diagnoses, etiologies, options for medical and surgical interventions, and probable outcomes. He was thoughtful and occasionally hesitant as he presented the possibilities of diagnosis and therapeutics relevant to the cases presented. However, the surgeons at Meadowbrook gave him low grades, and they did not choose him as a resident. They commented, "His knowledge is good and his judgment is good, but he did not act confident enough. He hesitated and thought too much before answering."

Another candidate was weak and occasionally wrong in his knowledge of, and presentation about, diagnoses, etiologies, options for medical and surgical interventions, and probable outcomes. However, he spoke with extreme confidence. He did not hesitate in answering with clear, direct, and assured tones, even when he guessed and gave answers which were wrong. In contrast to the way the senior surgeons evaluated the knowledgeable but hesitant candidate, they evaluated the assured candidate very highly. Even though he had inferior knowledge, he had displayed confidence and certainty. They chose him as one of their residents. They commented: "Your approach to answering questions is good. You were consistently composed, and you didn't get rattled. We want residents who don't get flustered, who can make decisions under pressure, and who can talk to the examiner as a peer." Similarly, Cassell reported that the surgeons she studied commented that a candidate for a surgical residency looked "frail," meaning that "he seemed to lack the confident, athletic, swashbuckling air exhibited by the more preferred candidates" (1991:17).

Surgeons appear to select those residents who fit into the traditional surgical image of confident, active, and optimistic demeanor, even when their knowledge was limited. Selecting surgical residents for their resemblance to the standard image of a surgeon perpetuated the culture of surgeons.

Residents learned to be full-fledged participants in the culture of surgery during the five to eight years of their surgical residency training. Much of that training, from ancient to modern times, has been through apprenticeship — learning by doing: "Surgery, like religion, is caught rather than taught, and it follows, therefore, that the personal relationship between the student and his chief is of greater importance than the details of an educational program" (Ross 1968).

Learning by doing is more important in surgery than in other fields of medicine, even though it is a component of clinical training in all medical fields. It is the same kind of training that artists and especially artisans have engaged in for centuries. Residents learned to be surgeons by simultaneously observing senior surgeons and by carrying out their surgical roles under the tutelage of surgeons. The criteria for resident selection and training not only perpetuate a past culture of surgeons but also inhibit change to a new culture of surgeons.

In the course of five to eight years of active participating and learning it is not surprising that the residents acquired not only the formal knowledge and techniques of surgery but also the full range of the culture of surgeons. They learned how to think and act like surgeons, how to communicate with patients and colleagues, make decisions, obtain referrals, and participate in research. In this process surgical residents are most influenced by the hospital(s) in which they serve, the surgeons at the hospital(s), and particularly by the chiefs of surgery, who are most responsible for establishing a specific cultural style (cf., Hermann 1990:4). Bahnson wrote: "The education of most surgeons is by the example of their chief" (1988).

SOME IMPLICATIONS OF THE CULTURE OF SURGEONS

The active posture — interventionist ethos — of surgeons has proved to be maladaptive in several respects. It has contributed toward the prolific rise in the cost of medical treatment, without showing a corresponding improvement in morbidity and mortality rates. The interventionist ethos has also influenced medical organizations, such as hospitals, the AMA, and the American College of Surgeons. It has influenced medical school curricula and student (including interns and residents) selection, as well as medical insurance funds and research allocations. Traditional fee-for-service medical insurance funds have until very recently been oriented toward active intervention and discourage waiting and inaction, and allocations for research favor comparisons of interventions (Ortiz de Montellano 1980). There is evidence that the mental and physical health of surgeons may be adversely affected by their culture, with greater incidences of mortality from ischemic heart disease, overall mental strain, inability to relax, and greater number of working hours than other physicians (Arnetz et al. 1988).

In spite of its shortcomings, the culture of surgeons has persisted over several centuries. Its characteristics attract people to the profession who find its tenets congenial and who are capable of handling the challenges and stresses of surgery. Many aspects of the culture of surgeons support its members and make it possible for them to persevere.

There are trends in the cultures of North America that may alleviate some of the burdens on surgeons and reduce the incidence of unprofessional behavior that have been distressing to the many diligent, honorable, and competent surgeons.

Table 1

CONTRASTS BETWEEN SURGICAL CULTURE AND CONTEMPORARY CULTURE OF MEDICAL CARE	
SURGICAL CULTURE	**CONTEMPORARY CULTURE OF MEDICAL CARE**
Active intervention and proclivity toward risk	Diagnostic scientific skills
Categorical thinking	Statistical/probabalistic thinking
Preference for technology	Cost-cutting consideration of technology
Definitive assured decision making	Thoughtful, questioning decision making involving the patient
Mystique of the confident, lone, heroic male	Preference for working in teams
Communication barriers with patients and colleagues	Emphasis upon communication with patients and colleagues
Emphasis on "cure"	Emphasis on care and (to some degree) prevention

One is a continuous growth in the medical sophistication of its patient population. In the past two decades at the end of this century challenges to the authority of all physicians have increased, together with the general level of education and knowledge about health (cf., Haug and Levin 1979). These challenges have been met with attempts on the part of all physicians, including surgeons, to inform patients more completely and engage them in a greater role in decision making. Understanding the culture of surgeons may encourage patients to be more active in demanding answers to their concerns from their surgeons.

Because most people are likely to be affected by decisions made by surgeons at some time in their lives, understanding the culture of surgeons can have important consequences for their participation as patients in the surgical culture. Patients who are knowledgeable about the proclivity of surgeons to make decisions without sufficiently communicating with their patients and colleagues and to evaluate risks with vastly different perspectives than their patients may be able to be more active and more effective collaborators in decisions affecting themselves as surgical patients.

Another trend is a reinterpretation of medical and surgical cultures. Many aspects of contemporary medical culture are different from those in traditional surgical culture (See Table 1). Contemporary medical culture emphasizes surgeons' diagnostic scientific skills over decisive action and risk-taking; modes of thinking that are more probabalistic than categorical and tending toward inquiry rather than certainty; a cost-cutting consideration of technology; a preference toward critical analysis of decisions, based on skepticism and appreciation of empirical evidence, and involving the patient in decision making; and a preference for greater teamwork.

Choosing residents on criteria that conform to the ideal image of the active, heroic certain surgeon may not be the most adaptive response to contemporary surgical challenges. Because of the differences between the traditional culture of surgeons and contemporary medical culture, surgeons may have to reconsider their criteria for choosing surgical residents and training residents so that they may be more adaptive to contemporary medical culture.

The surgeons at Meadowbrook University Hospital rejected many potential residents who did not fit into the traditional image of a surgeon, even when their knowledge was more comprehensive and their thoughtfulness was likely to indicate superior reasoning abilities. It is likely that such knowledge, hesitancy, and thoughtfulness would be valuable to a contemporary surgeon when he or she acquired more training and experience. Similarly, the emphasis in surgical training on "decision making under pressure" may only optimally be achieved after a period of time in which careful, thoughtful, patient-oriented, empirically-based decision making has been encouraged to mature.

CONCLUSION

Combining medical and surgical cultures would encourage reexamination of beliefs about the unquestioned virtues of action, certainty, and eschewing doubts, and it would increase surgeons' respect for the value of empirical clinical studies. It would encourage evaluating decisions for their *long-term* effects on patients.

The new surgical heroes may not be those who act with certainty, rush to "cure" even if they don't have sufficient knowledge or expertise, retain an extremely confident and optimistic manner while remaining distant in communicating with patients. And they need not be exclusively men.

The new surgical heroes may rather be those who can admit doubt and uncertainty when it exists, and can admit limits and be comfortable with palliation. They may communicate sensitively with patients in an effort to have patients participate in some of the decision making. They may communicate more openly with their colleagues. Given the new medical technologies, the characteristics of surgical decision making that were optimal in the past, such as decisive, active, confident decision making, may no longer be optimal for surgical practice. The new surgical heroes may not be those men who make decisions and take risks *for* their patients, but rather those men and women who make decisions and take risks *with* their patients.

Appendix A

CULTURE, MEDICAL ANTHROPOLOGY, AND BIOMEDICINE

~

An abbreviated explanation of the concepts of "culture," "medical anthropology," and the medical tradition called "biomedicine" is presented here for those who are not anthropologists.

Culture is used here as: implicit and explicit basic assumptions — beliefs, values, attitudes, and ideas — both about ways of viewing the world, emotionally and cognitively, as well as how to behave in that world with other people and with objects, such as tools. Culture is shared and learned. It includes skills for communicating through verbal and non-verbal language and other symbols. It also includes social arrangements for passing on skills to new generations (cf., Geertz 1984:125-126; Helman 1994; Levine 1984). The scale of a culture can be very large, such as Western culture or North American culture, or it can be more limiting (often termed subculture) such as Japanese-American culture, medical culture, biomedical culture, or surgical culture.

The field of medical anthropology has contributed to an "understanding of the cultural embeddedness of medical knowledge and practice, the dynamics of the healer's role, and the impact of the general political and economic forces between socio-cultural structures, ecological settings, and disease-causing agents" (Joralemon, personal comunication 1997). Most medical anthropologists acknowledge multiple cultural forces which determine medical beliefs and behavior (cf., Csordas and Kleinman 1996; Foster and Anderson 1978; Gaines 1991; 1992a; 1992b:191; B. Good 1994; B. Good and M. Good 1991; D. Gordon 1988; Hahn 1995; Hahn and Gaines 1985; Johnson 1995; Kaufman 1993; Kleinman 1980; Lindenbaum and Lock 1993; Lock and Gordon 1988; McElroy and Townsend 1996; Mishler et al. 1981; Rhodes 1996; Romanucci-Ross et al. 1991; Rubel and Hass 1996; Sargent and Johnson 1996; Stein 1990).

This study of the culture of surgeons is in this tradition of medical anthropology. It recognizes multiple cultural forces which impinge upon surgeons' beliefs and behavior, including the historical cultures of surgeons, physicians, and patients. They influence their present interactions with each other. It also includes the specific influences of hospitals, organization of Canadian and U.S. medicine, medical schools, insurance arrangements, fee structures, as well as social classes of patients and surgeons.

The perspective in this book departs from that of "critical medical anthropology." That approach interprets Western biomedical systems and the behavior of its practitioners as primarily influenced by the capitalist market economy and, therefore, is inherently class-related and exploitive (cf., Baer 1987; 1996; Baer, Singer and Johnson 1986; Frankenberg 1980; Morgan 1995; Scheper-Hughes 1990; Singer 1990; 1995;1996; Waitzkin 1979).

The culture of surgeons is embedded in Western "biomedicine," which includes beliefs about science, particularly biology, which explain disease, illness, expected kinds of treatment, and behavior of medical practitioners. Most of the basic values of biomedicine are rarely articulated by either its practitioners or patients; they are assumed to be an inevitable part of medicine because of its pervasiveness in North American culture (D. Gordon 1988; Rhodes 1996).

Appendix B

FELLOWSHIP PLEDGE OF AMERICAN COLLEGE OF SURGEONS

~

"Recognizing that the American College of Surgeons seeks to exemplify and develop the highest traditions of our ancient profession, I hereby pledge myself, as a condition of Fellowship in the College, to live in strict accordance with its principles and regulations.

I pledge myself to pursue the practice of surgery with honesty and to place the welfare and the rights of my patient above all else. I promise to deal with each patient as I would wish to be dealt with if I were in the patient's position, and I will set my fees commensurate with the services rendered. I will take no part in any arrangement, such as fee splitting or itinerant surgery, which induces referral or treatment for reason other the patient's best welfare.

Upon my honor, I declare that I will advance my knowledge and skills, will respect my colleagues, and will seek their counsel when in doubt about my own abilities. In turn, I will willingly help my colleagues when requested.

Finally, I solemnly pledge myself to cooperate in advancing and extending the art and science of surgery by my fellowship in the American College of Surgeons."

Appendix C

CYBERSURGERY: THE NEW SURGICAL TECHNOLOGIES

~

The culture of surgeons includes a love of technology. Surgeons have always been dependent on technology to practice their skills — scalpels, retractors, sutures from the earliest times, x-rays and anaesthesia since the nineteenth century, and fiber-optic endoscopes with video cameras, telesurgery, and computerized scans (i.e., MRI, CAT, and PET) at the end of the twentieth century.

"Cybersurgery," sometimes also called "robo-surgery," and "Nintendo surgery,"[1,2] refers to the surgical technologies of the new millennium. It encompasses a new relationship between surgeons and machines, particularly computers, and "the integration of diverse digital technologies into the full spectrum of surgical care" (Satava 1998a:4). The pioneers of cybersurgery talk about a "paradigm shift" in the profession in which there is a "shift in emphasis away from an art reliant upon simple tools, to a highly equipment-dependent discipline" (Sackier 1998:ix, xi).

NEW TECHNOLOGIES

The new technologies are basically those which permit surgeons to visualize the body in new ways in order to access the internal body through minimally invasive or non-invasive techniques for repairing the body. They involve advanced image displays, virtual reality, microelectromechanical systems, and computer-aided, image-guided surgery. The new technologies for visualization, also called "human interface technologies," allow surgeons to visualize inside the body in many dimensions. These technologies include endoscopes, virtual retinal displays, personal projection televison for intra-operative viewing, and 3-D holographic images (Barnett, et al. 1995; Satava 1998a). The 3-D holographic images can "represent the patient as a virtual holographic object" and are suspended in free space so that a hand can pass directly through it (Satava 1998b:18-23; 28).

Surgery depends most upon the feedback from the eye to the hand (Abernathy and Hamm 1995). In traditional open operative procedures surgeons are used to visualizing three-dimensionally, but they are limited by their vision that is restricted to the immediate surfaces of the areas exposed during an operation (Wyke 1997:99). When this last generation[3] of endoscopes (beginning with a 5 mm. tube with fiber-optic cables and a video camera at the end) was introduced they permitted visualization that equaled or exceeded that in traditional surgery. These endoscopes prevented surgeons from visualizing directly, and the visualization was in only two dimensions. The endoscopes permitted surgeons to perform procedures without physically touching the body through remote instruments within the cable to grasp, cut, and suture (cf., Gamradt 1997). As a result of these innovations in endoscopy, surgeons lost the immediacy of hand-to-eye coordination.

The new visualization technologies, one of which is represented by the Visible Human Project, can represent the body as high-density pixels on a screen. These representations are not only anatomically correct but also can display functional, biochemical, and physical parameters. Additionally, they can utilize information, including a patient's history as a medical chart. They allow surgeons to see the inside of an internal body structure, such as, for example, a colonoscope that allows visualization of the inside of a colon. These visualization technologies can also provide a simultaneous image of the outside of that colon. This virtual environment permits a surgeon to reconstruct a colon from a fly-through the inside and see both inside and out (Jones, personal communication 1997). Csordas discusses how this technology alters the human body's "being-in-the-world" (1997).

Such visualization permits surgical robots, which are computer-assisted, to enter the body precisely in the area needed. This experimental technology and others, such as image-guided microsurgery with a neuronavigational device, are used at the present time mostly in brain surgery (Satava 1998; Schaller, et al. 1997; Wirtz 1997). Some of these robotic technologies have been used in hip replacement surgery.

The most significant achievement of cybersurgery is that of the integration of visualization and therapeutic techniques (cf., Jolesz and Kikinis 1998:112). This involves, for example, MRI-guided endoscopy, surgical robots, telepresence surgery (also called telesurgery), energy delivery systems (e.g., lasers, super-ultrasound, cryosurgery), and computer-assisted interventional tools, with virtual reality simulators and virtual prototyping of surgical equipment (e.g., virtual scalpels and clamps) and operating rooms (Satava 1995).

Simulators which are data-bases providing a "synthetic world inside the body" with textured 3-D graphics and endoscopic controls are in use in a number of medical centers for training surgeons to perform specific procedures utilizing the new technologies (Prew 1997). Additionally, the experimental models of telepresence surgery have the promise of providing the surgeon with enhanced dexterity and remote access, in which the surgeon is in a central controlling console and receives enough sensory input to feel as if he were actually directly performing surgery upon the patient (Satava and Jones 1998:141-154).

NEW SKILLS REQUIRED BY NEW TECHNOLOGIES

The differences between traditional surgery and cybersurgery require significant adaptation for present-day surgeons. They have to learn new sensory and motor skills and coordination, and they have to adapt to new socio-cultural and organizational configurations. With regard to new sensory and motor skills, traditional surgery utilizes direct, real-time vision and manipulation, with feedback from touch. In contrast, cybersurgery depends upon virtual representation of both the body and the instruments in which both the representation of the body and the use of the instruments take place in delayed time. Thus, the new technologies shift the traditional skills used by surgeons, such as real-time visualization, hand-eye coordination and feedback, and reliance upon touch, to newer skills. The new skills require an intimate familiarity with computers and virtual reality. They require the ability to feel as comfortable in working with the image of a body instead of the body itself, including with the representation of movements upon the body into pixels in delayed time. Those surgeons who are likely to be more comfortable with these modalities are the younger ones who have grown up with computers.

With regard to adapting to new socio-cultural and organizational configurations, surgeons have to shift their orientation from that of representing themselves as self-reliant and controlling the operating room to that of being a member of a team who is highly dependent upon technicians for many procedures.

The language used in cybersurgery which describes surgeons and other human beings suggests that people are peripheral to the surgical enterprises described. The statement, "The human is a complex integration of the motor and sensory systems that provide the input and output to/from the environment" (Satava and Jones 1998:18) suggests the prominence of the mechanical quality of people. In describing robotic navigation the patient is often referred to as "the surgical object" — as opposed to the medical image which is the "virtual object" (Visarius 1997). Indeed, the new surgical technologies make surgeons *appear* to be superfluous. In discussing the new surgical technologies in *Twentieth Century Miracle Medicine*, Wyke wrote: "once progress has flung wide its tentacles of mechanization, there will be little need for the surgeon's human presence in the operating room" (1997:128). Similarly, when a surgeon familiar with the new technologies was asked about the abilities of present-day surgeons to adapt to the new technologies and incorporate them in everyday practice, he said, "We'll just have to wait until the old ones die off."

Even when the surgeon is present he is only one of a team of specialists. Moreover, he is frequently not the most knowledgeable among them about the new technologies, and he is dependent upon assistants to operate, maintain, and repair equipment (Gamradt 1997). For example, computer-assisted surgery when first introduced required the presence of at least one system engineer in the O.R., which resulted in lack of direct communication between the surgeon and the machine or software (Visarius et al. 1997). The language describing innovations, such as one in a new telesurgery software brochure, claims that: "By insulating the surgeon ... from the technical details of the infrastructure supporting telesurgery, the [software] will provide an intuitive and complete end-to-end platform ... that can be configured to meet specific surgical needs" (Data packets 1997:15).

ADAPTATIONS OF THE NEW TECHNOLOGIES BY SURGEONS

The literature on the new surgical technologies discusses the technical aspects and potentials of those technologies. It hardly discusses, however, ways in which these technologies become integrated into surgical practice. And it neglects to address how the culture of surgeons and the contexts in which they practice may influence the scope of receptivity and use of these technologies. The data from Meadowbrook

University Hospital suggests that there may be significant barriers to the acceptance and use of the new surgical technologies.

The culture of the hospitals in which surgeons trained and practiced is likely to play a major role in their propensity to learn, use, and eventually incorporate the new technologies into their practices. Indeed, the past and present resistance of surgeons to accept innovations[4] (such as Lister's theories and preoperative shaving practices, as described in Chapter 3, "Are Surgeons Scientists?") suggests that the requirements for drastically changing motor and sensory skills, as well as for changing their socio-cultural and organizational environments may precipitate many forms of serious resistance among surgeons.

All of the surgeons in Meadowbrook University Hospital had been concerned about the impact of the then new technologies upon their own practice. Some of them were eager to learn to use the then new emerging technologies of CT scans, MRIs, and endoscopes, and some of them were resistant. In informal conversation they worried that with so many hospitals purchasing CT scans (MRIs and PET scans were not yet in common use at the time) their surgical work load would decline. They worried whether the internists, such as gastroenterologists with their expertise of endoscopy, would "take away" their surgical patients (See Chapter 5, "Communication with Colleagues"). Similarly, although all of the surgeons in Meadowbrook University Hospital had been using staples for several years, many surgeons complained and insisted that their suturing skills were superior to staples. The differences in the "styles" of surgeons at Meadowbrook University Hospital resulted in differences in receptivity to new technologies. Chapter 4, "Styles of Surgeons," described the Meadowbrook University Hospital surgeons' varying responses to adopting a new, more effective technique for preventing post-operative infection in colon surgery.

The new emerging journals on cybersurgery (i.e., *Minimally Invasive Therapy, Surgical Endoscopy, Journal of Image Guided Surgery, Journal of Magnetic Resonance Imaging, Military Medical Technology, Computer Aided Surgery*) as well as the established surgical journals (of which there are over 300) publish critical articles in which the new technologies are used. In reporting the results of their trials or standard procedures, they discuss the technical reasons for their results. Few, if any surgeons, however, discuss the socio-cultural or organizational factors which influence the use of these technologies. Perhaps the next generation of surgeons who will be more familiar and comfortable with cybersurgery will consider the culture of surgeons to be not just an unnecessary "human factor" which interferes with the technology, but rather as an essential part of the process of integrating technical cultural components into a complex culture of surgeons and surgery.

NOTES

1. Most of the information in this appendix comes from interviews and demonstrations with the surgeons, Thomas E. Beam, Shaun B. Jones, Christopher Kaufman, Richard M. Satava, and from Satava (ed.) 1998 *Cybersurgery: Advanced Technologies for Surgical Practice.*

2. The leading pioneer of cybersurgery, Satava, reports that neologisms and a "realignment of thought processes" are necessary to define and understand the new surgical technologies (1998:3).

3. The actual first generation of endoscopes were introduced about a century ago and were tubes with a light bulb at the end (Thomas E. Beam, personal communication 1998)

4. Some surgeons also resisted x-rays in the early part of the nineteenth century, because they were used as arbiters of fault in malpractice cases (Reiser 1978:66).

BIBLIOGRAPHY

Abernathy, Charles M. and Robert M. Hamm. 1995. *Surgical Intuition: What it Is and How to Get it.* Philadelphia: Hanley and Belfus, Inc.

Aird, Ian. 1961. *The Making of a Surgeon.* London: Butterworth.

Alexander-Williams, J. 1979. "Introduction." In D.J.L. Strachan and R. Wise (Eds.) *Surgical Sepsis.* London: Academic Press.

Angell, M. 1994. "The doctor as a double agent." *Kennedy Institute Ethics Journal* 3:279-286.

Apelgren, Keith N., et al. 1990. "Intraoperative flexible videocholedochoscopy: An improved technique for evaluating the common duct." *The American Surgeon* 56:178-181.

Armstrong, David. 1977. "Clinical sense and clinical science." *Social Science and Medicine* 11:599-601.

Arndt, Margarete, et al. 1995. "Surgeon volume and hospital resource utilization." *Inquiry* 32(4):407- 411.

Arnetz, B.B., et al. 1988. "Comparison between surgeons and general practitioners with respect to cardiovascular and psychosocial risk factors among physicians." *Scandinavian Journal of Work and Environmental Health* 14(2):118-124.

Atkins, Hedley. 1965. *The Surgeon's Craft.* Manchester: Manchester University Press.

Atkinson, Paul. 1988. "Discourses descriptions and diagnoses: Reproducing normal medicine." In Margaret Lock and Deborah Gordon (Eds.) *Biomedicine Examined.* Dordrecht, Holland: Kluwer Academic Publishers. pp. 179-204.

Attiyeh, F. F. and M. Stearns. 1981. "Second-look laparotomy based on CEA elevations in colorectal cancer." *Cancer* 47: 2119-2125.

Auerbach, Stuart. 1996. "Picking a plan," *Washington Post Health*, November 12, 1996:16-17.

Baer, Hans A. (Ed.) 1987. *Encounters With Biomedicine: Case Studies in Medical Anthropology.* NY: Gordon and Breach.

Baer, Hans A. 1996. "Toward a political ecology of health in medical anthropology." *Medical Anthropology Quarterly* 10(4): 451-454.

Baer, Hans A., et al. 1986. "Introduction: Toward a critical medical anthropology." *Social Science and Medicine* 23(2):95-98.

Bahnson, H.T. 1988. "Presidential address: Education of a surgical chairman." *Annals of Surgery* 208:247-253.

Ballie, John and William J. Ravitch. 1993. "On endoscopic training and procedural competence." *Annals of Internal Medicine* 118(1):73-74.

Barley, Stephen R. 1988. "The social construction of a machine: Ritual, superstition, magical thinking and other pragmatic responses to running a CT scanner." In Margaret Lock and Deborah Gordon (Eds.) *Biomedicine Examined.* Dordrecht, Holland: Kluwer Academic Publishers pp. 497-539.

Barnett, Gene H., et al. 1995. "Adaptation of personal projection television to a head-mounted display for intra-operative viewing of neuroimaging." *Journal of Image Guided Surgery* 1:109-112.

Barrows, H.S. and D.L. Mitchell. 1975. "An innovative course in undergraduate neuroscience: Experiment in problem-based learning with 'problem boxes.'" *British Journal of Medical Education* 9:223-230.

Bell, Charles. 1821. *Illustrations of the Great Operations of Surgery: Trepan, Hernia, Amputation, Aneurism, and Lithotomy.* London: Longman, Hurst, Rees, Orme, and Brown.

Berggren, P., et al. 1996. "A cost-minimization analysis of laparoscopic cholecystectomy versus open cholecystectomy." *American Journal of Surgery* 172(4): 305-310.

Berggren, P., et al. 1997. "Intravenous cholangiography before 1000 consecutive laparoscopic cholecystectomies." *British Journal of Surgery* 84:472-476

Bergus, G.R., et al. 1995. "Clinical reasoning about new symptoms despite preexisting disease: Sources of error and order effects." *Family Medicine* 27(5): 314-320.

Bernard, Claude 1957 [1865]. *Introduction to the Study of Experimental Investigation Translated by Henry Copley Greene.* NY: Dover.

Bernays, Augustus Charles. 1906. *Golden Rules of Surgery: Aphorisms, Observations and Reflections on the Science and Art of Surgery.* St. Louis: C.V. Mosby.

Bernstein, Basil. 1971. *Class, Codes and Control: Theoretical Studies Towards a Sociology of Language.* NY: Schocken.

Birkmeyer, J.D. and N.O. Birkmeyer. 1996. "Decision analysis in surgery." *Surgery* 120(1):7-15.

Blalock, A. and E.M. Nanson. 1954. "Surgery." In *The Papers of Alfred Blalock.* Baltimore: The Johns Hopkins Press.

Bombardier, C. 1977. "Socioeconomic factors affecting the utilization of surgical operations." *New England Journal of Medicine* 297:699.

Bosk, Charles L. 1979. *Forgive and Remember: Managing Medical Failure.* Chicago: University of Chicago Press.

Bosk, Charles L. 1980. "Occupational rituals in patient management." *New England Journal of Medicine* 303: 71-76.

Boyd, William C. 1976. "Surgical infections." In R. D. Liechty and R. T. Soper (Eds.) *Synopsis of Surgery.* Third Edition. St. Louis: C.V. Mosby. pp. 78-95.

Boyer, L. Bryce, et al. 1986. "Crisis and continuity in the personality of an Apache shaman." *The Psychoanalytic Study of Society.* Vol. 11 Hillsdale, NJ: Analytic Press.

Braveman, P., et al. 1995. "Racial/ethnic differences in the likelihood of cesarean delivery." *American Journal of Public Health* 85(5): 625-630.

Brener, Bruce J. 1996. "Why am I still doing this?" *The American Journal of Surgery* 172(2):97-99.

Brett, Allan S. 1981. "Hidden ethical issues in clinical decision analysis." *New England Journal of Medicine* 305(19):1150-1152.
Brieger, Gert H. 1966. "American surgery and the germ theory of disease." *Bulletin of the History of Medicine* 40:135-145.

Brieger, Gert H. (Ed.) 1972. *Medical America in the Nineteenth Century: Readings from the Literature.* Baltimore: The Johns Hopkins Press.

Brieger, Gert H. 1984. "Mitral stenosis: A case study in the history of surgery." In A.H.M. Kerkhoff (Ed.) *De Novis Inventis: Essays in the History of Medicine in Honour of Daniel de Moulin.* Amsterdam: APA-Holland University Press.

Brieger, Gert H. 1986. "The development of modern surgery: Historical aspects important in the origin and development of modern surgical science." In David C. Sabiston (Ed.) *Textbook of Surgery: The Biological Basis of Modern Surgical Practice.* Philadelphia: W. B. Saunders. pp. 1-17.

Brieger, Gert H. 1987. "A portrait of surgery: Surgery in America, 1875-1889." *Surgical Clinics of North America* 67: 1181-1216.

Brieger, Gert H. 1992. "From conservative to radical surgery in the late nineteenth-century America." In Christopher Lawrence (Ed.) *Medical Theory, Surgical Practice: Studies in the History of Surgery.* London: Routledge. pp. 216-231.

Brown, Cynthia A. 1996. "What surgeons should know about the 1996 Medicare fee schedule." *Bulletin of the American College of Surgeons* 81(1):8-11.

Bunker, John P. 1970. "A comparison of operations and surgeons in the U.S. and in England and Wales." *New England Journal of Medicine* 282:135.

Bunker, John P. 1977. "Preface." J. P. Bunker (Ed.) *Costs, Risks, and Benefits of Surgery.* NY: Oxford University Press. pp. xiii-xvii.

Bursztajn, H. 1981. *Medical Choices, Medical Chances: How Patients, Families and Physicians can Cope with Uncertainty.* NY: Delacorte.

Byrne, P.S, and B.E. Long. 1976. *Doctors Talking to Patients.* London: Her Majesty's Stationary Office.

Carroll, B.J., et al. 1996. "Routine cholangiography reduces sequelae of common bile duct injuries." *Surgical Endoscopy* 10:1194-1197.

Cartwright, A. 1967. *Patients and Their Doctors.* London: Routledge and Kegan Paul.

Cartwright, Frederick. 1968. *The Development of Modern Surgery.* London: Arthur Barker.

Cassell, Joan. 1981. "Technical and moral error in medicine and in fieldwork." *Human Organization* 40:160-168.

Cassell, Joan. 1987. "On control, certitude, and the 'paranoia' of surgeons." *Culture, Medicine and Psychiatry* 11:229-249.

Cassell, Joan. 1989. "The fellowship of surgeons." *International Journal of Moral and Social Studies* 4:195-212.

Cassell, Joan. 1991. *Expected Miracles: Surgeons at Work.* Philadelphia: Temple University Press.

Celsus, Aulus Cornelius 1478. *De Medicina.* Volumes I, II, III.

Chalmers, Thomas C. and H.S. Sacks 1979. "Randomized clinical trials in surgery." *New England Journal of Medicine* 301(21):1182.

Christakis, Nicholas A. 1997. "The ellipsis of prognosis in modern medical thought." *Social Science and Medicine* 45:301-315.

Clarke, J.R. 1989. "Decision making in surgical practice." *World Journal of Surgery* 13(3): 245-251.

Cochrane, J.P.S., et al. 1980. "Value of outpatient follow-up after curative surgery for carcinoma of the large bowel." *British Medical Journal* 280:593-595.

Collins, H.M. 1994. "Dissecting surgery: Forms of life depersonalized." *Social Studies of Science* 24:311-333.

Coon, William W. 1990. "Iatrogenic splenic injury." *The American Journal of Surgery* 159:585-588.

Coyte, Peter C., et al. 1991. "Medical malpractice — The Canadian experience." *New England Journal of Medicine* 324(2):89-93.

Crane, V. 1988. "Economic aspects of clinical decision making: Applications of clinical decision analysis." *American Journal of Hospital Pharmacy* 45(3):548-553.

Criado, Francisco J. 1982. "The ideal cholecystectomy." *Surgical Rounds* February:70-75.

Crile, George. 1978. *Surgery: Your Choices. Your Alternatives*. NY: Delta/Seymour Lawrence.

Cruse, P.J.E. 1977. "Some factors determining wound infection: A prospective study of 30,000 wounds." In H.C. Polk, Jr. and H.H. Stone (Eds.) *Hospital Acquired Infections in Surgery*. Baltimore: University Park Press. pp. 79-85.

Csordas, Thomas J. (Ed.) 1994. *Embodiment and Experience: The Existential Ground of Culture and Self.* Cambridge: Cambridge University Press.

Csordas, Thomas J. 1997. "Computerized Cadavers: Shades of Being and Representation in Virtual Reality." Paper presented at the annual meeting of the American Anthropological Association. Washington, DC

Csordas, Thomas J. and Arthur Kleinman. 1996. "The therapeutic process." In Carolyn F. Sargent and Thomas M. Johnson (Eds.) *Medical Anthropology: Contemporary Theory and Method.* Revised Edition. Westport, CT: Praeger. pp. 3-20.

Curreri, P.W. 1974. "Survey of employment satisfaction in academic surgery." *Journal of Surgical Research* 17(3):215-218.

d'Aquili, Eugene G. 1975. "The biopsychological determinants of religious ritual behavior." *Zygon* 10(1):32-58.

"Data packets." 1997. *Military Medical Technology* 1(1):12-15.

Dawes, Robyn M. 1988. *Rational Choice in an Uncertain World.* NY: Harcourt Brace Jovanovich.

Dawes, Robyn M. 1989. "Clinical versus actuarial judgment." *Science* 43:1668-1674.

Deaver, John and Stanley Reimann. 1923. *Excursions into Surgical Subjects.* Philadelphia: W.B. Saunders.

Dennis, F.S. 1905. "The history and development of surgery during the past century." *American Medicine* 5:84.

Devereux, George. 1967. *From Anxiety to Method in the Behavioral Sciences.* The Hague: Mouton.

Dobson, Jessie R. and Milnes Walker. 1979. *Barbers and Barber-Surgeons of London: A History of the Barbers' and Barber-Surgeons' Companies.* London: Blackwell Scientific Publications.

Douglas, Mary. 1994. "The construction of the physician: A cultural approach to medical fashions." In Susan Budd and Ursula Sharma (Eds.) *The Healing Bond: The Patient-Practitioner Relationship and Therapeutic Responsibility.* London: Routledge. pp. 23-41.

Douglas, Mary and Aaron Wildavsky. 1982. *Risk and Culture: An Essay on the Selection of Technical and Environmental Dangers.* Berkeley: University of California Press.

Durkheim, Emile. [1933] 1947. *Division of Labor in Society.* Translated by George Simpson. Glencoe, Ill: The Free Press.

Eddy, David M. 1982a. "Clinical policies and the quality of clinical practice." *New England Journal of Medicine* 307:343-347.

Eddy, David M. 1982b. "Probabalistic reasoning in clinical medicine: Problem and opportunities." In D. Kahneman (Eds.) *Judgment under Uncertainty: Heuristics and Biases.* NY: Cambridge University Press. pp. 249-267 .

Edwards, W. and A. Tversky (Eds.) 1967. *Decision Making.* Baltimore: Penguin.

Egbert, Lawrence and Ilene Rothman. 1977. "Relation between the race and economic status of patients and who performs their surgery." *New England Journal of Medicine* 297:90-91.

Eibel, P. 1988. "Doctor or Mister: The correct appellation of British surgeons." *Canadian Journal of Surgery* 31(6):452-453.

Eichhorn, John H., et al. 1986. "Standards for patient montoring during anesthesia at Harvard Medical School." *Journal of the American Medical Association* 256(8):1017-1020.

Eisenberg, John M. 1979. "Sociological influences on decision-making by clinicians." *Annals of Internal Medicine* 90:957-964.

Eli, I. 1996. "Reducing confirmation bias in clinical decision making." *Journal of Dental Education* 60(10):831-835.

Escarce, Jose J., et al. 1997. "How practicing surgeons trained for laparoscopic cholecystectomy." *Medical Care* 35(3):291-296.

Estey, W.Z. 1978. "Medical litigation in Canada." *Canadian Journal of Surgery* 21(2):156-160.

Estroff, Susan. 1993. "Identity, disability, and schizophrenia: The problem of chronicity." In Shirley Lindenbaum and Margaret Lock (Eds.) *Knowledge, Power, and Practice: The Anthropology of Medicine and Everyday Life*. Berkeley: University of California Press. pp. 247-286.

Felker, Marcia Elliott. 1983. "Ideology and order in the operating room." In Lola Romanucci- Ross, et al. (Eds.) T*he Anthropology of Medicine: From Culture to Method*. NY: Praeger. pp. 349-365.

Fielding, L., et al. 1978. "Surgeon-related variables and the clinical trial." *Lancet* 809(3):778-779.

Finkler, Kaja. 1994. "Sacred healing and biomedicine compared." *Medical Anthropology Quarterly* 8(2):178-197.

Finney, J.M.T. 1940. *A Surgeon's Life: The Autobiography of J.M.T. Finney*. NY: P. Putnum.

Fisher, Bradley and Constance Peterson. 1993. "She won't be dancing much anyway: A study of surgeons, surgical nurses, and elderly patients." *Qualitative Health Research* 3(2):165-183.

Fisher, Sue. 1993. "Doctor talk/Patient talk: How treatment decisions are negotiated in doctor-patient communication." In Sue Fisher and Alexandra Dundas Todd (Eds.) *The Social Organization of Doctor-Patient Communication. Second Edition*. Norwood, NJ: Ablex Publishing Corporation. pp. 161-182.

Fisher, Sue and Alexandra Dundas Todd (Eds.) 1993. *The Social Organization of Doctor-Patient Communication. Second Edition*. Norwood, NJ: Ablex Publishing Corp.

Flood Ann Barry and W. Richard Scott. 1987. *Hospital Structure and Performance*. Baltimore: Johns Hopkins University Press.

Folse, R., et al. 1980. "Surgical manpower and practice patterns in nonmetropolitan areas." *Surgery* 87(1):95-100.

Fonealsoud, E.W. 1972. "Reassessment of surgical specialty training in the United States." *Archives of Surgery* 104:159-160.

Foster, George. 1976. "Disease etiologies in non-Western medical systems." *American Anthropologist* 78:773-782.

Foster, George and Barbara Gallatin Anderson. 1978. *Medical Anthropology*. NY: Wiley.

Fox, Nicholas J. 1992. *The Social Meaning of Surgery*. Milton Keynes Books: Open University Press.

Fox, Nicholas J. 1993. "Discourse, organisation and the surgical ward round." *Sociology of Health and Illness* 15(1):16-42.

Fox, Nicholas J. 1994. "Fabricating surgery: A response to Collins." *Social Studies of Science* 24:347-354.

Fox, Nicholas J. 1997. "Space, sterility and surgery: Circuits of hygiene in the operating theatre." *Social Science and Medicine* 45(5):649-657.

Frankenberg, Ronald. 1980. "Medical anthropology and development: A theoretical perspective." *Social Science and Medicine* 14:197-207.

Freidson, Eliot. 1976. *Doctoring Together: A Study of Professional Social Control*. NY: Elsevier.

Fuchs, Victor. 1974. *Who Shall Live?* NY: Basic Books.

Gaines, Atwood D. 1991. "Cultural constructivism: Sickness histories and the understanding ethnomedicines beyond critical medical anthropologies." In B. Pfleiderer and G. Bibeau (Eds.) *Anthropologies of Medicine*. Wiesbaden: Vieweg Verlag. pp. 221-257.

Gaines, Atwood D. (Ed.) 1992a. *Ethnopsychiatry: The Cultural Construction of Professional and Folk Psychiatries*. Albany: SUNY Press.

Gaines, Atwood D. 1992b. "Medical/psychiatric knowledge in France and the United States: Culture and sickness in history and biology." In Atwood D. Gaines (Ed.) *Ethnopsychiatry: The Cultural Construction of Professional and Folk Psychiatries*. Albany: SUNY Press. pp. 171-201.

Gamradt, Jan Armstrong. 1997. "Innovation, Risk, and the Anthropology of Learning in a Professional Community." Paper presented at the annual meeting of the American Anthropological Association. Washington DC.

Gamradt, Jan Armstrong and Susan Brandt Graham. 1993. "Knowledge Acquisition as Cultural Process: Studying Old Docs Who Are Learning New Tricks." Paper presented at the annual meeting of the American Anthropological Association. Washington DC.

Geer, Deborah A. 1993. "Women in surgery." *Journal of the American Medical Women's Association* 48(2):47-50.

Geertz, Clifford. 1984. "From the native's point of view: On the nature of anthropological understanding." In R.A. Shweder and R.A. LeVine (Eds.) *Culture Theory: Essays on Mind, Self, and Emotion.* Cambridge: Cambridge University Press. pp. 123-136.

Gius, John. 1972. *Fundamentals of Surgery.* Chicago: Yearbook Medical Publishers.

Glaser, Hugo. 1958. *The Road to Modern Surgery: The Advances in Medicine and Surgery During the Past Hundred Years.* London: Butterworth.

Gluckman, Max. 1970. *Custom and Conflict in Africa.* Oxford: Oxford University Press.

Goldberg, J.H. September 1989. "Are your earnings growing fast enough?" *Medical Economics* 8(9).

Golden, J.A. and G.D. Johnston. 1970. "Problems of distortion in doctor-patient communication." *Psychiatry in Medicine* 1:127-149.

Goldman, L., et al. 1988. "A computer protocol to predict myocardial infarchtion in emergency department patients with chest pain." *The New England Journal of Medicine* 318:797-803.

Good, Byron J. 1994. *Medicine, Rationality and Experience: An Anthropological Perspective.* Cambridge: Cambridge University Press.

Good, Byron. J. and Mary Jo Del Vecchio Good. 1981. "The semantics of medical discourse." In Everett Mendelsohn and Yehuda Elkana (Eds.) *Sciences and Cultures: Sociology of the Sciences.* Volume V. Dordrecht, Holland: D. Reidel Publishing Co. pp. 177-212.

Good, Byron J. and Mary Jo Del Vecchio Good. 1991. "The meaning of symptoms: A cultural hermeneutic model for clinical practice." In L. Eisenberg and A. Kleinman (Eds.) *The Relevance of Social Sciences for Medicine.* Dordrecht, Holland: D. Reidel Publishing Co. pp. 165-196.

Good, Mary Jo Del Vecchio, et al. 1990. "American oncology and the discourse on hope." *Culture, Medicine, and Psychiatry* 14(1):59-80.

Good, Mary Jo Del Vecchio. 1995. *American Medicine: The Quest for Competence.* Berkeley: University of California Press.

Goody, Jack. 1961. "Religion and ritual: The definition problem." *British Journal of Sociology* 12:142-164.

Gordon, David Paul. 1983. "Hospital slang for patients: Crocks, gomers, gorks, and others." *Language in Society* 12:173-185.

Gordon, Deborah. 1988. "Tenacious assumptions in western medicine." In Margaret Lock and Deborah Gordon (Eds.) *Biomedicine Examined.* Dordrecht, Holland: Kluwer Academic Publishers. pp. 19-56.

Gordon, Deborah. 1994. "The ethics of ambiguity and concealment around cancer: Interpretation of a local Italian ward." In P. Benner (Ed.) *Interpretive Phenomenology: Embodyment, Caring, and Ethics in Health and Illness.* Thousand Oaks, CA: Sage. pp. 279-322.

Greenberg, E.R., et al., 1988. "Social and economic factors in the choice of lung cancer treatment: A population-based study in two rural states." *New England Journal of Medicine* 318:612-617.

Hage, Jerold. 1983. "Communication and coordination." In S.M. Shortell and A.D. Kaluzny (Eds.) *Health Care Management.* NY: John Wiley. pp. 224-249.

Haggard, William D. 1935. *Surgery Queen of the Arts, And Other Papers and Addresses.* Philadelphia: W.B. Saunders.

Hahn, Robert A. 1982. "Culture and informed consent: An anthropological perspective." *President's Commission for the Study of Ethical Problems in Medicine and Biomedical and Behavioral Research. Appendix 3.* Washington, DC: U.S. Government Printing Office.

Hahn, Robert A. 1985. "A world of internal medicine: Portrait of an internist." In Robert A. Hahn and Atwood D. Gaines (Eds.) *Physicians of Western Medicine: Anthropological Approaches to Theory and Practice.* Dordrecht, Holland: D. Reidel. pp. 51-111.

Hahn, Robert A. 1995. *Sickness and Healing: An Anthropological Perspective.* New Haven, CN: Yale University Press.

Hahn, Robert A. and Atwood D. Gaines. (Eds.) 1985. *Physicians of Western Medicine: Anthropological Approaches to Theory and Practice.* Dordrecht, Holland: D. Reidel.

Hahn, Robert A. and Arthur Kleinman. 1983. "Biomedical practice and anthropological theory." *Annual Review of Anthropology* 12:305-333.

Halsted, William Stewart. 1904. "The training of the surgeon." *American Medicine* 8:69-75.

Halsted, William Stewart. 1913. "Ligature and suture material. The employment of fine silk in preference to catgut and the advantages of transfixion of tissue and vessels in control of hemorrhage. Also an account of the introduction of gloves, gutta-percha tissue and silver foil." *Journal of the American Medical Association* 60:1119-1126.

Hamburger, Jean. [1647] 1992. *The Diary of William Harvey: The Imaginary Journal of the Physician who Revolutionized Medicine.* Translated by Barbara Wright. New Brunswick, NJ: Rutgers University Press.

Hannan, Edward L., et al. 1989. "Investigation of the relationship between volume and mortality for surgical procedures performed in New York State hospitals." *Journal of the American Medical Association* 262 (4):485-510.

Hardy, J.D. 1959. *Total Surgical Management.* NY: Grune and Stratton.

Harvard Medical Practice Study. 1990. *Patients, Doctors, and Lawyers: Medical Injury, Malpractice Litigation and Patient Compensation in New York.* Cambridge, MA: Harvard University Press.

Haug, M.R. and B. Lavin. 1979. "Public challenge of physician authority." *Medical Care* 17(8):844-858.

Hauser, Stuart T. 1981. "Physician-patient relationships." In Elliott G. Mishler, et al. (Eds.) *Social Contexts of Health, Illness, and Patient Care.* Cambridge: Cambridge University Press. pp. 105-140.

Helman, Cecil G. 1994. *Culture, Health and Illness: An Introduction for Health Professionals: Third Edition.* Oxford: Butterworth-Heinemann, Ltd.

Herdt, Gilbert and Robert J. Stoller. 1990. *Intimate Communications: Erotics and the Study of Culture.* NY: Columbia University Press.

Hermann, Robert E. 1990. "Role models in the education of surgeons." *The American Journal of Surgery* 159:2-7.

Hilden, J. 199.1 "Intuition and other soft modes of thought in surgery." *Theoretical Surgery* 6:89-94.

Hirschauer, Stefan. 1991 "Manufacture of bodies in surgery." *Social Studies of Science* 21:279-319.

Hirschauer, Stefan. 1994. "Towards a methodology of investigations into the strangeness of one's own culture: A response to Collins." *Social Studies of Science* 24:335-346.

Holm, S. 1995. "The medical hierarchy and perceived influence on technical and ethical decisions." *Journal of Internal Medicine* 237(5):487-492.

Hsu, Francis. 1983. *Rugged Individualism Reconsidered.* Knoxville: University of Tennessee Press.

Huxley, Thomas Henry. 1896. *Darwiniana: Essays by T.H. Huxley.* London: D. Appleton.

Inglehart, John K. 1993. "The American health care system: Teaching hospitals." *New England Journal of Medicine* 329:1052-1056.

Israel, Lucien. 1982. *Decision-making, the Modern Doctor's Dilemma: Reflections On The Art of Medicine.* Translated by Mary Feeney. NY: Random House.

Johnson, Thomas M. 1995. "Managing patients." *Family Medicine* 27(7):460-462.

Jolesz, Ferenc A. and Ron Kikinis. 1998. "Image-guidance procedures and the OR of the future." In Richard S. Satava (Ed.) *Cybersurgery: Advanced Technologies for Surgical Practice.* NY: Wiley Liss, Inc. pp. 99-120.

Jollis, James G., et al. 1996. "Outcome of acute myocardial infarction according to the specialty of the admitting physician." *New England Journal of Medicine* 335(25):1880-1887.

Jordan, Brigitte. 1993. *Birth in Four Cultures: A Cross Cultural Investigation of Childbirth in Yucatan, Holland, Sweden, and the United States.* Revised and expanded by Robbie Davis-Floyd. Prospect Heights, IL: Waveland Press.

Jou, J. et al. 1992. "An information processing view of framing effects: The role of causal schemas in decision making." *Memory and Cognition* 24(1):1-15.

Kahneman, Daniel and Amos Tversky. 1979. "Prospect theory: An analysis of decision under risk." *Econometrica* 47(2):363-291.

Kassirer, Jerome P. 1989. "Our stubborn quest for diagnostic certainty: A case of excessive testing." *New England Journal of Medicine* 320(22):1489-1491.

Katz, Fred E. (Ed.) 1971. *Contemporary Sociological Theory.* NY: Random House.

Katz, Fred E. 1976. *Structuralism in Sociology.* Albany: SUNY Press.

Katz, Jay. 1984. *The Silent World of Doctor and Patient.* NY: The Free Press.

Katz, Pearl. 1981. "Ritual in the operating room." *Ethnology* 20:335-350.

Katz, Pearl. 1984. "Ritual in Psychoanalytic Practice." Paper presented at the annual meeting of the American Anthropological Association. New York, NY.

Katz, Pearl. 1985. "How surgeons make decisions." In Robert A. Hahn and Atwood D. Gaines (Eds.) *Physicians of Western Medicine: Anthropological Approaches to Theory and Practice.* Dordrecht, Holland: D. Reidel. pp. 155-175.

Katz, Pearl. 1988. "Ritual in Psychiatric Practice." Paper Presented in Grand Rounds, Department of Psychiatry, Walter Reed Army Medical Center. Washington, DC.

Katz, Pearl.   1990. "Emotional metaphors, socialization and roles of drill sergeants." *Ethos* 184:457-480.

Katz, Pearl. 1991. "How surgical rituals enhance surgical science." *Today's OR Nurse* 13:5-11.

Katz, Pearl and Faris R. Kirkland. 1988. "Traditional thought and modern western surgery." *Social Science and Medicine* 26:1175-1181.

Kaufman, Sharon R. 1993. *The Healer's Tale: Transforming Medicine and Culture.* Madison: University of Wisconsin Press.

Kelly, Joyce and Fred Hellinger. 1986. "Physician and hospital factors associated with mortality of surgical patients." *Medical Care* 24:785-800.

Kendylis, P.D. 1997. "Abnormal intraoperative cholangiography: Treatment options and follow-up." *Archives of Surgery* 132(4):347-350.

King, Lester S. 1982. *Medical Thinking: A Historical Preface.*   Princeton: Princeton University Press.

Kitahama, A., et al. 1986.   "Routine intraoperative cholangeogram." *Surgery Gynecology, Obstetrics* 164:316-322.

Klapp, Orin. 1962.   *Heroes, Villains, and Fools: The Changing American Character.* Englewood Cliffs: Prentice-Hall.

Kleinman, Arthur 1980.   *Patients and Healers in the Context of Culture: An Exploration of the Borderland between Anthropology, Medicine and Psychiatry.* Berkeley: University of California Press.

Knafl, Kathleen and Gary Burkett. 1975. "Professional socialization in a surgical specialty: Acquiring medical judgement." *Social Science and Medicine* 9:397-404.

Koenig, Barbara A. 1988. "The technological imperative in medical practice: The social creation of a 'routine' treatment." In Margaret Lock and Deborah Gordon (Eds.) *Biomedicine Examined.* Dordrecht, Holland: Kluwer Academic Publishers. pp. 465-496.

Kondylis, P.D., et al. 1997. "Abnormal intraoperative cholangiography. Treatment options and long-term follow-up." *Archives of Surgery* 132(4):347-350.

Konner, Melvin. 1987. *Becoming a Doctor: A Journey of Initiation into Medical School.* NY: Penguin Books.

Koo, K.P. and L.W. Traverso. 1996. "Do preoperative indicators predict the presence of common bile duct stones during laparoscopic cholecystectomy?" *American Journal of Surgery* 171(5):495-499.

Kordes de Vaal, J.H. 1996. "Intention and the omission bias: Omissions perceived as nondecisions." *Acta Psychology Amsterdam* 93(1-3):161-172.

Korsch, Barbara and V.F. Negrete. 1972. "Doctor-patient communication." *Scientific American* 227:66-74.

Kuhn, Thomas S. 1970. *The Structure of Scientific Revolutions Second Edition* Enlarged. Chicago: University of Chicago Press.

L'Hommedieu, Elizabeth. 1991. "Walking out on the boys." *Time* July 8, 1991:52-53.

Lau, Wan-yee, et al. 1988. "Influence of surgeons' experience on postoperative sepsis." *The American Journal of Surgery* 155:322-326.

Lawrence, Christopher. 1992. "Introduction." In Christopher Lawrence (Ed.) *Medical Theory, Surgical Practice: Studies in the History of Surgery.* London: Routledge.

Lawrence, Christopher and Richard Dixey. 1992. "Practising on principle: Joseph Lister and the germ theories of disease." In Christopher Lawrence (Ed.) *Medical Theory, Surgical Practice: Studies in the History of Surgery.* London: Routledge. pp. 153-215.

Leach, Edmund R. 1968. "Ritual." *International Encyclopedia of the Social Sciences* 13:520-526.

Legorretta, Antonio P., et al. 1993. "Increased cholecystectomy rate after the introduction of laparoscopic cholecystectomy." *Journal of the American Medical Association* 240(12):1429-1432.

LeMaitre, George and Janet Finnegin. 1975. *The Patient in Surgery: A Guide for Nurses. Third Edition.* Philadelphia: W.B. Saunders.

Levine, Robert A. 1984. "Properties of culture: An ethnographic view." In Richard A. Shweder and Robert A. LeVine (Eds.) *Culture Theory: Essays on Mind, Self, and Emotion.* Cambridge: Cambridge University Press. pp. 67-87.

Lewis, C. 1969. "Variations in the incidence of surgery." *New England Journal of Medicine* 281:880.

Lex, Barbara. 1979. "The neurobiology of ritual trance." In E. G. D'Aquili, et al. (Eds.) *The Spectrum of Ritual.* NY: Columbia University Press.

Lindenbaum, Shirley and Margaret Lock (Eds.) 1993. *Knowledge, Power, and Practice: The Anthropology of Medicine and Everyday Life.* Berkeley: University of California Press.

Lock, Margaret and Deborah Gordon. 1988. "Relationship between society, culture, and biomedicine: Introduction to the essays." In Margaret Lock and Deborah Gordon (Eds.) *Knowledge, Power, and Practice: The Anthropology of Medicine and Everyday Life.* Berkeley: University of California Press. pp.11-16.

Loewenthal, John. 1968. "The design of operating theatres." In C. Rob and R. Smith (Eds.) *Operative Surgery: General Principles and Breast.* London: Butterworth. pp. 3-13.

LoGerfo, J.P. 1977. "Variation in surgical rates: Fact vs. fantasy." *New England Journal of Medicine* 29(7):387-389.

Lorenz, W. and M. Rohmund. 1989. "Theoretical surgery: A new specialty in operative medicine." *World Journal of Surgery* 13:292-299.

Lynch, Michael. 1994. "Collins, Hirschauer and Winch: Ethnography, exoticism, surgery, antisepsis and dehorsification." *Social Studies of Science* 24:354-369.

Lyons, Joseph P. 1994. "The American medical doctor in the current milieu: A matter of trust." *Perspectives in Biology and Medicine* 37(3):442-459.

Major, R.H. 1954. *A History of Medicine.* Volume II. Springfield, IL: Charles C Thomas.

Malterud, K. 1995. "The legitimacy of clinical knowledge: Towards a medical epistemology embracing the art of medicine." *Theoretical Medicine* 16(2):183-198.

Margalith, Ilana and Amos Shapiro. 1997. "Anxiety and patient participation in clinical decision-making: The case of patients with ureteral calculi." *Social Science and Medicine* 45(3):419-427.

Marteau, Theresa M. 1989. "Framing of information: Its influence upon decisions of doctors and patients." *British Journal of Social Psychology* 28:89-94.

Martin, Emily. 1992. *Flexible Bodies: Tracking Immunity in American Culture: From the Days of Polio to the Age of AIDS.* Boston: Beacon Press.

Maynard, C., et al. 1986. "Institutional differences in therapeutic decision making in the coronary artery surgery study." *Medical Decision Making* 6:127-135.

Mazur, D.J. and D.H. Hickam. 1996. "Five-year survival curves: How much data are enough for patient-physician decision making in general surgery?" *European Journal of Surgery* 162(2):101-104.

McElroy, Ann and Patricia K. Townsend (Eds.) 1996. *Medical Anthropology in Ecological Perspective. Third Edition.* Boulder, CO: Westview Press.

McPeek, B. 1991. "Intuition as a strategy of medical decision making." *Theoretical Surgery* 6:83-84.

Merton, Robert. 1968. *Social Theory and Social Structure.* Enlarged Edition, NY: The Free Press.

Miller, J.M. 1982. "William Stewart Halsted and the use of the surgical rubber glove." *Surgery* 92:1119-1126.

Millman, Marcia. 1976. *The Unkindest Cut: Life in the Backrooms of Medicine.* NY: William Morrow.

Mirza, D.F., et al. 1997. "Bile duct injury following laparoscopic cholecystectomy: Referral pattern and management." *British Journal of Surgery* 84:786-790.

Mishler, Elliot G. 1981. "The health care system: Social contexts and consequences." In Elliot G. Mishler, et al. (Eds.) *Social Contexts of Health, Illness, and Patient Care.* Cambridge: Cambridge University Press. pp. 195-217.

Mishler, Elliot G., et al. 1981. "Viewpoint: Critical perspectives on the biomedical mode." In Elliot G. Mishler, et al. (Eds.) *Social Contexts of Health, Illness, and Patient Care.* Cambridge: Cambridge University Press. pp. 1-23.

Mizrahi, Terry. 1986. *Getting Rid of Patients: Contradictions in the Socialization of Physicians.* New Brunswick, NJ: Rutgers University Press.

Morgan, Lynn A. 1995. "Comment on Singer's 'Beyond the ivory tower: Critical praxis in medical anthropology.'" *Medical Anthropology Quarterly* 9(1):120-122.

Moynihan, Sir Berkeley. 1920a. *Addresses on Surgical Subjects.* Philadelphia: W.B. Saunders.

Moynihan, Sir Berkeley. 1920b. "The ritual of a surgical operation." *British Journal of Surgery* 8.

Moynihan, Sir Berkeley. 1928. *Essays on Surgical Subjects.* Philadelphia: W. B.Saunders.

Muller, Jessica H. and Barbara A. Koenig. 1988. "On the boundary of life and death: The definition of dying by medical residents." In Margaret Lock and Deborah Gordon (Eds.) *Biomedicine Examined.* Dordrecht, Holland: Kluwer Academic Publishers. pp. 351-337.

Mustard, R. 1970. "A survey of techniques and results of hiatus hernia repair." *Surgery, Gynecology, and Obstetrics.* 130:131-136.

National Opinion Research Center. 1991. *General Social Survey.* Chicago: National Opinion Research Center.

Nolen, William A. 1970. *The Making of a Surgeon.* NY: Pocket Books.

O'Connor, G.T., et al. 1996. "A regional intervention to improve the hospital mortality associated with coronary artery bypass graft surgery: The Northern New England cardiovascular disease study group." *Journal of the American Medical Association* 275(1):841-846.

Ortiz, Bernard de Montellano. 1980. "Minorities and the medical professional monopoly." *Grito del Sol Quarterly Books* 2:27-70.

Osler, William. 1914. *The Leaven of Science: Aequanimitas with Other Addresses.* Philadelphia: Blakiston's.

Osler, William. 1919. *A Way of Life: An Address Delivered to Yale Students Sunday Evening, April 20, 1913.* Springfield, IL: Charles C Thomas.

Paget, Marianne A. 1993. "On the work of talk: Studies in misunderstandings." In Sue Fisher and Alexandra Dundas Todd (Eds.) *The Social Organization of Doctor-Patient Communication.   Second Edition.* NY: Ablex Publishing Corporation. pp. 107-126.

Parker, G. 1920. *The Early History of Surgery in Great Britain: Its Organization and Development.* London: A. and C. Black, Ltd.

Parsons, Talcott. 1951. *The Social System.* Glencoe, IL: The Free Press.

Pear, R.A. and E. Eckholm. 1991. "When healers are entrepreneurs: A debate over costs and ethics." *The New York Times* June 2,1991:1.

Pernick, Martin. 1985. *A Calculus of Suffering: Pain, Professionalism, and Anesthesia in Nineteenth-Century America.* NY: Columbia University Press.

Peters, Larry G. and Douglass Price-Williams. 1980. "Towards an experiential analysis of shamanism." *American Ethnologist* 7(3):397-413.

Peterson, Clare Gray. 1972. *Perspectives in Surgery.* Philadelphia: Lea and Febiger.

Pichot, Anedee. 1860. *The Life and Labours of Sir Charles Bell.* London: Richard Bentley.

Plaja, A. and S. Cohen. 1968. "Communication between physicians and patients in out-patient clinics: Social and cultural factors." *Milbank Memorial Fund Quarterly* 46:161-213.

Politser, Pam and Diane Schneidman (Eds.) 1990. *Socio-Economic Factbook for Surgery 1990.* Chicago: American College of Surgeons.

Polk, Hiram C., Jr. 1977. "A brief history of surgical infection." In L. M. Flint and D. E. Fry (Eds.) *Surgical Infections.* Garden City, NY: Medical Examination Publishing Co. pp. 1-7.

Posen, , M.W. et al. 1984. "A predictive instrument to imporve coronary-care-unit admission practices in acute ischemic heart disease: A prospective multicenter clinical trial." *New England Journal of Medicine* 310:1273-1278.

Posner, K.L., et al. 1995. "Changes in clinical practice in response to reductions in reimbursement: Physician autonomy and resistance to bureaucratization." *Medical Anthropology Quarterly* 9(4):476-492.

Power, D'Arcy. 1933. *A Short History of Surgery.* London: John Bale and Danielson.

Prew, Sarah-Jane. 1997. "Laparoscopic simulator developed by Centre for Human Sciences." *Military Medical Technology* 1(1):12-13.

Ravitch, Mark M. 1981. *A Century of Surgery, 1880-1980: The History of the American Surgical Association* Volumes I and II. Philadelphia: J.B. Lippincott.

Reading, Anthony E. 1981. "Psychological prepararation for surgery: Patient recall of information." *Journal of Psychosomatic Research* 25:57-72.

Redelmeier, D. A., et al. 1995. "Probability judgement in medicine: Discounting unspecified possibilities." *Medical Decision Making* 15(3):227-230.

Regnier, Stephen J. 1995. "Symposium explores OR efficiency." *Bulletin of the American College of Surgeons* 80(9):53-59.

Reiser, S.J. 1978. *Medicine and the Reign of Technology.* Cambridge: Cambridge University Press.

Relman, A. 1985. "The United States and Canada: Different approaches to health care." *New England Journal of Medicine* 315:117-118.

Rhee, Sang-O. 1977. "Relative importance of physicians' personal and situational characteristics for the quality of patient care." *Journal of Health and Social Behavior* 18:10-15.

Rhodes, Lorna Amarasingham. 1996. "Studying biomedicine as a cultural system." In Carolyn F. Sargent and Thomas M. Johnson (Eds.) *Medical Anthropology: Contemporary Theory and Method.* Revised Edition. Westport, CT: Praeger. pp. 165-180.

Richardson, Robert G. 1964. *The Story of Modern Surgery.* NY: Collier.

Richardson, Robert G. 1968. *Surgery: Old and New Frontiers.* NY: Charles Scribner.

Robson, Martin C. 1980. "Biology of infection." In M.D. Kerstein (Ed.) *Management of Surgical Infections*. Mount Kisco, NY: Futura. pp. 15-26.

Rogers, Carolyn M. and William F. Seward. 1996. *Socio-Economic Factbook for Surgery 1996-1997*. Chicago: American College of Surgeons.

Romanucci-Ross, Lola, et al. (Eds.) 1991. *The Anthropology of Medicine: From Culture to Method. Second Edition*. Waltham, MA: Bergin and Garvey.

Romanucci-Ross, Lola and Daniel E. Moerman. 1991. "The extraneous factor in western medicine." In Romanucci-Ross, Lola, et al. (Eds.) *The Anthropology of Medicine: From Culture to Method. Second Edition*. Waltham, MA: Bergin and Garvey.

Rosenbaum, Edward E. 1988. *A Taste of My Own Medicine: When the Doctor is the Patient*. NY: Random House.

Rosenberg, Charles. 1987. *The Care of Strangers: The Rise of America's Hospital System*. NY: Basic Books.

Rosenberg, Steven A. 1984. "The organization of surgical oncology in university departments of surgery." *Surgery* 95(5):632-634.

Ross, J.P. 1968. "On teaching by example." *Surgery, Gynecology, and Obstetrics*. 127:1317-1318.

Roush, T.S. and L.W. Traverso. 1995. "Management and long-term follow-up of patients during laparoscopic cholecystectomy." *American Journal of Surgery* 169(5):484-487.

Routh, D.K. and K.M. King. 1972. "Social class bias in clinical judgment." *Journal of Consulting Clinical Psychology* 38:415-419.

Rubel, Arthur J. and Michael R. Hass. 1996. "Ethnomedicine." In Carolyn F. Sargent and Thomas M. Johnson (Eds.) *Medical Anthropology: Contemporary Theory and Method*. Revised Edition. Westport, CT: Praeger. pp. 113-130.

Sagan, Carl. 1996. Television Broadcast of Interview. May 27, 1996, PBS.

Sackier, Jonathan M. 1998. "Series preface." In Richard S. Satava (ed.) 1998 *Cybersurgery: Advanced Technologies for Surgical Practice*. NY: Wiley Liss, Inc. pp. ix-xi.

Salem-Schatz, Susanne R., et al. 1990. "Influence of clinical knowledge, organizational context, and practice style on transfusion decision making: Implications for practice change strategies." *Journal of the American Medical Association* 264(4):476-484.

Sankar, Andrea. 1988. "Patients, physicians and context: Medical care in the home." In Margaret Lock and Deborah Gordon (Eds.) *Biomedicine Examined.* Dordrecht, Holland: Kluwer Academic Publishers. pp. 155-178.

Sargent, Carolyn F. and Thomas M. Johnson (Eds.) 1996. *Medical Anthropology: Contemporary Theory and Method.* Revised Edition. Westport, CT: Praeger.

Satava, Richard S. 1995. "Virtual reality, telesurgery, and the new world order of medicine." *Journal of Image Guided Surgery* 1:12-16.

Satava, Richard S. (Ed.) 1998. *Cybersurgery: Advanced Technologies for Surgical Practice.* NY: Wiley Liss, Inc.

Satava, Richard S. 1998. "Cybersurgery: A new vision for general surgery." In Richard S. Satava (Ed.) *Cybersurgery: Advanced Technologies for Surgical Practice.* NY: Wiley Liss, Inc. pp. 3-15.

Satava, Richard S. and Shaun B. Jones. 1998. "Human interface technology." In Richard S. Satava (Ed.) *Cybersurgery: Advanced Technologies for Surgical Practice.* NY: Wiley Liss, Inc. pp. 17-32.

Schaller, Carlo, et al. 1997. "Image guided microsurgery with a semifreehand neuronavigational device." *Computer Aided Surgery* 2:162-171.

Scheeres, D.E., et al. 1990. "Endoscopic retrograde cholangiopancreatography in a general surgery practice." *American Surgeon* 56(3): 185-191.

Scheper-Hughes, Nancy. 1990. "Three propositions for a critically applied medical anthropology." *Social Science and Medicine* 30(2):189-198.

Schumacker, H. 1985. "What do we want in a surgical chairman?" *American Journal of Surgery* 150:291-294.

Schwartz, Seymour. 1983. "The scalpel and the baton." *Contemporary Surgery* 23:13.

Schwarzbart, Gunter. 1982 "The romantic aspects of being a surgeon." *Medical News* 22.

Selzer, Richard. 1982. *Letters to a Young Doctor.* NY: Simon and Schuster.

Seropian, R. and B.M. Reynolds. 1971. "Wound infections after preoperative depilatory versus razor preparation." *American Journal of Surgery* 121:251-254.

Shively, Eugene H., et al. 1990. "Operative cholangiography." *American Journal of Surgery* 159:380-385.

Shortell, Stephen M. 1974. *A Model of Physician Referral Behavior: A Test of Exchange Theory in Medical Practice.* Chicago: Center for Health Administration Studies, University of Chicago.

Shortell, Stephen M. and Odin W. Anderson. 1971. "The physician referral process: A theoretical perspective." *Health Services Research* 6:39-48.

Shryock, Richard Harrison. 1936. *The Development of Modern Medicine: An Interpretation of the Social and Scientific Factors Involved.* NY: Alfred A. Knopf.

Shweder, Richard A. 1972. "Aspects of cognition in Zinacanteco shamans: Experimental results." In William A. Lessa and Evon Z. Vogt (Eds.) *Reader in Comparative Religion: An Anthropological Approach. Third Edition.* NY: Harper and Row, Publishers. pp. 407-412.

Siegler, Miriam and Humphrey Osmond. 1974. *Models of Madness, Models of Medicine.* NY: Harper and Row.

Singer, Merrill. 1990. "Postmodernism and medical anthropology: Words of caution." *Medical Anthropology* 12:289-304.

Singer, Merrill. 1995. "Beyond the ivory tower: Critical praxis in medical anthropology." *Medical Anthropology Quarterly* 9(1):80-106.

Singer, Merrill. 1996. "Farewell to adaptationism: Unnatural selection and the politics of biology." *Medical Anthropology Quarterly* 10(4):496-515.

Souba, W.W., et al. 1995. "Strategies for success in academic surgery." *Surgery* 117(1):90-95.

Soumerai, Stephen B., et al. 1993. "A controlled trial of educational outreach to improve blood transfusion practice." *Journal of the American Medical Association* 270(8):961-966.

Spencer, Frank Cole. 1978. "Teaching and measuring surgical techniques: The technical evaluation of competence." *Bulletin of the American College of Surgeons* 63:9-12.

Spencer, Frank Cole. 1979. "Competence and compassion: Two qualities of surgical excellence." *Bulletin of the American College of Surgeons* 64:15-22.

Stein, Howard F. 1990. *American Medicine as Culture.* Boulder: Westview Press.

Tancredi, Laurence R. 1982. "Competency for informal consent: Conceptual limits of empirical data." *International Journal of Law and Psychiatry* 5:51-63.

Taylor, Kathryn M. 1988. "Physicians and the disclosure of undesirable information." In Margaret Lock and Deborah Gordon (Eds.) *Biomedicine Examined.* Dordrecht, Holland: Kluwer Academic Publishers. pp. 441-463.

Temkin, Owsei. 1951. "The role of surgery in the rise of modern medical thought." *Bulletin of the History of Medicine* 25:135-145.

Timmermans, D.T., et al. 1996. "How do surgeons' probability estimates of operational mortality compare with a decision analytic model." *Acta Psychology Amsterdam* 93:107-120.

Tobias, J.S., et al. 1981. "Who should treat cancer?" *The Lancet* 8225:884-886.

Trotter, Wilfred. 1946. *The Collected papers of Wilfred Trotter.* London: Oxford University Press.

Tversky, A. and D. Kahneman. 1984. "Judgement under uncertainty: Heuristics and biases." *Science* 185:1124-1131.

Vayda, E. 1976. "Surgical rates in the Canadian provinces, 1968-1972." *Canadian Journal of Surgery* 19(3):235-242.

Vayda, E. 1984. "Five-year study of surgical rates in Ontario counties." *Canadian Medical Association Journal* 131(2):111-115.

Vayda, E., et al. 1981. "Use of hypothetical cases to investigate indications for surgery." *Canadian Journal of Surgery* 24(1):19-21.

Vayda, E., et al. 1981. "Use of hypothetical cases to investigate indications for surgery." *Canadian Journal of Surgery* 24(1):19-21.

Visarius, H., et al. 1997. "Man-machine interfaces in computer assisted surgery." *Computer Aided Surgery* 2:102-107.

Waiztkin, Harold. 1979. "Medicine superstructure and neuropolitics." *Social Science and Medicine* 13:601-609.

Wangensteen, Owen H. 1975. "The surgical amphitheatre: History of the origins, functions, and fate." *Surgery* 77:403-418.

Wangensteen, Owen H. and Sarah D. Wangensteen. 1978. *The Rise of Surgery: From Emperic Craft to Scientific Discipline.* Minneapolis: University of Minnesota Press.

Wartofsky, M.W. 1986. "Clinical judgement, expert programs, and cognitive style: A counter-essay in the logic of diagnosis." *The Journal of Medical Philosophy* 11(1):81-92.

Weinberg, A.D., et al. 1981. "Informal advice and information seeking between physicians." *Journal of Medical Education* 56:174-180.

Weintraub, Walter. 1982. *Verbal Behavior: Adaptation and Psychopathology.* NY: Springer.

Welch, Claude and Ronald Malt. 1987. "Surgery of the stomach, duodenum, gallbladder, and bile ducts." *New England Journal of Medicine* 316:999-1008.

Wennberg, J. and A. Gittelsohn. 1973. "Small area variation in health care delivery." *Science* 182:1102.

West, Candace. 1993. *Routine Complications: Troubles with Talk Between Doctors and Patients.* Bloomington, IN: Indiana University Press.

Wheeler, Brent R., et al. 1990. "Choledochoscopy and common bile duct exploration." *The American Surgeon* 56:182-184.

Wikan, Unni. 1991. "Toward an experience-near anthropology." *Cultural Anthropology* 6(3):285-305.

Williams, Ben T. (Ed.) 1981. *Computer Aids to Clinical Decisions. Volume I.* Boca Raton, Florida: CRC Press.

Williams, Robin. 1963. *American Society: A Sociological Interpretation. Second Edition, Revised.* NY: Alfred A. Knopf.

Wilson, Donald R. 1977. "The Canadian Association of General Surgeons." *The Canadian Journal of Surgery* 20:196-197.

Wilson, Robert N. 1954. "Teamwork in the operating room." *Human Organization* 12:9-14.

Wirtz, C. Rainer, et al. 1997. "Intraopeative magnetic resonance imaging to update interactive navigation in neurosurgery: Method and preliminary experience." *Computer Aided Surgery* 2:172-179.

Wolfe, Samuel and Robin F. Badgley. 1974. "How much is enough? The payment of doctors: Implications for health policy in Canada." *Journal of Health Services* 4(2):245-264.

Wright, James G., et al. 1996. "Practice guidelines in surgery." *Surgery* 119:7-6-709.

Wyke, Alexandra. 1997. *21ˢᵗ Century Miracle Medicine: RoboSurgery, Wonder Cures, and the Quest for Immortality.* NY: Plenum.

Yancy, J.M. 1992. "Response to letter to the editor." *American Journal of Surgery* 163:365.

Yates, J.L. 1905. "An experimental study of the local effects of peritoneal drainage." *Surgery, Gynecology, Obstetrics* 1:473.

Young, Allan. 1982. "The anthropologies of illness and sickness." *Annual Review of Anthropology* 11:257-285.

Young, Katherine. 1989. "Disembodiment: The phenomenology of the body in medical examinations." *Semiotica* 731-2:43-66.

Zimmerman, Leo M. and Ilza Veith. 1961. *Great Ideas in the History of Surgery.* Baltimore: Williams and Wilkins Co.

INDEX